PREACHING JESUS

Preaching Jesus

New Directions for Homiletics in Hans Frei's Postliberal Theology

Charles L. Campbell

WILLIAM B. EERDMANS PUBLISHING COMPANY
GRAND RAPIDS, MICHIGAN / CAMBRIDGE, U.K.

© 1997 Wm. B. Eerdmans Publishing Co.
255 Jefferson Ave. S.E., Grand Rapids, Michigan 49503 /
P.O. Box 163, Cambridge CB3 9PU U.K.
All rights reserved

Printed in the United States of America

02 01 00 99 98 97   7 6 5 4 3 2 1

Library of Congress Cataloging-in-Publication Data

Campell, Charles L., 1954-
Preaching Jesus : new directions for homiletics in
Hans Frei's postliberal theology / Charles L. Campbell.
p.   cm.
Includes bibliographical references.
ISBN 0-8028-4156-2 (alk. paper)
1. Preaching. 2. Frei, Hans W. I. Title.
BV4211.2.C26   1997
251 — dc21   96-53633
CIP

For Dana

Contents

PART II
NARRATIVE HOMILETICS: A POSTLIBERAL CRITIQUE

PART III
NEW DIRECTIONS FOR PREACHING

Acknowledgments

The seeds of this book were planted more than ten years ago when Union Theological Seminary in Virginia asked me to study homiletics while I was serving a pastorate in Stuttgart, Arkansas. In the mysterious providence of God, my journey has taken a number of unexpected twists and turns during these past ten years, and many people have helped me along the way.

The late Wellford Hobbie, formerly of Union Theological Seminary, is the person most responsible for my entering the field of homiletics. Although he did not live to see the fruit of his labor, I have thought of him often along the way; he remains for me a model prophet-pastor-teacher. James L. Mays introduced me to the literary criticism of the gospels, the field of hermeneutics, and the work of Hans Frei. He has been a valuable teacher, wise counselor, and constant support over the years. The congregation of First Presbyterian Church in Stuttgart, Arkansas, not only made sacrifices so their pastor could study homiletics but also taught me more about preaching than I ever learned from books.

Many other people contributed more directly to this book. Stanley Hauerwas directed my dissertation, on which the book is based. His commitment to his students; his efficient, direct, and insightful feedback; and his passion for the gospel have been invaluable to my work — and my life. Richard Lischer has been equally supportive and helpful in the field of homiletics. He has not only been an invaluable role model as a teacher and scholar but has also kept me focused on important theological matters in a field in which it is all too easy to become enamored with peripheral concerns. Without the support of these two mentors and friends, this book would never have been written.

Others have also offered encouragement and support. The trustees of Hans Frei's papers provided me with a manuscript of *Types of Christian Theology* prior to its publication. John Woolverton provided valuable biographical information about Frei and helpful insights into Frei's own preaching. George Hunsinger encouraged my work and supplied me with a number of Frei's unpublished papers. William Placher not only provided invaluable materials and support but also read earlier versions of this book and offered extremely helpful suggestions. Geoffrey Wainwright, Mary McClintock Fulkerson, Richard Hays, George Stroup, and Walter Brueggemann also read and commented upon an earlier draft of the book. Finally, William B. Eerdmans, Jr., saw the potential in my dissertation, and Jennifer Hoffman graciously walked me through the publication process. To all of these people I am extremely grateful.

I am also grateful to the folks at Columbia Theological Seminary. Colleagues, students, and friends at Columbia have challenged my thinking and enriched my life since I first set foot on the campus in 1991. President Douglas Oldenburg and Dean James Hudnut-Beumler have provided tangible and intangible support for my work, including a sabbatical in 1995, which enabled me to complete the revisions of my manuscript. Lucy Rose, my colleague and friend in the homiletics department, has been a blessing. Her faithful life and her homiletical wisdom have challenged and encouraged me time and again. Hannah Brawley, a Columbia student, provided invaluable assistance with the last-minute details of publication, including the index.

Finally, and most importantly, I need to thank my family. Charles and Johnsye Campbell, my parents, generously supported me and my family through too many years of school. Lydia and Thomas, my children, were patient with Daddy's hours in the study — "the black hole," they call it — and at least tried to remind me that there is more to life than work. Dana, my wife, put up with a student husband for almost half of our twenty years of marriage. Somehow she understood why I needed to pursue this work, loved me through it, and kept me from taking myself too seriously along the way. She has unquestionably sacrificed the most for this book, and I dedicate it to her.

Introduction

Over the past twenty-five years homiletics has enjoyed growing vitality.[1] And today the field seems to be as strong as ever. New books are published almost daily. Homiletical conferences, journals, and resources multiply. Doctoral programs turn out specialized professors who are in demand in the seminaries. New theories and forms of preaching abound at every turn. These are unquestionably exciting days for homiletics.

Beneath the surface, however, signs of trouble can be discerned. The new preaching theories and resources do not appear to have brought new life to the church. Over the same period that homiletics has enjoyed a resurgence, mainline Protestant churches have been in decline. The multiplication of preaching theories and resources has taken place alongside a growing sense of concern, even despair, about the life and future of the church. Recent homiletical developments seem to have accomplished little more than to rearrange the proverbial deck chairs on the Titanic. And many local pastors recognize this fact. They know something is lacking in their preaching. They've tried inductive preaching, story preaching, dialogue sermons, and homiletical plots. While these new methods have been exciting for the moment, many preachers sense something is still missing, and they have not found amid

1. Wellford Hobbie described the resurgence of preaching since the 1960s very well in his inaugural lecture at Union Theological Seminary in Virginia. See Wellford Hobbie, "Out of the Shadows: The Resurgence of Homiletics/Preaching Since the Sixties," *Affirmation* 1 (1980): 21-37.

the myriad books, articles, and conferences an articulation of the problem or a direction for the future.

In a paper presented at the Academy of Homiletics, Ronald Allen touched on the primary root of the current trouble: "Preaching is preeminently a theological act," Allen affirmed, "yet, there is a near lacuna in our literature: we give little attention to theological analysis of the preaching event."[2] Allen went on to argue that theological reflection about preaching should be at the top of the homiletical agenda in the coming years.

Allen's paper is disturbing. If preaching is "preeminently a theological act," one has to wonder why serious theological reflection has been neglected in recent years. Apart from such reflection, it is doubtful that homileticians have much of importance to contribute to preachers or the church. Looking back over the past twenty years, during which homiletical reflection has focused primarily on sermon form, rather than theological content, I am reminded of the haunting words of the historian, Yngve Brilioth: "One of the marks of spiritually impoverished times is too great a concern for external form."[3]

Allen's paper is also surprising. Although affirming the theological character of preaching, Allen overlooks the fact that every homiletical position explicitly or implicitly embodies theological presuppositions. Theology is not a discipline that can be added to or subtracted from preaching, although current divisions in the seminary curriculum might suggest that possibility. The issue is not simply the absence of theological reflection, but rather the character and quality of the theology that is present. Consequently, future theological reflection about preaching will necessarily include an examination of the theological presuppositions implicit in contemporary homiletical theory and practice, as well as the development of richer theological alternatives.

It is just this task that I undertake in this book. I agree with Allen that the trouble with homiletics today is fundamentally theological, including both the lack of explicit theological reflection about

2. Ronald Allen, "Agendae in Homiletics," *Papers of the Annual Meeting of the Academy of Homiletics* (Fuller Theological Seminary, December 5-7, 1991), 35. An abbreviated version of this paper has been published as "New Directions in Homiletics," *Journal For Preachers* 16 (Easter 1993): 20-26.

3. Yngve Brilioth, *A Brief History of Preaching*, trans. Karl E. Mattson (Philadelphia: Fortress Press, 1965), 61.

preaching and the inadequacy of the theology implicit in contemporary homiletics. In what follows I will address both sides of this matter. Using as an example the most popular recent homiletical development, narrative preaching, I will demonstrate that contemporary homiletical theory and practice remain dependent on modern, liberal theological presuppositions, which have serious limitations for preaching in the contemporary context. As an alternative, I will develop the homiletical implications of Hans Frei's postliberal theology, which suggests important new directions for preaching and can contribute to the enrichment of the Christian pulpit and the renewal of the church.

Although Frei's work lies "quietly at the center of much contemporary theological debate in North America,"[4] his theology has had little impact on recent homiletical developments. His work on biblical narrative has indirectly influenced the turn to narrative in preaching, but his postliberal theological and hermeneutical position has remained a virtually untapped resource. This failure to take Frei's work seriously reflects the different theological and hermeneutical presuppositions that have shaped contemporary homiletics. Frei is kept at arm's length because his position is at odds with the dominant homiletical paradigms. In fact, Frei's carefully developed alternative to modern, liberal theology exposes and critiques the theological and hermeneutical presuppositions of contemporary homiletics. And Frei's distinctive approach to biblical narrative also raises serious issues about the appropriation of "story" in contemporary preaching. Consequently, Frei's work offers an excellent location from which to critique current homiletical presuppositions and offer an alternative to them.

Prior to this critique and alternative, however, a detailed examination of Frei's at times dense and difficult work is required. Part One of this book focuses on the specifics of Frei's theological position. The first chapter examines the historical context in which Frei developed his position, as well as the important influences on his theology. Chapter Two treats Frei's critique of modern theological liberalism and his alternative to it. Chapters Three and Four examine Frei's later work, which he himself called "a continuation as well as revision" of his earlier

---

4. John Webster, "Response to George Hunsinger," *Modern Theology* 8 (April 1992): 129.

position.[5] Frei's turn to a cultural-linguistic model of Christianity and a communal hermeneutic, as well as his increasing appreciation for variety in interpretation, are all discussed.

In Part Two I provide a critique of contemporary homiletics in light of three central dimensions of Frei's theology. Based on Frei's cultural-linguistic model of Christianity, I critique the current homiletical emphasis on individual, experiential events (Chapter Five). From the perspective of Frei's postliberal, communal hermeneutic, I raise issues about the understanding of the relationship between Scripture and the contemporary world in narrative preaching (Chapter Six). Finally, drawing on Frei's understanding of the distinctive logic of the gospel narratives, I critique appropriations of narrative in contemporary preaching (Chapter Seven).

In Part Three I suggest new directions for preaching based on Frei's theological position. Chapter Eight develops the implications of Frei's work for the content, form, and "performance" of the sermon. The final chapter examines the communal character of preaching from the perspective of Frei's cultural-linguistic theology. The result is a distinctive understanding of the language of preaching, a renewed emphasis on the communal context of preaching, and a fresh appreciation for figural interpretation in the pulpit.

Several years ago in the journal *Homiletic*, George Stroup rather cryptically suggested that Hans Frei's work should be of great interest to homileticians: "Frei's position has significant consequences for readers of this journal, for those for whom the interpretation of biblical narrative is not simply a matter of theological and literary theory but also a matter of praxis."[6] In what follows I will demonstrate that Stroup is right — and why.[7]

---

5. Hans W. Frei, *Types of Christian Theology*, ed. George Hunsinger and William C. Placher (New Haven: Yale Univ. Press, 1992), 6. Frei's "later work" consists of his writings during the 1980s, prior to his untimely death in 1988.

6. George Stroup, review of *The Bible and the Narrative Tradition*, ed. Frank McConnell, *Homiletic* 12, no. 1 (1987): 24.

7. A word about language is in order at this point. Although I have tried to use inclusive language throughout the book, I have quoted from authors who, largely because of their historical context, were not sensitive to this issue. While I have chosen neither to alter the quotations nor to use "[sic]" after each non-inclusive term, I am aware of the limitations of this quoted material. I hope readers will be patient with my uneasy compromise.

PART ONE

Hans Frei's Theology

". . . as Barth's Dogmatics developed past the prolegomena . . . the doctrines of the person and work of Christ, Christology and soteriology, moved closer to each other, the bond between them being a concept of personhood as self-enacted agency or performative project rather than the epistemic notion of revelation as existentially imparted and appropriated knowledge or understanding. In that sense and that alone, one can say that Barth became a 'narrative' theologian: Jesus was what he did and underwent, and not simply his understanding or self-understanding."

Hans W. Frei, "Barth and Schleiermacher:
Divergence and Convergence," 71-72.

"In the next life, if I have any choice, there will be two terms that I shall eschew, one is 'hermeneutics,' the other is 'narrative!'"

Hans W. Frei, "Conflicts in Interpretation," 346.

Chapter One

Frei's Theological Background:
The American Context

Within the North American theological context Hans Frei has been recognized primarily for his contributions in three areas. First, along with his colleague, George Lindbeck, Frei was instrumental in the development of the "postliberal" theology of the "Yale School." Over the past decade this approach to theology has become a significant and distinctive voice in the pluralistic theological conversation in the United States. Representing a fresh appropriation of Barth's work, postliberal theology has usually been set over against "revisionist" approaches to theology, which have drawn on the liberal tradition of Schleiermacher and have generally been associated with the University of Chicago. Indeed, much of the recent theological debate in the United States has been framed in terms of the "postliberal"-"revisionist" or Yale-Chicago dichotomy.[1] Frei's work has been at the center of this debate.

Second, Frei has been closely associated with the development of a literary approach to biblical interpretation in the United States. His two major works, *The Eclipse of Biblical Narrative* and *The Identity of*

---

1. Major representatives of the "revisionist" approach are David Tracy in theology and James Gustafson in ethics. George Lindbeck's book *The Nature of Doctrine: Religion and Theology in a Postliberal Age* (Philadelphia: Westminster Press, 1984) is the programmatic work on postliberal theology. As will become clear in what follows, however, there are important differences between Frei's and Lindbeck's work. For a good comparison of "postliberal" and "revisionist" approaches to theology, see William C. Placher, *Unapologetic Theology: A Christian Voice in a Pluralistic Conversation* (Louisville: Westminster/John Knox Press, 1989).

Jesus Christ, made a significant contribution to a "postcritical," literary reading of the Bible.[2] Finally, because of his work on biblical narrative, Frei has been one of the main figures associated with the development of "narrative theology," though he himself would have had reservations about being lumped in this category.

While each of these characterizations of Frei's work is accurate, the situation is considerably more complex. To discern Frei's distinctive contribution to American theology and his distinctive approach to narrative theology, it is important to examine the historical context within which he developed his position. The keys to understanding that context are the rise and fall of "neo-orthodoxy" and "biblical theology" in mid-century American theology and the related faith-and-history debate that preoccupied theologians and biblical scholars during that period.[3]

Two significant forces in Protestant theology at the middle of the twentieth century, when Frei was developing his theological agenda, were "neo-orthodoxy" and the "Biblical Theology Movement."[4] Significantly, however, neither of these movements adequately understood or appreciated the theology of Karl Barth, despite the affinities that each should have had with Barth's work. During the sixties, both these move-

2. Hans W. Frei, *The Eclipse of Biblical Narrative: A Study in Eighteenth and Nineteenth Century Hermeneutics* (New Haven: Yale Univ. Press, 1974); Hans W. Frei, *The Identity of Jesus Christ: The Hermeneutical Bases of Dogmatic Theology* (Philadelphia: Fortress Press, 1975). *The Identity of Jesus Christ* was first published as "The Mystery of the Presence of Jesus Christ," Unit I, *Crossroads* (January-March 1967): 69-96; Unit II, *Crossroads* (April-June 1967): 69-96.

3. I place "neo-orthodoxy" in quotation marks because, though it is a label frequently applied to the theology of that period, it is a confusing one. There were many significant differences among the theologians labeled "neo-orthodox," among them Emil Brunner, Karl Barth, Reinhold Niebuhr, H. Richard Niebuhr, and even Paul Tillich. In fact, Frei himself, with his particular understanding of Barth, rejected all of the others (with the highly qualified exception of H. Richard Niebuhr) as "liberal theologians under the skin." Hans W. Frei, "H. Richard Niebuhr on History, Church, and Nation," in Hans W. Frei, *Theology and Narrative: Selected Essays,* ed. George Hunsinger and William C. Placher (New York: Oxford Univ. Press, 1993), 220. On the basic characteristics of "neo-orthodoxy," see William Deane Ferm, "American Protestant Theology, 1900-1970," *Religion in Life* 44 (Spring, 1975): 65-68.

4. For a discussion of the broader theological picture, of which "neo-orthodoxy" and biblical theology were a part, see John Macquarrie, *Twentieth Century Religious Thought,* 4th ed. (London: SCM Press, 1988; Philadelphia: Trinity Press International, 1988), 253-372; and John B. Cobb, Jr., *Living Options in Protestant Theology: A Survey of Methods* (Philadelphia: Westminster, 1962).

ments collapsed, and the work of Barth was generally dismissed along with them. Theologians returned to more liberal theological emphases and to the new "secularism."[5] Paul Tillich was the outstanding systematic theologian, and the work of Bultmann and his "second generation" students was coming more into prominence. John A. T. Robinson's *Honest To God* and Harvey Cox's *The Secular City* were the most popular theological works.[6] It was in this context that Frei developed his "post-liberal" theology, which represented a distinctive interpretation and appropriation of the theology of Karl Barth and, simultaneously, a new biblical theology. An examination of Frei's relation to "neo-orthodoxy" and the Biblical Theology Movement in the United States helps to clarify his contribution to American theology and provide the context of his turn to narrative.

"Neo-Orthodoxy"

In 1918 Karl Barth's *Epistle to the Romans* burst onto the theological scene in Europe, followed three years later by the even more radical and explosive second edition. This single work, with its challenge to the tradition of liberal theology and its radical understanding of the otherness of God and justification by faith, gave birth to the new "dialectical" or "crisis" theology on the continent.

Barth's early dialectical theology soon found a number of important adherents in Europe, the most important for the American context being Emil Brunner. However, in the early part of the century American theology remained virtually untouched by Barth's work. In fact, it was not until the

5. Some of the "secularlist" and "death of God" theologians did appeal to Barth's theology for support. Although Frei recognized Barth's "secular sensibility," he rightly argued that these theologians misappropriated Barth's work. See Hans W. Frei, "Karl Barth: Theologian," in *Karl Barth and the Future of Theology: A Memorial Colloquium Held at the Yale Divinity School, January 28, 1969*, ed. David L. Dickerman (New Haven: Yale Divinity School Association, 1969), 8-9, 13-14. The major portion of Frei's contribution to this colloquium (though not all of his comments on Barth's secular sensibility) has been reprinted in Frei, *Theology and Narrative*. See also Hans W. Frei, "German Theology: Transcendence and Secularity," in *Postwar German Culture*, ed. Charles E. McClelland and Stephen P. Scher (New York: E. P. Dutton, 1974), 98-112.

6. John A. T. Robinson, *Honest To God* (Philadelphia: Westminster, 1963); Harvey Cox, *The Secular City* (New York: Macmillan, 1965).

thirties and forties, and not fully until the postwar period, that dialectical theology began to make a serious impact on American theology.

Even then, the American appropriation of Barth's theology was quite limited. In the first place, it was generally Barth's early "dialectical" theology that was read; and even where Barth's later materials were studied, they were generally understood in light of the earlier work. Not surprisingly, "neo-orthodox" theology in the United States was often virtually equated with "dialectical" or "crisis" theology.[7] The significance of Barth's move through the book on Anselm to the *Church Dogmatics* was not widely recognized in the United States at that time. In the preface to the 1958 edition of the Anselm volume Barth himself noted that few people, even in Europe, had understood the significance of that book for his theology.[8] The English translation of the work, *Anselm: Fides Quaerens Intellectum,* was not even published until 1960.

In addition, even this early Barth was appropriated primarily through the work of Emil Brunner. However, as their debate over "natural theology" made clear, there were significant differences between Barth and Brunner.[9] Brunner's theology remained very much within an existentialist, dialectical framework and emphasized the uniqueness of existential, personal understanding.[10] In addition, as Frei himself re-

---

7. See, for example, Van A. Harvey, "Neo-Reformed Theology," in *A Handbook of Theological Terms* (New York: Macmillan, 1964), 162-64.

8. Karl Barth, *Anselm: Fides Quaerens Intellectum,* trans. Ian W. Robertson, Pittsburgh Reprint Series (London: SCM Press, 1960), 11.

9. See the famous (or infamous) debate between Brunner and Barth over "natural theology": Emil Brunner, "Nature and Grace," and Karl Barth, "No!" in *Natural Theology,* trans. Peter Fraenkel (London: Centenary Press, 1946).

10. Brunner's existentialism, with its emphasis on "personal encounter," was informed more by Martin Buber than by Heidegger, who was the primary influence on Bultmann and his followers. Whereas existentialism played a central role in American "neo-orthodoxy," Barth, with the Anselm volume, had eschewed existentialism, a philosophical orientation that would continue to be the target of much of Frei's work. See Hans W. Frei, "Religion: Natural and Revealed," in *A Handbook of Christian Theology: Definition Essays on Concepts and Movements of Thought in Contemporary Protestantism,* ed. Marvin Halverson and Arthur A. Cohen (Cleveland: World Publishing Co., 1958), 315. As Frei notes even in this early essay, it was Barth, often viewed as a theological "irrationalist" in the United States, who was actually more open to the use of philosophy in theology. Unlike Brunner and other existentialists, Barth, and Frei like him, would not "separate philosophy and theology by making God's grasp upon us subject to a unique religious or existential apprehension" ("Religion: Natural and Revealed," 315-17). Brunner, in this respect, was closer to Schleiermacher than to Barth.

peatedly noted, Brunner continued with a basically anthropological starting point; he simply did not grasp the theocentric focus of Barth, which prevented the two men from even getting on the same "wavelength."[11]

Thus, "neo-orthodox" theology in the United States generally drew at best upon the early dialectical Barth at second hand through Brunner. Nevertheless, when "neo-orthodoxy" collapsed in the great theological upheaval of the sixties, Barth went down with it. John A. T. Robinson, for example, mentions Barth only once, indirectly, in his popular and influential book, *Honest to God.* However, what "went down with the ship" of "neo-orthodoxy" was a very limited understanding of Barth's theology. As Frei himself noted, "In this country Barth was identified with 'neo-orthodoxy,' and its demise as a result of the radical sixties meant that his own complex, massive reflections were submerged and left to an array of residual Barthians."[12]

Precisely during this period Frei, in his dissertation, was examining Barth's break with liberalism in great detail.[13] Unlike most other interpreters, Frei understood the significance of the book on Anselm. In the dissertation he traces Barth's break with liberalism through the first two editions of *Romans.* Then he notes that Barth went on, in the book on Anselm, to move beyond the existentialism, idealism, and dialectic of *Romans* toward an appreciation of analogy.[14] Anselm's method of "faith seeking understanding," Frei argued, enabled Barth to move "beyond the *Problematik* posed for him by Schleiermacher and Kant," that is, the

11. Hans W. Frei, "Niebuhr's Theological Background," in *Faith and Ethics: The Theology of H. Richard Niebuhr,* ed. Paul Ramsey (New York: Harper and Brothers, 1957), 44.

12. Hans W. Frei, "An Afterword: Eberhard Busch's Biography of Karl Barth," in *Karl Barth in Re-View: Posthumous Works Reviewed and Assessed,* ed. H.-Martin Rumscheidt, Pittsburgh Theological Monograph Series 30 (Pittsburgh: Pickwick Press, 1981), 95.

13. Hans W. Frei, *The Doctrine of Revelation in the Thought of Karl Barth, 1909-1922: The Nature of Barth's Break With Liberalism* (Ann Arbor, Mich.: University Microfilms, 1956).

14. This was Barth's *analogia fidei,* "in which it is God who is the analogue and man who is the analogate," rather than the traditional *analogia entis* (Frei, *Doctrine of Revelation,* 200). See also Graham White, "Karl Barth's Theological Realism," *Neue Zeitschrift für systematische Theologie und Religionsphilosophie* 26, no. 1 (1984): 54-70; and George Hunsinger, "Beyond Literalism and Expressivism: Karl Barth's Hermeneutical Realism," *Modern Theology* 3, no. 3 (1987): 209-23.

problem of "how to elevate thought from the creature to the Creator other than by taking for granted their 'religious' togetherness or sundering faith and reason."[15]

> It was St. Anselm's *Proslogion* that helped Barth solve his dilemma. Here Barth finds faith completely girded for a rational task. No extrinsic, non-rational considerations intrude, a fact that appeals to him because he, too, wants to speak in and from faith, without sundering faith and reason as the nineteenth-century tradition had done. Barth's book on Anselm is absolutely indispensable for a knowledge of the revolution in his thought between the two editions of *The Doctrine of God*.[16]

This was written in 1956. Two years later, as I noted above, Barth would write that few people had understood the importance of the Anselm volume for his work. Frei was on the way to a fresh understanding of Barth in the American context. However, long before he could develop the implications of his discovery, Barth's theology, along with "neo-orthodoxy," went into decline in the United States. It is a tribute to Frei that he persevered and developed his distinctive appropriation of Barth's theology in the Anselmian direction.

This work on Barth would lead to Frei's most significant contribution to American theology: his appropriation of Barth's Anselmian theology as a viable theological option, and his development of a distinctive theological position consistent with it. Frei, as Jeffrey Stout has written, provided "a reading of Barth, which, though not entirely novel, secured a hearing for him as the great Anselmian theologian of our time."[17] In so doing, Frei not only would contribute to a renaissance in Barth studies and challenge the liberalism of the "revisionist" school, but, equally significantly, would demonstrate the lingering liberalism of American "neo-orthodoxy" itself. Indeed, it is in large part through the work of Frei and his students that "Barthian" theology occupies a sig-

---

15. Frei, *Doctrine of Revelation*, 193.
16. Frei, *Doctrine of Revelation*, 193-94.
17. Stout calls Frei the "leading Anselmian theologian of his generation." See Jeffrey Stout, "Hans Frei and Anselmian Theology" (paper presented at the annual meeting of the American Academy of Religion, Boston, 1987, TMs [photocopy]), 7-9. I will discuss Frei's appropriation of Barth's "Anselmian" theology in more detail in Chapter Two.

nificant place in the pluralistic, postmodern American theological context today. However, as I will argue later, contemporary homiletics has not followed Frei at this point.

The Biblical Theology Movement

During the same period that "neo-orthodoxy" flourished in Protestant theological circles in the United States, a related movement exercised significant influence in the field of biblical studies: the Biblical Theology Movement. A distinctive American development, the Biblical Theology Movement sought to recapture the theological dimension of Scripture (which many felt had been lost in the details of historical criticism), without, however, giving up historical criticism itself.[18]

In addition to the primary aim of recapturing the theological dimension of Scripture while retaining the historical-critical method, several specific elements characterized the Biblical Theology Movement.[19] First, the movement emphasized the unity of the Bible. However, there was no consensus about how this unity was to be understood, though both a Christological and a typological unity were rejected. Usually, as Childs points out, some form of "unity in diversity" was affirmed. Second, the movement emphasized revelation as the "acts of God" in history, though, again, there was little consensus on the way history was understood or the way an "act of God" was conceived. In fact, because of the concern to maintain the independence and integrity of the historical-critical method, historical "acts of God" were usually conceived as perfectly "natural" occurrences, which were interpreted as "acts of God" by the Hebrew

18. My discussion of the Biblical Theology Movement is dependent on the work of Brevard Childs, *Biblical Theology in Crisis* (Philadelphia: Westminster, 1970). However, Childs should *not* be understood as defining the entire field of "biblical theology." Indeed, his book reflects a particular perspective that was based on his own project and proposals. Other scholars would argue that there never was anything so formal as a "biblical theology movement" that could be said to have collapsed for the reasons Childs cites. Nevertheless, the Biblical Theology Movement, as interpreted by Childs, provided the context for the work of Frei, his colleague at Yale. For Childs's discussion of the distinctiveness of the American movement and its close association with Reformed Protestantism, see Childs, 13-31.

19. My discussion is based on Childs's analysis of the "elements of the consensus." See Childs, 32-50.

people; "event plus interpretation" became the key framework within
which this issue was understood. Third, the movement stressed the distinctiveness of the "biblical mentality," particularly the "Hebrew mind,"
which was viewed as historical and dynamic in opposition to the static and
abstract thinking of the Greeks. In particular, the nonmythical character
of the biblical mind was emphasized over against the mythical thinking of
the ancient world. Often this characteristic of the movement took the
form of a "word study" approach to the Bible, which highlighted the
distinctiveness of biblical concepts. Fourth, the movement sought to
highlight, through archaeological study, the distinctiveness of the biblical
material in its original context, arguing for its unique perspective in the
ancient Near East.

Despite its force during the forties and fifties, the Biblical Theology
Movement, along with neo-orthodoxy, faced a crisis by the early sixties.[20] While a number of factors, including the changing theological
climate in the United States, contributed to the troubles of the movement,[21] ultimately the inherent tensions within the Biblical Theology
Movement itself led to its demise. Most basically, the contradictions
between the movement's grand theological assertions and its reliance
on historical criticism were never adequately defended. The approach
to the Bible was fundamentally schizophrenic, divided between careful
historical inquiry on the one hand and "rhetorical" theological assertions on the other — a split that is evident in the *The Interpreter's Bible*.[22]
Finding a method that was both "theological" and "critical" proved to
be an intractable problem. However, there appeared to be no clear
alternative to historical criticism concerning either the context or the
subject matter of interpretation.[23]

For various reasons, not least among them the lingering specter
of fundamentalism, the Biblical Theology Movement failed to recognize
the significance of Barth's exegesis. Because Barth objected to the critical
attempt to go behind the text, his work in this area was dismissed as
"precritical."[24] For the adherents of the Biblical Theology Movement

20. Again, my account is dependent on that of Childs: Childs, 51-87.
21. Childs, 82-87.
22. On this point see also James Barr, "Story and History in Biblical Theology,"
The Journal of Religion 56 (January 1976): 3.
23. Childs, 52.
24. Childs, 110.

something more important than the actual biblical text lay behind it, whether that was understood as historical event, "original meaning," or something else.[25] In terms that Frei himself would later employ, the Biblical Theology Movement sought to use the Bible as both a histori-cal-critical "source" and a theological "text," but without resorting to myth. However, as Frei himself argued, Strauss and, later, Troeltsch had already demonstrated the virtually insuperable difficulties of such an attempt.[26] It is not surprising that Bultmann's project of demythologiz-ing enjoyed increased popularity as the Biblical Theology Movement waned or that the New Hermeneutic, developed by Bultmann's students, came to prominence in the sixties.[27]

In addition to this fundamental problem, the specific elements of the movement crumbled under a devastating critique. As the position came under increasing scrutiny, it simply did not have the resources to meet the criticisms. Langdon Gilkey's important essay, "Cosmology, Ontology, and the Travail of Biblical Language," provided one of the crucial blows to the movement.[28] In a compelling critique, Gilkey simply pointed out the inner contradictions in the movement's "liberal" reli-ance on historical criticism and its "conservative" (i.e. univocally refer-ential) use of theological language. This tension came to a head, for Gilkey, in the event-plus-interpretation understanding of the acts of God in history:

> In sum, therefore, we may say that for modern biblical theology the Bible is no longer so much a book containing a description of God's actual acts and words as it is a book containing Hebrew interpreta-tions, "creative interpretations" as we call them, which, like the parable of Jonah, tell stories of God's deeds and man's response to express

25. Childs, 52.

26. Hans W. Frei, "David Friedrich Strauss," in *Nineteenth Century Religious Thought in the West,* ed. Ninian Smart et al. (New York: Cambridge Univ. Press, 1985), vol. 1, 215-60.

27. The New Hermeneutic, which has exercised enormous influence on contem-porary homiletics, had its sources in the work of Gerhard Ebeling and Ernst Fuchs in Germany and was introduced in the United States primarily by James Robinson. See James M. Robinson and John B. Cobb, eds., *New Frontiers in Theology,* vol. 2, *The New Hermeneutic* (New York: Harper and Row, 1964).

28. Langdon Gilkey, "Cosmology, Ontology, and the Travail of Biblical Language," *The Journal of Religion* 41 (July 1961): 194-205.

the theological beliefs of Hebrew religion. Thus the Bible is a book descriptive not of the acts of God but of Hebrew religion. . . . For us, then, the Bible is a book of the acts Hebrews believed God might have done and the words he might have said had he done and said them — but of course we recognize that he did not.[29]

Frei himself also critiqued this aspect of the movement, though from a different angle. In *The Eclipse of Biblical Narrative* Frei focused on the referential assumptions about meaning that historical criticism embodied. For historical criticism, according to Frei, a text "meant" by referring to historical events or to some history behind the text; the text became, in short, a "source." Further, Frei pointed out the referential confusion at the heart of the Biblical Theology Movement, which approached Scripture in a doubly referential way. The Bible was understood as referring not only to historical events, but to the historically developing communal interpretation of them.[30] The result, as Gilkey had argued, was confusion. Frei's challenge, however, unlike Gilkey's, came not at the philosophical level of ontology and cosmology, but at the literary level: it was directed at the historical-critical assumption about the referential character of meaning in the biblical narrative.

Thus, from various directions the problems inherent in the notion of the acts of God, which lay at the heart of the Biblical Theology Movement, were revealed. Other elements of the position also came under critique. In several crucial articles James Barr not only pointed out the problems with the notion of the acts of God in history, but raised internal questions about the centrality of the concept of historical revelation itself.[31] In addition, Barr, along with others, both discredited the assertion of the uniqueness of the "Hebrew mind" and refuted

---

29. Gilkey, 197.

30. Frei, *Eclipse*, 181-82; 219-20.

31. James Barr, "Revelation Through History in the Old Testament and in Modern Theology," *Interpretation* 17 (April 1963): 193-205. Barr argues that the emphasis on historical revelation was in many ways an apologetic response to the nineteenth-century concern with history; revelation in history, he points out, is not the only means, and possibly not even the primary means, of divine revelation in the Old Testament. In one of his later articles Barr suggests a turn from history to story as the primary category for biblical theology. Barr's proposal regarding the Old Testament paralleled Frei's work with the New Testament during the same period. Indeed, Barr even cites approvingly Frei's *The Eclipse of Biblical Narrative*. See Barr, "Story and History," 5.

claims about the distinctiveness of the Bible in its original setting.[32] Further, with the development of redaction criticism, the whole question of the unity of the Bible was thrown into chaos; diversity was emphasized more than unity.

By the early sixties, in short, the Biblical Theology Movement faced a crisis. And in 1970 Frei's colleague at Yale, Brevard Childs, not only interpreted this crisis, but began the "quest" for a new biblical theology; he sought an approach that took theological interpretation seriously but avoided the problems of the old Biblical Theology Movement. Childs noted several directions that this new biblical theology should take.[33] First, the church's use of Scripture — the normative function of Scripture within the church — should be the primary context within which the Bible is interpreted.[34] Second, the final, canonical form of the text, rather than its earlier stages or traditions, should be the focus of interpretation. Rather than going "behind" the text, biblical interpretation should focus on the text itself as the church uses it. Third, literary approaches should be given a more prominent role in biblical interpretation. Finally, the tradition of precritical exegesis, which often represented a profound theological exposition of Scripture, should be recovered.

Childs thus set an agenda for the development of a new biblical theology. Moreover, the theologian inspiring this agenda was none other than Karl Barth. As Childs wrote of Barth in a revealing comment: "Barth remained invulnerable to the weaknesses of the Biblical Theology Movement. He would have nothing to do with *Heilsgeschichte*, Hebrew mentality, or unity in diversity in the Bible."[35] Childs thus suggested that in Barth's approach to Scripture lay the future direction of a new biblical theology.

It is in the context of this development of a new biblical theology that Frei's theological project needs to be understood. And it is here that another of his significant contributions to theology in the United States can be recognized. He not only helped to recover the theology of Karl

32. Childs, 71-72.

33. Childs, 97-122.

34. For a discussion of the authoritative function of Scripture within the church, which was important for Frei's work, see the book by Frei's other colleague at Yale, David Kelsey, *The Uses of Scripture in Recent Theology* (Philadelphia: Fortress Press, 1975).

35. Childs, 110.

Barth after the decline of "neo-orthodoxy," but he also helped to appropriate Barth's approach to Scripture (which, of course, was inseparable from his theology). Frei recognized and appreciated the literary character of Barth's exegesis, which treated the Bible as a "text," rather than as a "source."[36] Indeed, before Childs's *Biblical Theology in Crisis* appeared, Frei had not only explicitly linked Barth's exegesis with the literary realism of Erich Auerbach,[37] but had even begun employing this literary approach theologically in his "Theological Reflections on the Gospel Accounts of Jesus' Death and Resurrection" and *The Identity of Jesus Christ.*[38] Frei's other major work of this period, *The Eclipse of Biblical Narrative,* provided an extended critique of historical criticism and argued for a "postcritical," literary approach to biblical narrative along the lines of Barth's exegesis. As Frei wrote in the preface,

> It seems to me that Barth's biblical exegesis is a model of the kind of narrative reading that can be done in the wake of the changes I describe in this book. He distinguishes historical from realistic reading of the theologically most significant biblical narratives without falling into the trap of instantly making history the test of the *meaning* of the realistic form of the stories.[39]

Frei's *Eclipse* was unquestionably a crucial work that provided the intellectual and historical support for a literary approach to Scripture and a new biblical theology.

Not surprisingly, Frei's work addresses, almost point for point, the crucial issues that caused the demise of the Biblical Theology Movement.

36. Frei, *Types,* 81, 11.

37. Frei, "Karl Barth: Theologian," 5-7.

38. Hans W. Frei, "Theological Reflections on the Gospel Accounts of Jesus' Death and Resurrection," *The Christian Scholar* 49 (Winter 1966): 263-306. This is one of Frei's most important essays. It is an earlier version of *The Identity of Jesus Christ* and is in some ways superior to the later work, primarily because it is not concerned with the rather confusing matter of "presence." The essay has been reprinted in Frei, *Theology and Narrative.*

39. Frei, *Eclipse,* viii. Frei cites in particular Barth's "remarkable use" of figural interpretation in the *Church Dogmatics,* II, 2, *The Doctrine of God,* ed. G. W. Bromiley and T. F. Torrance, trans. G. W. Bromiley et al. (Edinburgh: T & T Clark, 1957), 340-409; and Barth's narrative treatment of the gospel story in *Church Dogmatics,* IV, 1, *The Doctrine of Reconciliation,* ed. G. W. Bromiley and T. F. Torrance, trans. G. W. Bromiley (Edinburgh: T & T Clark, 1956), 224-28.

Most basically, his turn to a "non-referential" literary reading of Scripture challenged the old dichotomy between theology and historical criticism. The notion of the acts of God in history was accordingly rejected in explorations of the *meaning* of the biblical text.[40] More specifically, as I will discuss below, Frei's literary approach sought to overcome the old dichotomy between the "Jesus of History" and the "Christ of Faith," which was itself a result of the rift between historical criticism and theology.

This characteristic of Frei's work was immediately noted by readers. In a comment on Frei's "Theological Reflections," Amos Wilder wrote, "Frei is taking a literary approach, rather than a historical or a theological approach."[41] Wilder's comment reveals both the dominance of the other two categories and the new direction that Frei took. For Frei, a literary approach, unlike historical criticism, enabled a theological interpretation of Scripture, as he tried to demonstrate in *The Identity of Jesus Christ*. Frei's "narrative theology" is in fact primarily a biblical theology focused on the gospel narratives.

In addition, Frei's literary reading provided a way of dealing with other problems inherent in the older Biblical Theology Movement. For example, Frei's narrative approach offered a specific interpretation of the unity of Scripture. Frei focused on the final form of the text, rather than on the variety of "pieces" that went into the composition of the Bible. In addition, like Barth, he not only stressed the Christological unity of Scripture, but defended typology (or figuration) as the vehicle through which this unity is manifested in the biblical narrative.[42]

Frei's theological approach to biblical narrative also avoided claims about the uniqueness of the "Hebrew mentality" or of biblical concepts. Biblical theology, as Frei understood it, always involved "conceptual redescription," rather than merely a rote repetition of the biblical language or concepts. For Frei it was the specific "logic" of the biblical narrative that was crucial, not the particular concepts in which that logic was embodied. As he tried to demonstrate in *The Identity of Jesus Christ*,

---

40. That is, the *meaning* of the text was different from its historical or ideal referent. Questions of history and truth, which, for Frei, were of a different order from questions of meaning, could be raised only after the necessary literary analysis had helped one discern the proper way of raising them.

41. Amos Wilder, "Comment," *The Christian Scholar* 49 (Winter 1966): 307.

42. Frei's concern for the unity of Scripture and his defense of typology as a unitive device are in evidence throughout *Eclipse*.

it was possible, in a modest, *ad hoc* fashion, to employ contemporary descriptive categories in theological interpretation.[43]

Frei does seem to make stronger claims for the uniqueness of the biblical materials in their Ancient Near East setting. He repeatedly sets the "realistic narrative" of the gospels over against the savior myths of the ancient world.[44] However, his approach does not depend on grand generalizations about the uniqueness of the Bible in this respect. Rather, his focus is on the specific character of a particular narrative. The appearance of other "realistic narratives" in the ancient world would not present a challenge to his position.

Thus, Frei's literary approach to Scripture explicitly or implicitly addressed the various issues that had plagued the Biblical Theology Movement. Within the American context, Frei's work needs to be understood as a search for a new biblical theology. Once again, largely because of Frei's work, it was Karl Barth who served as the catalyst for the development of this new biblical theology. In the intimately related areas of theology and biblical interpretation, Frei's distinctive interpretation and appropriation of Barth's work represents his most significant contribution to theology in the United States.

Faith and History

The question of the relationship between faith and history, inherited from nineteenth-century academic theology, was a central concern of

---

43. I will examine this matter in detail in Chapter Two.

44. Drawing on Erich Auerbach's influential book, *Mimesis*, Frei highlights four basic characteristics of "realistic narrative." First, the narrative shape, including chronological sequence, is indispensable to the meaning, theme, or subject matter of the story. Second, "subject and social setting belong together, and characters and external circumstances fitly render each other. Neither character nor circumstance separately, nor yet their interaction, is a shadow of something else more real or more significant." Third, in light of the first and second characteristics, realistic narrative is "history-like" (but not historically referential at the level of meaning, a confusion which created the problems that Frei examines in *Eclipse*). Fourth, realistic narrative is a style in which "the sublime or at least the serious effect mingles inextricably with the quality of what is casual, random, ordinary, and everyday" (Frei, *Eclipse*, 13-14). See Erich Auerbach, *Mimesis: The Representation of Reality in Western Literature,* trans. Willard R. Trask (Princeton, New Jersey: Princeton Univ. Press, 1953; Princeton Paperback Edition, 1974).

American theology in the middle of the twentieth century. As I noted above, the Biblical Theology Movement ran into problems largely because of its inability to deal with this issue. In addition, "neo-orthodox" theology was also occupied with the faith-and-history question, as the work of the Niebuhrs reveals. The issue was part of the theological air that Frei breathed, particularly at Yale University, where, under the influence of H. Richard Niebuhr, the question was at the very center of the theological agenda. It is thus not surprising that the relationship between faith and history was a central concern of Frei's throughout his theological career.

For Frei the issue took two forms. First, there was the question of the relationship between theology and the historical-critical method, which I discussed in examining Frei's relationship to the Biblical Theology Movement. Frei's best known work, *The Eclipse of Biblical Narrative*, focused on this aspect of the problem. Second, there was the issue of the relationship between the "Jesus of history" and the "Christ of faith," a problem that had plagued theology since the introduction of the historical method. Frei's constructive theological work was directly addressed to this second issue.[45]

This second form of the issue is my concern in this section, not only because of its importance for understanding Frei's work in general, but because of its significance for appreciating Frei's distinctiveness within the American context. Frei sought to move beyond the old categories ("Jesus of history"–"Christ of faith") and to offer a new approach to this issue. In the process he not only tried to address the issue more directly and substantively than had Barth, but he also challenged the particular existentialist treatment of this question that had been dominant in the American context, specifically in the New Quest of the Historical Jesus.[46] I will thus address this aspect of Frei's work by examining both the unique method by which he sought to deal with the problem and the challenge he presented to existentialist approaches.

In his essay "Theological Reflections on the Gospel Accounts of Jesus' Death and Resurrection" and in his later book *The Identity of*

---

45. By "constructive work" I have in mind "Theological Reflections" and *Identity*. Frei also dealt with this second issue historically in his essay "David Friedrich Strauss."

46. Frei clearly felt that Barth had not adequately dealt with the historical question (Frei, *Types*, 6, 90-91).

Jesus Christ, Frei is clearly concerned with the question of the relationship between the "Jesus of history" and the "Christ of faith." In "Theological Reflections" Frei concludes with an "Excursus" in which he directly critiques the New Quest of the Historical Jesus. In *Identity* Frei explicitly sets his understanding of Jesus' "identity" and "presence" over against earlier positions that had virtually equated identity with the "Jesus of history" and presence with the "Christ of faith."[47] In both works Frei sought to move beyond the old categories and to challenge the presuppositions that created the problem in the first place.

The approach Frei takes is strikingly original. He does not draw at all on historical method. He does not seek to discern the true "historical Jesus" in the manner of the "old quest." Nor does he employ any kind of "external evidence," after the manner of Wolfhart Pannenberg.[48] Nor does Frei accept the approach of the New Quest, which sought the historical Jesus in the self-understanding expressed in his authentic words (especially the parables) with the aid of an esoteric combination of existentialism and ontology drawn from the later Heidegger.[49] Rather, Frei seeks to address this issue on the basis of the internal logic of Christian belief through a literary analysis of the gospel narratives. More specifically, Frei undertakes an Anselmian "proof" to demonstrate that disbelief in the resurrection is rationally impossible for Christians.[50] Indeed, it is within this Anselmian framework that the subtitle of *Identity,* "The Hermeneutical Bases of Dogmatic Theology," makes sense. The book seeks to examine as formally and analytically as possible the hermeneutical logic of the church's *Credo* as it is embodied in the structure of the gospel narratives.[51]

The character of *Identity* as an Anselmian "proof" is evident throughout, revealing the extraordinary influence of Anselm, through

47. Frei, *Identity,* 86.

48. Frei, "Theological Reflections," 264. Frei's work can be seen in conjunction with Pannenberg's and Moltmann's early work as a response to the virtual equation of resurrection with Christian faith in Bultmann's project. Thus, Frei's adamant rejection of myth in both "Theological Reflections" and *Identity.* See Frei, "German Theology," 109-10.

49. For Frei's most concise discussion of Fuchs's and Ebeling's work, see "German Theology," 108-9.

50. Frei, *Identity,* 152.

51. I have borrowed the term *Credo* from Barth, *Anselm.*

Barth, on Frei. To begin with, the framework of Frei's argument is that of faith seeking understanding. Like Anselm in the *Proslogion,* Frei both begins and ends by affirming the centrality of worship and praise to his undertaking. As Frei writes, "By and large, then, reflection about the presence of Christ is, for the believer, a pleasurable exercise in arranging or, as I should prefer to say, ordering his thinking about his faith and — in a certain sense — praise of God by the use of analytical capacities"; it is "an exercise of ordering and of praise."[52] In addition, as the emphasis on praise makes clear, Frei asserts that he is engaged in "reflection within belief." He seeks to examine the way believers talk about their relation to Christ: ". . . we talk about the relation to Christ as if it were already established and I simply wanted a kind of descriptive expansion."[53] Frei's work is not "neutral,"

52. Frei, *Identity,* 5.

53. Frei, *Identity,* 4. Frei understood Anselm's *Proslogion* to be a "reflection on the *grammar* of the word *God* as it is used in the Christian Church" (Frei, *Types,* 79). In a parallel way Frei is reflecting on the "grammar" of the way the words "presence" and "identity" are used about Jesus Christ in the church. I will discuss Frei's Anselmian theological method in more detail in Chapter Two. However, at this point in *Identity* one finds a key to the issue of "reference" in Frei's work. The question of reference cannot be considered apart from the church. Two points need to be emphasized. First, Frei here suggests that it is not the biblical text that "refers," but rather speakers in the community of faith who witness to the risen Christ. The text renders the identity of the risen Christ who is present in the church, and in that sense may "refer" indirectly by helping the church to speak of Christ. However, as Stanley Hauerwas has astutely argued with regard to Frei's work, "the narrative does not refer, but rather people do." Stanley Hauerwas, "The Church as God's New Language," in *Christian Existence Today* (Durham, North Carolina: Labyrinth Press, 1988), 59-60. The question of reference must be located not at the level of the text, but at the level of speakers. Second, the "performative" function of Scripture in the church must also be taken into account. As James William McClendon has argued on the basis of speech-act theory, the primary function of Scripture is not a referential one, but the performative one of forming a people. See James William McClendon, *Systematic Theology: Ethics* (Nashville: Abingdon Press, 1986), 334-46. Frei himself has written provocatively in this vein: ". . . when Christians speak of the Spirit as the indirect presence now of Jesus Christ and of the God who is one with him, they refer to the church. The church is both the witness to that presence and the public and communal form the indirect presence of Christ now takes, in contrast to his direct presence in his earthly days" (Frei, *Identity,* 157). Here Frei suggests that Christian speech about the presence of Christ actually *refers* to the *church.* Again, the emphasis is on speakers, rather than on a text. And the suggestion is that the identity of Jesus Christ is rendered for the upbuilding of the people who are called to embody his presence in and for the world. Thus, the speech of the church both witnesses to Jesus

but is embedded within the larger framework of Christian belief and practice.[54]

The parallels to Anselm, however, run even deeper than this general faith-seeking-understanding method. In fact, the similarities between Frei and Anselm occur at every point in the book. For example, *within the framework of belief,* Frei, like Anselm, seeks to carry out his project as formally and analytically as possible. The main difference from Anselm is that Frei is guided not simply by abstract, logical reflection, but by an analysis of the structure of the gospel narratives through particular categories of identity description.[55]

Moreover, Frei's argument and conclusions run parallel to those of Anselm's *Proslogion.* Indeed, the aim of the work is difficult to understand apart from these parallels. For example, toward the end of "Theological Reflections" Frei consciously imitates Anselm's argument — even incorporating a dialogical dimension so customary with Anselm — to summarize his point:

> In a sense (if I may put it in a manner totally uncongenial to them) the synoptic Gospel writers are saying something like this: "Our argument is that to grasp what *this* identity, Jesus of Nazareth, is, is to believe that, in fact, he has been raised from the dead. Someone may reply that in that case the most perfectly depicted character, the most nearly life-like fictional identity ought also in fact to live a factual historical life. We answer that the argument holds good only in this one and absolutely unique case where the described identity (the "WHAT" of him) is totally identical with his factual existence. He *is* the resurrection and the life; how can he be conceived as not resurrected?

Christ and refers to itself as the embodiment of his presence in and for the world. The function of the gospel narratives in rendering Jesus' identity is connected with both of these kinds of speech.

54. George Hunsinger, "Hans Frei As Theologian: The Quest for a Generous Orthodoxy," *Modern Theology* 8 (April 1992): 114. A revised version of this essay appears in Frei, *Theology and Narrative.*

55. In this respect, Frei's work is even less apologetic than Anselm's; it is closer to dogmatics. As Hunsinger notes, Frei's project involves "clarifying the place of certain literary and logical considerations within a larger if mostly tacit dogmatic framework" (Hunsinger, "Hans Frei as Theologian," 117). Frei states at the beginning of *Identity* that he is doing neither apologetics nor dogmatics, which is a fitting characterization of an Anselmian "proof" (Frei, *Identity,* 1, 3).

It may be dubious wisdom to make Luke or John speak like a late eleventh-century theologian. But something like this argument seems to me to be present in the resurrection account.[56]

Frei concludes, "There is a kind of logic in a Christian's faith that forces him to say that disbelief in the resurrection of Jesus is rationally impossible."[57]

The Identity of Jesus Christ, then, is an Anselmian "proof" for the reality of the resurrection based on the logic of Christian belief. In contemporary terms, for believers the resurrection is a "fact," though a unique one.[58] Having established this point on the basis of the internal logic of Christian belief, Frei then addresses the historical question.[59] And he clearly affirms the historical character of the Christian faith and, indirectly at least, the *unique* historical character of the resurrection. Although the resurrection, because it is a unique event, can never be verified by historical methods, it *could* conceivably be *disproven* by his-

---

56. Frei, "Theological Reflections," 299; italics mine. Frei employs the same argument in *Identity,* though he leaves out the reference to late eleventh-century theologians (*Identity,* 145-46). Kevin J. Vanhoozer summarizes Frei's point here in a helpful way: "The Gospel narratives are unique: they break out of their fictional description to a factual claim." Vanhoozer also recognizes the Anselmian character of Frei's argument in *Identity:* "Where Anselm asks us to consider the identity of God, the 'being-than-which-nothing-greater-can-be-conceived,' Frei asks us to consider the identity of the risen Jesus, the 'one-who-cannot-be-thought-of-except-as-now-present.'" Kevin J. Vanhoozer, *Biblical Narrative in the Philosophy of Paul Ricoeur* (Cambridge: Cambridge Univ. Press, 1990), 163-64. Significantly, Frei keeps his point in the negative: Jesus' "nonresurrection" is "inconceivable" for believers. This, of course, does not mean that the resurrection, which is a unique, eschatological event, is *conceivable* (Frei, *Identity,* 145).

57. Frei, "Theological Reflections," 302; Frei, *Identity,* 151-52.

58. Frei was very much aware that the concept of a "fact" is a modern one, and certainly not a transcultural or "theory neutral one." Here Frei is simply saying that if one thinks in terms of "facts," then Jesus' resurrection cannot be conceived as not being one. See Frei's brief but important late essay "Response to 'Narrative Theology: An Evangelical Appraisal,'" *Trinity Journal* 8 (Spring 1987): 24. This essay has been reprinted in Frei, *Theology and Narrative.*

59. One of Frei's central arguments is that the historical question is different from the question of meaning; it cannot be addressed until the logic of the narratives is understood. Otherwise, the historical question will be addressed in the wrong way. Frei's argument, as I will discuss below, is that the historical question becomes both possible and necessary at the point of the resurrection. Frei's move is not a simplistically referential one, but an indirect one based on the logic of Christian belief and the gospel narratives.

torical investigation. The Christian faith remains a risky historical venture.[60]

Frei's argument is quite complex and highly qualified; I have hardly done it justice in this brief treatment. And, of course, there are numerous points at which the argument could be criticized.[61] However, the key point is that Frei's concern here is to find a path beyond the old categories of "Jesus of history" and "Christ of faith," as these had been understood for generations. Indeed, part of Frei's theological contribution lies just here, in his ability to discern the ways in which the conceptions of certain problems limit the discussion of them and lead theological reflection down dead-end streets.

Equally important, however, is the way in which Frei relocates the question of "historicity." He not only moves it from "external" considerations to the "internal" logic of Christian belief, but within that "logic," he locates the issue at the point of the resurrection. Here, Frei argues, Jesus is most truly "historical" — in the sense of most uniquely himself;[62] here, according to the logic of the gospel narratives, is the point at which the question of historicity becomes both possible and necessary.[63] In this way, too, Frei shifts the focus of the debate significantly. The historical question arises not in relation to the details of Jesus' earthly life, as it had in the "old quest"; nor does it arise in relation to Jesus' linguistically expressed, existential self-understanding, as it did for the New Quest; nor is it linked with Jesus' consciousness or self-understanding, as it often was in both "quests." Rather, the crucial historical question arises first and foremost at the point of the resurrection, which presents a challenge not only to

---

60. Frei, "Theological Reflections," 302; Frei, *Identity*, 150-52.

61. For example, Frei would do better, I think, to discuss the resurrection in eschatological terms, rather than in terms of "unique historical fact," though I think he has the eschatological dimension of the resurrection in mind here. Frei's decision to speak, however uneasily, of a "unique historical fact" simply reveals his concern to address the "Jesus of history"–"Christ of faith" issue. In addition, Frei clearly makes a huge jump from the "necessity" of the resurrection to the necessity of Christ's "presence" to the believer. Further, questions could be raised about his use of Ryle's philosophy of mind in his description of Jesus' identity. And one does have to wonder if Frei takes Jesus' life and ministry seriously enough. However, these criticisms do not have to be developed here. I am simply seeking to demonstrate Frei's concern for a particular issue and the distinctive way in which he treated it.

62. Frei, "Theological Reflections," 292-96.

63. Frei, "Theological Reflections," 298-99; Frei, *Identity*, 143-47.

Bultmann's demythologization of the resurrection, but also to earlier conceptions of the historical issue. Frei's project may or may not be successful. Indeed, Frei himself recognized that he had hardly solved the problem.[64] However, Frei did seek to address the historical question; and he did so in a way that broke fresh ground for future reflection.

In addition to Frei's distinctive methodological challenge to the basic categories of the "Jesus of history"–"Christ of faith" debate, his approach also offered a specific critique of existentialist treatments of this problem. Indeed, it was over against the "post-Bultmannian" New Quest of the Historical Jesus that Frei developed his distinctive position. Further, it is in this debate that the significance of Frei's appropriation of Gilbert Ryle's work can be seen. At a time when existentialism was the dominant philosophy appropriated by Protestant theologians in America, Frei turned to the analytical philosophy of Ryle. Frei's rejection of existentialism and his "modest" appropriation of Ryle's philosophy in his understanding of human identity further suggest Frei's distinctive theological position in the American context at the middle of the century. His combination of the continental theology of Barth and the Anglo-American philosophy of Ryle distinguishes him from other American Protestant theologians of the period.[65]

Frei rejected two forms of the existentialist approach to the faith-and-history question, that of Bultmann himself and that of the "post-Bultmannians." First of all, throughout his work he criticized the position of Bultmann, which posited two histories, one "objective," one "existential." For Frei this attempt to find a middle ground between an "unrevelational history" and an "unhistorical revelation" was a false solution to the problem.[66] Further, although Frei is considerably more

---

64. Frei, "Strauss," 1: 255.

65. Frei's application of Ryle's category of intention-action to Jesus' identity was closely related to his interpretation of Barth's own view of personhood as "self enacted agency or performative project." Hans W. Frei, "Barth and Schleiermacher: Divergence and Convergence," in *Barth and Schleiermacher: Beyond the Impasse,* ed. James O. Duke and Robert F. Streetman (Philadelphia: Fortress Press, 1988), 72. This essay has been reprinted in Frei, *Theology and Narrative.*

66. Frei, "Religion: Natural and Revealed," 318. This position, as is characteristic of liberal theology, loses the unique, unsubstitutable identity of Jesus and offers an inadequate reading of the realistic narrative of the gospels. In addition, Bultmann's existentialist anthropology was too individualistic and ahistorical. See also Frei, "German Theology," 109.

sympathetic to H. Richard Niebuhr's "internal" and "external" history, Frei ultimately rejected that position as well.[67] Niebuhr's lingering, existentialist "faith method" tended too much toward critical idealism to be acceptable to Frei.[68] Niebuhr, Frei concluded, was "more sympathetic to Bultmann than to Barth."[69] Frei himself explicitly rejected any notion of "two histories."[70]

In fact, Frei's project was in many ways increasingly an attempt to move from the subjective elements of idealism and existentialism to more public approaches to identity, the church, and history.[71] In *The Identity of Jesus Christ*, for example, Frei interprets the identity of the historical church just as he interprets the identity of Jesus — in a public way. He applies the categories of intention-action and self-manifestation

67. For Niebuhr's account of "internal" and "external" history see *The Meaning of Revelation* (New York: Macmillan, 1941; Macmillan Paperbacks Edition, 1960), 32-66.

68. Frei, "H. Richard Niebuhr on History, Church, and Nation," 223-24. Frei was nevertheless very appreciative of the complexity of Niebuhr's thought and the tensions within it; he refused to lump Niebuhr simplistically with other liberal theologians. For Frei, however, Niebuhr never made the decision between a "narrative and a transnarrative universal understanding of God's acts in history." Niebuhr always sought to go beyond the particular to more general, universal frameworks, despite his profound appreciation for historical particularity. This was the source of the deep tensions in Niebuhr's work. Finally, however, in his quest for universal frameworks, Niebuhr remained too "modern." Frei did, however, appreciate Niebuhr's confessionalism and the way he tried to relate story and concept. Frei's early and late criticisms of *The Meaning of Revelation*, one of the seminal works for "narrative theology," may account for the fact that Frei actually appears to have been little influenced in his approach to narrative by Niebuhr's book. Frei was actually more impressed by Niebuhr's treatment of history, including the significance of language, narrative, and tradition, in *The Kingdom of God in America*. As I will discuss below, Frei was also profoundly influenced by Niebuhr's treatment of Christology in *Christ and Culture*. See Frei, "H. Richard Niebuhr on History, Church, and Nation."

69. Frei, "H. Richard Niebuhr on History, Church, and Nation," 228.

70. Frei, *Identity*, 160-61.

71. Although Frei never clarified the problems with idealism in any extended way, he reacts against characteristics of several kinds of idealism. First, he rejects the "turn to the subject," with its often attendant assertions about the "transcendent ego," which is present in some forms of idealism. Second, Frei rejects the tendency of idealism toward grand theories and systems. Finally, Frei rejects the tendency of idealism to make the theory of knowledge central in philosophy and theology, whether it takes the form of an epistemology in philosophy or an account of Christian experience or the like in theology. His rejection of idealism at this point is closely related to his rejection of the liberal theology inspired by it. See White, "Barth's Theological Realism," 55.

both to Jesus and to the church, which receives its identity from him.[72] Later in his life, as Frei turned to a cultural-linguistic model of religion, he would move even further in this direction; he would conceive religion itself not as a dimension of consciousness or experience, but as a public, social phenomenon.[73]

Second, Frei rejected the "post-Bultmannian" New Quest of the Historical Jesus.[74] Indeed, the descriptive categories of intention-action and self-manifestation, which Frei employed in "Theological Reflections" and *Identity*, were an integral part of his critique of the New Quest. Through both of these categories he challenged a "ghost-in-the-machine" approach to human identity, which, he argued, was still present in existentialism.[75] The intention-action model, borrowed from Ryle, located human identity at the public level, rather than in some inner consciousness or self-understanding "behind the scene."[76] Frei, however, did not argue this point on general, anthropological grounds. Rather, he argued that this approach to identity was more faithful to the character of the "realistic narrative" of the gospels, which rendered Jesus' identity through the interplay of character and incident.[77] At-

---

72. Frei, *Identity*, 154-65.

73. I will discuss Frei's cultural-linguistic model of religion in detail in Chapter Three.

74. The primary American work on the New Quest is James M. Robinson, *A New Quest of the Historical Jesus* (London: SCM Press, 1959; repr., Philadelphia: Fortress Press, 1983). This "quest" was intimately related to the New Hermeneutic of Gerhard Ebeling and Ernst Fuchs. Robinson (*New Quest*, 7) contends that the New Quest reached its most valid formulation in Gerhard Ebeling's response to Bultmann in *Theology and Proclamation: Dialogues With Bultmann*, trans. John Riches (Philadelphia: Fortress Press, 1966).

75. Frei, "Theological Reflections," 278; Frei, *Identity*, 41.

76. Frei adopted Ryle's categories for modest, descriptive purposes. He was aware of the limitations of Ryle's position and certainly did not subscribe to it in all its details or as a general, systematic theory. He simply used the categories descriptively. For Ryle's position see his major work, *The Concept of Mind* (London: Hutchinson, 1949; repr., Chicago: Univ. of Chicago Press, 1984).

77. Frei was fond of quoting Henry James: "What is character but the determination of incident? What is incident but the illustration of character?" (Henry James, "The Art of Fiction," in *The Future of the Novel*, ed. Leon Edel [New York: Vintage Books, 1956], 15-16; cited in Frei, *Identity*, 88; Frei, *Eclipse*, 14). Here the influence of Auerbach is also important. Indeed, Frei's appropriation of Ryle and Auerbach in the service of a Barthian theology goes a long way toward clarifying the distinctiveness of his work. For an excellent discussion of the convergence of Barth, Ryle, and Auerbach in Frei's work,

tempts to get at Jesus' consciousness in the nineteenth century or at his self-understanding in the New Quest were all of one piece; they had to go "behind" the gospels in order to infer Jesus' true identity.[78] They did not take seriously the character of the gospels as "realistic narratives."

The self-manifestation category also challenged a fundamental presupposition of existentialism: the alienation of the true self from its public enactment. Again, this presupposition required an inference about Jesus' true identity "behind" the interplay of character and incident in the gospels.[79] Frei, however, rejected the self-alienation approach, not only because he felt it was in conflict with the gospel narratives, but also because he thought the position contained within it an implicit "ghost-in-the-machine" view of human identity.[80] While Frei recognized the elusive character of any self-manifestation, he nevertheless affirmed a positive connection between the enacted, public self and the real self.[81]

Thus, Frei's more public understanding of human identity, grounded fundamentally in the "realistic narrative" of the gospels, led to his direct challenge to existentialist views of human identity and to his critique of the New Quest of the Historical Jesus. As he succinctly summarized his concern,

> The implication of what I want to suggest is that those who endeavor old and new "quests" for the historical Jesus as well as their opponents have looked for Jesus' identity with a faulty, one-sided understanding of identity. They end with abstractions of their own making, in which

---

see William C. Placher, "Introduction," in Hans W. Frei, *Theology and Narrative: Selected Essays,* ed. George Hunsinger and William C. Placher (New York: Oxford Univ. Press, 1993), 3-25.

78. As Robinson states, the New Quest was concerned to penetrate the "deeper" reality of the historical Jesus — "the depths at which the reality of history lies"; the "depths beneath the surface at which man actually exists"; "his understanding of existence behind what he does" (Robinson, *New Quest,* 28-29; 39-40).

79. Frei, "Theological Reflections," 303-6.

80. Frei, "Theological Reflections," 286-89. Frei, like Barth, wants to move from the identity of Jesus to human identity in general. Therefore, he does not argue for his conception of identity primarily on general anthropological grounds, though those are certainly implicit, but on the basis of the character of the gospels as "realistic narratives."

81. Frei himself expressed doubts about the category of self-manifestation in his later preface to *The Identity of Jesus Christ* (vii-ix). The category smacked too much of idealism. Increasingly, Frei emphasized the social character of selves.

the being of Jesus is finally not intrinsically connected with narratable occurrences and such events therefore have no genuine significance. Moreover, both have looked for Jesus' identity with a faulty, one-sided view of the New Testament narrative as *purely* historical and/or kerygmatic — never literary.[82]

Considering the enormous influence of various forms of existentialism on Protestant theology at midcentury, Frei's departure was a significant one indeed.

In sum, although Hans Frei published only two books during his lifetime, he made an extraordinary contribution to American theology. His distinctive interpretation and appropriation of Barth's theology helped to secure a place for Barth in contemporary theology following the collapse of "neo-orthodoxy." In addition, his literary approach to Scripture, which sought to overcome the old dichotomy between theology and historical criticism, not only contributed to the development of a new biblical theology, but also challenged the dominance of the historical-critical method and helped to secure a place for a literary approach to Scripture. Frei's own literary interpretation of the gospel narratives represents his most significant contribution to the development of "narrative theology" in the United States. Finally, Frei not only suggested a new Christological path beyond the old "Jesus of history"–"Christ of faith" debate, but in the process challenged the dominant, existentialist philosophical orientation of midcentury American theology.

All of these contributions are woven into a unified fabric in Frei's rich and complex thought, so that it is quite difficult to disentangle individual pieces. Moreover, all of the strands come together in Frei's Christology, where his theological project, his literary approach to Scripture, and his understanding of identity bore particularly rich fruit. As George Stroup has written,

---

82. Frei, "Theological Reflections," 290. The "opponents" Frei refers to are Schubert Ogden and Van Harvey, who wrote an important critique of Robinson's book: "How New Is the 'New Quest of the Historical Jesus'?" in *The Historical Jesus and the Kerygmatic Christ: Essays on the New Quest of the Historical Jesus*, ed. Carl E. Braaten and Roy A. Harrisville (Nashville: Abingdon Press, 1964), 197-242. According to Frei, Ogden and Harvey shared Robinson's basic presuppositions about identity (Frei, "Theological Reflections," 303-6).

Frei's "experiment" in [*The Identity of Jesus Christ*] is a bold attempt
to reconstruct Christology and the doctrine of God, not in terms of
the classical categories of nature, substance, and being, but in terms
of the categories of intention and action. For Frei, Jesus "becomes
who he is in the story by consenting to God's intention and by
enacting that intention in the midst of the circumstances that devolve
around him as the fulfillment of God's purpose." That is an exciting
proposal. It suggests that a new reading of the Gospels might provide
not only new information about Jesus and the One he calls "Father,"
but a new construal of the reality of both.[83]

In somewhat different terms, David Ford has also noted Frei's contribution in this area. In citing key marks of the "Yale School," Ford mentions
first of all the "emphasis on the unsubstitutable identity of Jesus Christ,
rendered primarily in narrative form, as the main way of doing justice
to Christian particularity. . . ."[84] Although applied to the "Yale School,"
this comment is appropriately applied to Frei himself. For it is here, in
his emphasis on the unique, unsubstitutable identity of Jesus Christ,
that the various strands of Frei's work come to their most significant
juncture. And it is here that Frei's larger theological project, his challenge
to modern theological liberalism, finds its focus.

---

83. George Stroup, "Theology of Narrative or Narrative Theology? A Response
to *Why Narrative?*" *Theology Today* 47 (January 1991): 429. Stroup quotes Frei, *Identity*,
107.

84. David Ford, "Hans Frei and the Future of Theology," *Modern Theology* 8 (April
1992): 207.

Chapter Two

Frei and Modern Theological Liberalism

During the sixties American theology had generally rejected "neo-orthodoxy" and "biblical theology" and was embracing forms of liberalism and the new "secularism." In this context Frei labored away in obscurity with little intellectual support or encouragement from others. Nevertheless, despite the lack of interest in his work, Frei went quietly and carefully about his research, pursuing those matters that seemed intrinsically important to him and developing his distinctive theological position.[1] Indeed, in thinking about Frei the theologian during this period, I have been reminded of words that Karl Barth spoke to his students in the summer of 1933 as the situation in Germany deteriorated: "only quite serious theological work can have any real significance."[2]

As has already become evident, it was in fact Karl Barth who most profoundly influenced Frei's theology. In his massive dissertation on Barth's break with liberalism, Frei highlighted the issues that were to be intrinsically important for him and signaled the direction that his own work would take. In fact, both the critical and the constructive dimensions of Frei's own project are already evident in his dissertation, revealing the close connection between Barth's theological position and Frei's own. On the critical side, Barth's break with liberalism, the focus

---

1. George Lindbeck, "Hans Frei and the Future of Theology in America," December 2, 1988, TMs [photocopy], p. 26.
2. Eberhard Busch, *Karl Barth: His Life From Letters and Autobiographical Texts,* trans. John Bowden (Philadelphia: Fortress Press, 1976), 225.

of the dissertation, would be taken up by Frei in his own work. Like
Barth, Frei was concerned with the sovereign freedom of God.[3] *Soli Deo
gloria* was for him the first and last concern of the theologian, as he
reminded his colleagues in his final lecture:

> Why, we might ask of H. Richard Niebuhr, be a theologian in our
> utterly untheological times? I think he would have made short shrift
> of that question. He would have asserted, I believe, that our responsi-
> bility to affirm the glory of the Lord, and his glory alone, has not
> been altered one whit, and that this remains our duty in propitious
> and unpropitious times.[4]

As David Ford has written of Frei, "One thing is clear: however it
happened, one tended to come away from any thorough theological
engagement with Frei with the impression that God mattered more than
anything. . . ."[5] Here was the affinity with Barth at the deepest level.
And here was Frei's ultimate reason for rejecting liberalism.

On the constructive side, Barth's turn to Anselm and biblical realism would play a central role in Frei's own theological project, even
as he interpreted and appropriated Barth's work in a "postmodern,"
linguistic direction.[6] Frei's Anselmian approach to theology, which he

---

3. As will become clear in what follows, Frei's theocentrism, following that of
Barth, was more Christocentric than that of H. Richard Niebuhr, a fact that does not
make Frei's position any less theocentric than Niebuhr's "radical monotheism." In fact,
one could say that Barth and Frei are theocentric enough to let God be "self-focused"
in Jesus Christ because God has freely and sovereignly chosen to do that. See Hans W.
Frei, "Karl Barth: Theologian," in *Karl Barth and the Future of Theology: A Memorial
Colloquium Held at the Yale Divinity School, January 28, 1969,* ed. David L. Dickerman
(New Haven: Yale Divinity School Association, 1969), 8. The distinction between theocentric and Christocentric is a false issue for Frei.

4. Hans W. Frei, "H. Richard Niebuhr on History, Church, and Nation," in Hans W.
Frei, *Theology and Narrative: Selected Essays,* ed. George Hunsinger and William C.
Placher (New York: Oxford Univ. Press, 1993), 231. This was Frei's final essay, which was
read at the Niebuhr conference by someone else because Frei was too ill to be present.

5. David Ford, "Hans Frei and the Future of Theology," *Modern Theology* 8 (April
1992): 211.

6. In his dissertation Frei argued that Anselm and biblical realism provided the two
critical pieces of Barth's constructive theology. On biblical realism see Hans W. Frei, *The
Doctrine of Revelation in the Thought of Karl Barth, 1909-1922: The Nature of Barth's Break
With Liberalism* (Ann Arbor, Michigan: University Microfilms, 1956), 386-98, 487-503.
Biblical realism is consistently associated with *preaching* in the dissertation, suggesting

learned from Barth, and his interpretation of the gospels as "realistic narratives" (a postcritical development of biblical realism) serve as Frei's main constructive tools not only for challenging liberalism, but for dealing with the other concerns that he encountered in his theological context. In many ways, then, Frei set out his own agenda in the dissertation.[7] Following the completion of his dissertation Frei spent many years quietly and carefully developing his own distinctive theological approach based on this initial study of Barth.

Frei's Critique of Liberalism

Although Frei was an irenic spirit, who has been characterized as possessing a "diffident definiteness,"[8] and although most of his work — not to mention his writing style — lacks the polemical edge of Barth, one should not take lightly the radicalness of Frei's theological project. From the beginning, as his dissertation suggests, he was drawn to Barth's bold break with liberalism, and time and again he relishes Barth's daring theological moves. Frei's work, in its own way, also represented a significant break with the liberal theological tradition. As George Hunsinger has written of Frei's main theological work, *The Identity of Jesus Christ:*

> Frei has nothing less far-reaching in view than to break with the entire modern liberal tradition in theology, while still remaining within the purview of that tradition to the extent that he does not wish merely to relapse into the pitfalls of the older orthodoxy. He wishes to accept and yet subvert the liberal tradition by simultaneously correcting and outbidding it.[9]

---

that Frei's approach to the gospels as realistic narratives may be particularly important for the Christian pulpit, even though Frei himself did not develop these implications.

7. Even some of the more specific concerns that would occupy Frei are explored in the dissertation. For example, the question of the relationship between literary form, content, and intention occupies a significant place in Frei's examination of the two editions of Barth's *Romans* (Frei, *Doctrine of Revelation*, 91-105). This issue is closely related to that of the relationship between philosophical concepts and theology, which also occupies an important place in the dissertation.

8. Ford, 203.

9. George Hunsinger, "Hans Frei As Theologian: The Quest for a Generous Orthodoxy," *Modern Theology* 8 (April 1992): 104.

Through his careful study of theological and hermeneutical developments in the eighteenth and nineteenth centuries, Frei sought unapologetically to develop a "postliberal" theology, which would overcome
the deficiencies of liberalism without returning to the problems associated with orthodoxy.[10]

However, simply to assert in a general way that Frei sought to
"correct and outbid" the liberal theological tradition is inadequate. "Liberalism" is a large term that is used in various ways; and the critique of
liberal theology has come from various directions. For example, in the
United States one of the most outspoken critics of liberal theology was
Reinhold Niebuhr, who focused on the optimism of the liberal tradition
and its lack of appreciation for the seriousness and the depths of sin.
Frei, however, viewed Niebuhr, who had no sympathy with Barth, as a
liberal.[11] In addition, Frei regularly referred to other "supposedly neo-
orthodox" theologians, such as Emil Brunner and Paul Tillich, as "liberal
theologians under the skin."[12]

What, then, constituted the modern liberal theology that Frei

10. The term "postliberal theology" has taken on a specific meaning in recent
years following George Lindbeck's book *The Nature of Doctrine: Religion and Theology
in a Postliberal Age* (Philadelphia: Westminster Press, 1984). This recent form of "postliberal" or "cultural-linguistic" theology, to which Frei himself turned in his later work,
will be discussed in Chapter Three. However, as early as his dissertation, finished in
1956, Frei was using the term "post-liberal" to refer to the theology of Karl Barth. Frei
has in mind here a theology that moves beyond the experiential liberalism or "relationalism" of nineteenth-century theology, while at the same time taking seriously the
concerns of that theology and not going back to the "external" cognitive, propositional
theology of eighteenth-century Protestant Orthodoxy, which was itself too dependent
on philosophical presuppositions demolished by Kant. See Frei's essay "Religion: Natural
and Revealed," in *A Handbook of Christian Theology: Definition Essays on Concepts and
Movements of Thought in Contemporary Protestantism,* ed. Marvin Halverson and Arthur A. Cohen (Cleveland: World Publishing Co., 1958), where he sets forth the history
of eighteenth- and nineteenth-century theology very much along the lines of Lindbeck.
Long before *The Nature of Doctrine,* Frei had clearly staked out Lindbeck's "types":
"cognitive-propositional," "experiential-expressive," and "post-liberal." Frei, however,
rarely used these general categories, preferring to look more closely at specific positions.

11. Frei, "H. Richard Niebuhr on History, Church, and Nation," 226-28. Frei and
Lindbeck part company where Reinhold Niebuhr is concerned. Lindbeck, unlike Frei,
views Niebuhr as the last great "intratextual" theologian (Lindbeck, *Nature of Doctrine,*
124). This difference alone should make one uneasy about simplistically lumping Frei
and Lindbeck together.

12. Frei, "H. Richard Niebuhr on History, Church, and Nation," 220.

sought to correct and outbid?[13] For Frei, liberal theology was fundamentally apologetics, a term that Frei understood in an "extended sense."[14] Apologetics, according to Frei, does not involve primarily the attempt to prove the truth of the Christian faith; few theologians ever claim that as their purpose. Rather, liberal, apologetic theology has consistently had the goal of defending the religious and moral *meaningfulness* of the Christian faith in relation to general human needs or common human experience.[15] That is, liberal theology has basically sought to relate or "correlate" the Christian message with dimensions of human existence that can be discerned apart from the "linguistic world" of the Christian faith itself. Once these anthropological needs or experiences have been discerned, then the Christian message is made meaningful for modern people by being expressed in terms of those independently discovered human needs and experiences. Liberal theology, Frei could assert, moves inductively from human experience to theological assertions, in contrast to orthodoxy, which (in equally problematic fashion) moved deductively to human life from abstract, external propositions.[16] As Frei often put it, modern theology has focused on the *possibility* of faith, on the "order of coming to faith," rather than on the "order of belief."[17] Modern liberal

13. In this section I have been helped tremendously by the insightful essay of George Hunsinger, "Hans Frei as Theologian."

14. Hans W. Frei, *The Eclipse of Biblical Narrative: A Study in Eighteenth and Nineteenth Century Hermeneutics* (New Haven: Yale Univ. Press, 1974), 117.

15. Frei, *Eclipse*, 117.

16. Hans W. Frei, "Niebuhr's Theological Background," in *Faith and Ethics: The Theology of H. Richard Niebuhr*, ed. Paul Ramsey (New York: Harper and Brothers, 1957), 37-38, 40, 45. Frei, like Barth, simply did not believe that these were the only two options. However, whereas for Barth the "object" of theology (The Word of God) broke down these categories, for Frei the language and practices of the community, which are prior to both ideas and experience (to deduction and induction), provided the alternative. This distinction between inductive and deductive movement is important because contemporary homiletical theory, including narrative preaching, has been heavily influenced by the inductive method of Fred Craddock in reaction against the older style of deductive, propositional preaching. See Fred Craddock, *As One Without Authority: Essays on Inductive Preaching*, 3rd ed. (Nashville: Abingdon Press, 1979). Contemporary homiletics has simply not yet moved beyond a liberal response to "cognitive-propositionalism."

17. Hans W. Frei, *The Identity of Jesus Christ: The Hermeneutical Bases of Dogmatic Theology* (Philadelphia: Fortress Press, 1975), x-xii.

theology, in short, has concentrated on explanation rather than on description.[18]

Frei succinctly stated his understanding of apologetics or "mediating theology" in his most important book, *The Eclipse of Biblical Narrative.*

> To the mediating theologians, the unique truth of Christianity is actually discoverable only by divine, self-communicating grace (or revelation). And this, in turn, has to be grasped through the venture of an act of faith which remains just as risky and uncertain as the grace or revelation, to which it refers, stays indemonstrable. But the possibility of such a miracle — for it is nothing less — and the meaningfulness of what is communicated by it, involve more than an appeal to divine authority. They involve an appeal to the appropriateness of this miracle to the human condition; and that condition is one that all right-thinking men can or should be able to recognize. In other words, there is an area of human experience on which the light of the Christian gospel and that of natural, independent insight shine at the same time, illumining it in the same way. The degree to which and the manner in which the one mode of insight has to be bolstered by the other is a matter of difference among various mediating theologians, and they have invented a wide variety of often very complex ways of stating their views on this subject. But on the substantive point that both modes must be present and correlated they are all agreed. There is no such thing as revelation without someone to receive it, and receive it, moreover, as a significant answer to or illumination of general life questions.
>
> I have used the term apologetics to cover (among other things) this appeal to a common ground between analysis of human experience by direct natural and by some distinctively Christian thought. This has been the chief characteristic of the mediating theology of modernity.[19]

Liberal theology, in this sense, can take many forms. It may, for example, take the form of a positive, constant relation between God and

---

18. Hans W. Frei, *Types of Christian Theology*, ed. George Hunsinger and William C. Placher (New Haven: Yale Univ. Press, 1992), 27. Frei's distinction is between a general explanation of how people may come to believe, which may be the same across religions, and a religion-specific description of Christian belief.

19. Frei, *Eclipse*, 128-29.

human beings that is inherent in human life itself. The human being may be viewed as a "religious creature who by virtue of that fact has a natural contact with God."[20] This was the form of liberal theology or "relationalism" that Frei discerned in various forms in the nineteenth century. Schleiermacher and, in this century, Tillich are the supreme examples; for them, according to Frei, the human being "has a primordial, inward, and constant relation to God given with his very being, more profound than all changing articulations of it, whether social or individual."[21] It was this form of liberalism that Barth challenged in his *Epistle to the Romans*.

However, liberal theology could and did take other, less constant and positive forms as well. It could take the form of Brunner's relational theology, with its "negative contact point," in which the existential despair of human beings provides the occasion for the meaningfulness of revelation. Indeed, Frei was highly critical of Brunner, who, he argued, never really understood Barth and continued to approach theology from a fundamentally anthropological starting point. According to Frei, Barth and Brunner could not even share a common basis for disagreement.[22]

Liberal theology could also take the form of Reinhold Niebuhr's "natural theology" of sin, in which the human condition, existentially interpreted as the dizzying anxiousness of life in the tension between finitude and transcendence, reveals the human need for God and provides the terms in which God's work in Jesus Christ can be meaningful

20. Hans W. Frei, "German Theology: Transcendence and Secularity," in *Postwar German Culture*, ed. Charles E. McClelland and Stephen P. Scher (New York: E. P. Dutton, 1974), 103.

21. Frei, "German Theology"; Frei, "Karl Barth: Theologian," 10. This is basically Lindbeck's "experiential-expressivism." Frei's evaluation of Schleiermacher, particularly in his later work, is far more nuanced and appreciative than this single, early comment would suggest.

22. Frei, "Niebuhr's Theological Background," 44; Frei, "Religion: Natural and Revealed," 317. The "point of contact" for Barth and Frei is Jesus Christ, in whom God and the human being are inextricably related, not on the basis of a general understanding of human nature, but in the specific person of Jesus of Nazareth, who alone defines that relationship. Anthropology (and an understanding of human identity), Frei repeatedly asserted with Barth, begins not with a general understanding of human nature, but with Jesus (Hans W. Frei, "Theological Reflections on the Gospel Accounts of Jesus' Death and Resurrection," *The Christian Scholar* 49 (Winter 1966): 287, 297; Frei, *Types*, 135).

to modern people.[23] To cite yet another example, this theological approach can take the form of Bultmann's existentialist project of demythologizing, in which theological language necessarily becomes language about human existence because God is so transcendent that one can only speak of God's "effects" on human beings in the existential decision of faith.[24]

Behind all these forms of liberalism, Frei suggests, lies not only the anthropological orientation of philosophy since Kant's "turn to the subject," but also a tendency within Protestant theology itself — the tendency to make the relation between God and human beings central to the theological enterprise. Rather than speaking about God, Protestant theology, Frei argued, has tended to focus instead on faith, with the result that theology, in Barth's terms, has tended to become *Glaubenslehre*.[25] As Frei wrote,

> The common heritage of neo-orthodox and liberal theologians — from their Protestant origins, as they saw it . . . — is that it is not God "in himself" but only "God revealed," or rather our relation with God, that is the object of our communion with God. "Faith" not only removes into a special, self-based kind of insight, but gradually, by a kind of merciless Kantian or perhaps Fichtean logic, is deconstructed into a totally originative human construction, in which the moment of divine revelation is no more than a self-positing move of the constructive intellectual capacity, in which the mind imagines or sets over against itself a transcendent "other" for its own regulating and constructing purposes.[26]

23. See Niebuhr's most important work, *The Nature and Destiny of Man,* 2 vols. (New York: Charles Scribner's Sons, 1941-43). Chapter 5, the initial constructive chapter in the book, is entitled "The Relevance of the Christian View of Man." This starting point captures in a nutshell Frei's understanding of liberal theology.

24. For Frei's specific discussion of Bultmann, see "German Theology," 106-7. For a clear statement of Bultmann's project see *Jesus Christ and Mythology* (New York: Charles Scribner's Sons, 1958).

25. Frei, "Niebuhr's Theological Background," 45.

26. Frei, "H. Richard Niebuhr on History, Church, and Nation," 223-24. For Barth's similar comment about Protestant theology, see Karl Barth, "An Introductory Essay," trans. James Luther Adams, in Ludwig Feuerbach, *The Essence of Christianity,* trans. George Eliot (New York: Harper and Row, 1957), xxii-xxiii. Frei is not saying that "faith" is unimportant for theology — or better, faithfulness (Frei consistently wants to emphasize the faithfulness of discipleship in the church, rather than the internal, in-

As Frei saw it, this tendency of Protestant theology, combined with philosophical pressures, opened the door all too easily to a confusion between theology and anthropology — and to the consequent problems of liberalism.

Integrally related to apologetic theology, Frei contended, is a similar approach to biblical interpretation, which grew out of the eighteenth-century concern for the religious meaningfulness of the Bible.[27] Throughout most of the church's tradition, Frei argued in *Eclipse,* believers had read the Bible "intratextually."[28] The "world of the Bible" had been the one "real world" within which life was interpreted. Erich Auerbach's characterization of the biblical narrative was important for Frei and captured his understanding of the church's traditional reading of Scripture:

> The Bible's claim to truth is not only far more urgent than Homer's, it is tyrannical — it excludes all other claims. The world of the Scripture stories is not satisfied with claiming to be a historically true reality — it insists that it is the only real world, is destined for autocracy. All other scenes, issues, and ordinances have no right to appear independently of it, and it is promised that all of them, the history of all

---

dividual, existentialist understanding of faith). Nor is he suggesting that knowledge of God is possible apart from the particular language of the Christian community. Nor is Frei discounting the mystery of God. Rather, Frei's point is, first, that faith does not provide a unique, existential way of knowing; and second, that theology can, on the basis of Scripture, speak analogically about God in Christ and not simply about the "faith relation." As Frei suggested in his final essay on H. Richard Niebuhr, it is the Christian language itself that points in this direction; the logic or "grammar" of this language points to the otherness of God and the "radical realism" of theology. By "radical realism" Frei does not have in mind a general epistemological realism in which God is "available" outside a particular linguistic community to the neutral, objective observer. Rather, Frei's emphasis on "radical realism" is a theological assertion, emphasizing the reality of God apart from the relation of faith, an assertion that depends, nonfoundationally, upon the linguistic community of the church. See Frei, "H. Richard Niebuhr on History, Church, and Nation," 225.

27. Frei, *Eclipse,* 122, 124, 127-28. For Frei, theology and biblical interpretation are always related. Different approaches to Scripture affect theology and vice versa. Frei touches briefly on this relationship in *Eclipse,* but explores it in much more detail in *Types,* 56-69.

28. Hans W. Frei, "The 'Literal Reading' of the Biblical Narrative in the Christian Tradition: Does It Stretch or Will It Break?" in *The Bible and the Narrative Tradition,* ed. Frank McConnell (New York: Oxford Univ. Press, 1986), 71-73.

mankind, will be given their due place within its frame, will be subordinated to it. The Scripture stories do not, like Homer's, court our
favor, they do not flatter us that they may please us and enchant us
— they seek to subject us, and if· we refuse to be subjected we are
rebels.[29]

During the eighteenth and nineteenth centuries, however, this understanding of Scripture was lost; a great reversal took place. The "biblical
world" ceased to provide the primary frame of reference, but rather
came to be interpreted into a purportedly "wider" modern framework.[30]
More specifically, the Bible began to be read primarily as a source of
historical information or philosophical ideas known independently of
Scripture. Biblical interpretation became "a matter of fitting the biblical
story into another world with another story rather than incorporating
that world into the biblical story."[31] Such an approach to Scripture was
the natural counterpart to liberal, apologetic theology.[32]

Frei's critique of theological and hermeneutical liberalism can thus
be summarized in terms of aim, method, and content.[33] According to
Frei, the apologetic *aim* of liberal theology is to to explain and defend
the religious and moral meaningfulness of the Christian faith in relation
to general human needs and common human experience. The *method*
of this apologetic or "mediating" theology generally involves some form
of correlation. The Christian message is correlated with dimensions of
human existence discerned independently of Christian beliefs and practices. The result of this theological aim and method, according to Frei,
is that the primary *content* of theology becomes anthropology. Jesus

29. Erich Auerbach, *Mimesis: The Representation of Reality in Western Literature,*
trans. Willard R. Trask (Princeton, New Jersey: Princeton Univ. Press, 1953; Princeton
Paperback Edition, 1974), 14-15.

30. For an excellent critique of the notion of a "wider" modern world into which
the Bible should be interpreted, see John Howard Yoder, "But We Do See Jesus," in *The
Priestly Kingdom* (Notre Dame, Indiana: Univ. of Notre Dame, 1984), 46-62.

31. Frei, *Eclipse*, 130.

32. Not surprisingly, contemporary hermeneutical theory, drawn on by "revisionist" theologians such as David Tracy, became the target of Frei's critique of liberal
theology in his later work, as I will discuss in Chapter Four. For Frei, general hermeneutical theories, within which Scripture is subsumed, are the guise under which apologetic theology is pursued today.

33. I am indebted to George Hunsinger for this summary of Frei's critique. See
George Hunsinger, "Hans Frei as Theologian," 105-6.

Christ becomes little more than a cipher for an independent under-standing of human existence, which sets the terms for his significance. Theologically, Christology becomes a function of an independently generated soteriology. That is, an analysis of the human situation shapes the understanding of what salvation can mean, and then Jesus Christ is provided as the answer to that soteriological question. A general an-thropology, which delineates the human need for salvation, determines the understanding of Christology.[34] As a consequence, Jesus gets ab-sorbed into human experience and loses his unique, unsubstitutable identity.

These theological and hermeneutical consequences stem, accord-ing to Frei, from liberal theology's failure to take seriously the "logic" of the gospel stories about Jesus. According to Frei, the logic of the stories is "ascriptive," rather than descriptive. That is, the focus of the stories is the person of Jesus, to whose unique, unsubstitutable person the various titles, characteristics, and actions are ascribed. The ascriptive subject, Jesus of Nazareth, is primary, rather than the particular predi-cates used to describe him. The stories, as the church has traditionally read them in their "literal sense," are quite simply about Jesus.[35] When theology ignores this logic, the result is not only an arbitrary interpreta-tion of the stories about Jesus, but also a Christology in which Jesus of Nazareth becomes a mere cipher either for the predicates describing him, as usually happens in the "Christ figures" of contemporary litera-ture, or for general truths about human existence, which is the case in mythological or symbolic interpretations of the gospel stories.[36]

---

34. Hunsinger, "Hans Frei as Theologian," 119-20.

35. Frei, *Types,* 124-26. At this point, I have to leave open Frei's carefully nuanced understanding of the "literal sense." I will examine this matter in detail in Chapter Four.

36. Frei, "Theological Reflections," 268-72, 297-98; Frei, *Identity,* 54-84. The issue here is closely related to that of historical reference and historical method. For example, Frei contended in his later work that Schleiermacher *could* have taken seriously the ascriptive logic of the gospel stories, but, because he was intent on relating the historical Jesus, discovered by historical method, to the Christ of faith, his project broke down and the particulars of the gospel stories — especially the death and resurrection — became unnecessary. Jesus' consciousness, rather than the identity rendered in the gospel narratives, became the link between the historical Jesus and the Christ of faith (Frei, *Types,* 65-78). In "Theological Reflections" and *Identity* Frei critiques both the mytho-logical interpretation of the New Testament and the "Christ figures" of contemporary literature, both of which are linked to liberal approaches to the New Testament and

This concern for the unique ascriptive subject, Jesus of Nazareth, is precisely the issue at stake in Frei's rather enigmatic discussion of the priority of "identity" over "presence" in *The Identity of Jesus Christ*. According to Frei, Jesus' unique, unsubstitutable identity is lost, diffused into human experience, when the question of his presence, the question of meaningfulness, takes priority over the question of his identity. In order to be truly present, Jesus must have a self-focused identity that he can "turn" and "share" with us. Consequently, apart from a consideration of that identity, there is no direct way to discuss his presence. Although in Jesus Christ identity and presence are inseparable, the question, "Who is Jesus Christ?" must precede the question, "How is he present?" Jesus' presence, his salvific meaningfulness, is a function of his identity and not vice versa. As George Hunsinger has succinctly put it: hermeneutically, the meaningfulness of the gospel narratives is a function of their sense; theologically, soteriology is a function of Christology.[37]

A Homiletical Illustration: Paul Tillich's "You Are Accepted"[38]

In order to suggest the homiletical significance of Frei's understanding of theological liberalism, I will briefly analyze one of the most well-known sermons of the twentieth century, Paul Tillich's "You Are Accepted." Tillich's work serves as an appropriate illustration of the liber-

---

both of which lose the unique ascriptive subject, Jesus of Nazareth. Frei's critique of liberalism will remain fundamentally the same throughout his work, though it will be nuanced considerably in his later writings, particularly *Types of Christian Theology*. In this work Frei is more specific about the various ways in which theology has been related to philosophy and human experience, an analysis that leads him to a more positive evaluation of Schleiermacher, though Frei himself ultimately sides with Barth.

37. Hunsinger, "Hans Frei as Theologian," 103-7, 119-20. In his later preface to *Identity* Frei expressed dissatisfaction with the category of "presence," which, he came to feel, was too closely connected to the concept of revelation as "personal encounter" and too much a part of the idealistic, liberal tradition that he was critiquing. He would discontinue using the concept in that form in his later work. Indeed, in some of his later work, he would even use Derrida to "deconstruct" the notion of "presence" in phenomenological hermeneutics. See Frei, "Literal Reading," 36-77. For this reason I think the hermeneutical categories of "sense" and "meaningfulness" and the theological categories of Christology and soteriology are more helpful than identity and presence.

38. Paul Tillich, "You Are Accepted," in *The Shaking of The Foundations* (New York: Charles Scribner's Sons, 1948), 153-63.

alism that Frei sought to correct and outbid. Tillich was the most influential theologian in the United States during the period in which Frei developed his theological position. The first volume of Tillich's *Systematic Theology* was published while Frei was working on his dissertation; and the third volume, with its emphasis on presence, came out shortly before the *Crossroads* edition of *Identity,* which was entitled "The Mystery of the Presence of Jesus Christ." Frei unquestionably had Tillich in mind as the focus of much of his critique of liberal theology.

In addition, it was not only Tillich's volumes of systematic theology, but also his sermons, particularly those in *The Shaking of the Foundations,* that were influential. For example, in *Honest to God,* as everyone recognizes, John A. T. Robinson drew heavily from the work of Tillich. However, what is easily overlooked is the fact that Robinson frequently cites not Tillich's *Systematic Theology,* but his sermons.[39] In addition, Tillich's theology and preaching exercised an important influence during the early stages of the development of narrative homiletics. One of the most important early works on narrative preaching, Charles Rice's *Interpretation and Imagination,* not only explicitly rejects the approach of Barth, but draws extensively on the work of Tillich.[40]

In light of Tillich's influence not only on American theology and homiletics in general, but on the early stages of narrative homiletics in particular, it is significant to discover that his most well-known sermon embodies precisely the three elements that Frei critiqued about modern

39. John A. T. Robinson, *Honest To God* (Philadelphia: Westminster, 1963), 46, 55, 57-59, 80, and 82. Tillich's three volumes of sermons, *The Shaking of the Foundations, The New Being* (New York: Charles Scribner's Sons, 1955), and *The Eternal Now* (New York: Charles Scribner's Sons, 1963), are related both temporally and thematically to the three volumes of the *Systematic Theology* (Chicago: Univ. of Chicago Press, 1951-63).

40. Charles Rice, *Interpretation and Imagination: The Preacher and Contemporary Literature* (Philadelphia: Fortress Press, 1970). Rice would later co-author, with Edmund Steimle and Morris Niedenthal, one of the most important books on narrative preaching, *Preaching the Story* (Philadelphia: Fortress Press, 1980). Significantly, Niedenthal did his dissertation on Tillich's preaching, concluding that "Tillich's method [of correlation] probably offers the best approach for dealing with the difficulties of speaking of God's presence." Morris Niedenthal, *Preaching the Presence of God* (Ann Arbor: University Microfilms International, 1969), 103. Tillich's influence on contemporary homiletics — and on narrative homiletics — has been inadequately explored and deserves further consideration. Along with Gerhard Ebeling — the focus of Frei's early hermeneutical critique — Tillich would be one of the major theological influences.

liberal theology: an apologetic aim, a correlationist method, and an anthropological content (which takes the form of a radical subordination of Christology to an independently developed soteriology). Tillich's sermon not only serves as a good example of the liberalism that Frei critiqued, but also as an example of some of the homiletical issues inherent in liberal theology.

Tillich is explicit about the apologetic aim of his sermons. Indeed, the desire to illustrate "apologetic preaching" was the most important reason for the publication of *The Shaking of the Foundations*. As Tillich states in the preface to the book,

> A large part of the congregation at the Sunday services came from outside the Christian circle in the most radical sense of the phrase. For them, a sermon in traditional Biblical terms would have had no meaning. Therefore, I was obliged to seek a language which expresses in other terms the human experience to which the Biblical and ecclesiastical terminology point. In this situation, an "apologetic" type of sermon has been developed. And, since I believe that this is generally the situation in which the Christian message has to be pronounced today, I hope that the publication of some attempts to meet this situation may not be useless.[41]

Tillich's aim, like that of liberal theology, was to make the Christian message meaningful by relating it to the "general human experience" that it expresses.

This aim, combined with Tillich's method of correlation, determines the movement of "You Are Accepted." The sermon begins with a general analysis of the human situation, which poses the question of salvation in a certain way, and then uses the gospel to answer that question in the terms in which it has been posed. Interestingly, the movement of the sermon is very much like that of the "problem-solution" sermon popularized by the most famous of the liberal preachers, Harry Emerson Fosdick, which begins with a problem in general human experience and uses the gospel to "solve" it.[42]

---

41. Tillich, *Shaking*, iii.

42. This fact will be significant when I turn to examine narrative homiletics in Part Two. Some forms of narrative preaching are little more than the old "problem-solution" method in a new shape.

"You Are Accepted" opens with the basic question: How are we to recapture the meaningfulness of the terms "sin" and "grace"?[43] In order to establish their meaningfulness, Tillich turns to a general analysis of human existence, drawing on the tools of philosophy and "depth psychology." This analysis of "the human situation" provides the questions that point to the real meaning of the two ancient terms. The way to recapture the meaningfulness of this traditional language is not to look at Jesus Christ or the logic of Christian belief, but rather to follow the path that

> leads us down into the depth of our human existence. In that depth these words [sin and grace] were conceived; and *there* they gained power for all ages; *there* they must be found again by each generation, and by each of us for himself.[44]

In these depths the human situation is found, in good existentialist fashion, to be one of estrangement — from self, from others, from the "Ground of Being" itself. "Sin is separation."[45] Inherent in this sense of separation, however, is also an understanding of grace, of the reunion and reconciliation that is missing from human life.[46] The question of human existence is raised in the form of separation and reunion.

As a result, the correlative answer to the human question is *acceptance,* which brings the desired reunion that is beyond human power. However, the life, death, and resurrection of Jesus Christ play no essential role in this answer.[47] In the sermon Jesus has no unique, unsubstitutable identity; at best his "presence" is diffused throughout general human experience. Indeed, the only mention of Christ occurs in relation to Paul's "experience of acceptance" on the Damascus road, when the "picture of Jesus as the Christ appeared to him at the moment of his greatest separation from other men, from himself, and from God. . . ."[48] The picture of Jesus as the Christ appears to Paul as *one medium* through

43. Tillich, "You Are Accepted," 153.
44. Tillich, "You Are Accepted," 159.
45. Tillich, "You Are Accepted," 54-55.
46. Tillich, "You Are Accepted," 156, 159.
47. The *symbols* of crucifixion and resurrection appear only as the general form that the experience of acceptance takes in human life. The experience surprises us at the moments of our deepest separation.
48. Tillich, "You Are Accepted," 160.

which this powerful experience of acceptance has taken place.[49] Otherwise the experience of acceptance is a general one that is divorced
completely from the particulars of Jesus' life, death, and resurrection.
The correlationist method has forfeited the particularity of Jesus of
Nazareth.

By the end of the sermon the reader is invited simply to *"accept
the fact that you are accepted."* [50] The sermon concludes Christologically
empty. The content is thoroughly anthropological:

> . . . sometimes it happens that we receive the power to say "yes" to
> ourselves, that peace enters into us and makes us whole, that self-
> hatred and self-contempt disappear, and that our self is reunited with
> itself. Then we can say that grace has come upon us.[51]

In "You Are Accepted" Jesus Christ becomes the function of an
independently developed understanding of salvation; he becomes the
form for an anthropologically determined content. In fact, for all practical purposes, he disappears. The implications of liberal theology for
preaching are extraordinary. Similarly, as I will demonstrate in what
follows, Frei's theological alternative to liberalism suggests a different
approach to preaching.

Frei's Alternative to Liberalism

Although Frei's work undergoes some important changes, the general
direction of his theological alternative to liberalism remains remarkably
consistent. In terms of the earlier categories — aim, method, and content — Frei's theology may be described, in direct opposition to liberal
theology, as having a dogmatic aim, an Anselmian method, and a Christological content. A look at each of these emphases will help both to

---

49. Here the form of the human question (separation), derived from "general
human experience," requires that Paul's experience on the Damascus road be described
as one of "acceptance," an interpretation that is not only present nowhere in Acts, but
is also quite different from the way in which Paul himself interprets this incident in
Galatians 1:15-16. The issue here is not the acceptance of the individual, but the mission
to the Gentiles and the formation of a new community.

50. Tillich, "You Are Accepted," 162.

51. Tillich, "You Are Accepted," 163.

clarify Frei's alternative to liberalism and to indicate some of the important influences on his work.

A Dogmatic Aim: Conceptual Redescription

For Frei theology has a dogmatic, rather than an apologetic, aim.[52] The goal of theology is the second-order description of the logic and content of Christian belief, as they are embodied in the first-order language and practices of the Christian community, particularly, but not exclusively, in the Scripture that functions authoritatively within the church.[53] The category of "description" sets theology, as Frei understands it, apart from apologetics, which, as noted above, seeks to *explain* belief in terms of some independent anthropological theory. The aim of theology, in distinction from apologetics, is Christian self-description; theology is "religion-specific," internal to the Christian community, and not subsumed under general theories of meaning or meaningfulness. Exercising both a normative and a critical function, Christian theology seeks to clarify and critique

---

52. Frei, *Identity,* x-xiii; see also Frei, *Types,* 38-46.

53. Frei, *Identity,* xiii; Frei, *Types,* 124. For Frei, "logic" refers to the "the basis and mutual coherence of Christian concepts" (Frei, *Identity,* xiii). Although Frei, influenced by Wittgenstein, can sometimes use "grammar" metaphorically as a synonym for "logic," Frei prefers the latter term. Here one can discern the influence of Ryle, who focuses on the logic of concepts, which are embodied in linguistic practices but distinguished from "rules of grammar" (Gilbert Ryle, *The Concept of Mind* [London: Hutchinson, 1949; repr., Chicago: Univ. of Chicago Press, 1984], 8, 79). For an example of what Frei has in mind by logic, see his discussion of the Chalcedonian formula in *Types,* 124-25. It is important to remember that "concepts" for Frei are not simply "inner mental ideas," but skills that are practiced in the Christian community; they are performative, related to "forms of life" (Frei, *Types,* 42). For example, "love" as a concept is not primarily an idea, but a "skill" that is practiced. Similarly, the identity of Jesus Christ as the crucified and resurrected Redeemer is not just a matter of cognitive content, though it is that, but also involves the faithfulness of discipleship. The influence of Gilbert Ryle, as well as Wittgenstein, is also evident here. See Ryle, 25-61.

The issue of the relation between first- and second-order theology is important and somewhat fuzzy in Frei's work (isn't it always?). For example, Frei's main distinction is that first-order language involves assertions ("This is so"), whereas second-order theology examines the internal logic implicit in these assertions (Frei, *Types,* 124); like Lindbeck, Frei, in his later work, can speak of doctrines as rules. In addition, Frei also suggests that first-order language is more "self-involving." However, Frei notes that in Barth's theology this distinction between first- and second-order theology is fuzzier than in other types of theology; Barth tends to collapse the two.

the church's self-understanding embodied in its language and practices, rather than to explain how some aspect of the "human condition" makes belief meaningful.[54] As Frei came to stress, the primary cognate discipline of this kind of theology is not philosophy, but rather "interpretive social science," particularly anthropology and sociology.[55] Like these disciplines, Christian theology seeks "thick description" of the Christian "semiotic system," parallel to Clifford Geertz's thick description of a culture.[56]

For Frei, Barth's theology best exemplified this aim. In particular, Frei was drawn to Barth's descriptive explication of the biblical narrative, which became increasingly central in Barth's later work. In the *Dogmatics,* Frei argued, Barth pursued the descriptive task of theology while still giving the primary place to the temporal, narrative "world" of the Bible. As Frei wrote in his review of Eberhard Busch's biography of Barth:

> Barth was about the business of conceptual description. He took the classical themes of communal Christian language molded by the Bible, tradition, and constant usage in worship, practice, instruction and controversy, and he restated or redescribed them, rather than evolving arguments on their behalf. . . .
>
> Barth's theology proceeds by narrative and conceptually descriptive statement rather than by argument or by way of an explanatory theory undergirding the description's real or logical possibility. . . . he set forth a textual world which he refused to understand by paraphrase, or by transposition or "translation" into some other context but interpreted in second-order reflection with the aid of an array of formal technical tools.[57]

54. Frei, *Types,* 124.

55. Frei, *Types,* 2.

56. See Clifford Geertz, *The Interpretation of Cultures* (New York: Basic Books, 1973), 3-30. Frei's later work was influenced by Geertz, through his colleague George Lindbeck. Interestingly, Geertz got the term "thick description" from Gilbert Ryle (Geertz, 6). The move from Ryle to Geertz (i.e. from analytical philosophy to interpretive social science as the appropriate cognate discipline of theology) was not a radical shift of direction, but an enrichment of Frei's position. Both approaches were primarily tools for Frei's overarching Anselmian, descriptive understanding of theology.

57. Hans W. Frei, "An Afterword: Eberhard Busch's Biography of Karl Barth," in *Karl Barth in Re-View: Posthumous Works Reviewed and Assessed,* ed. H.-Martin Rumscheidt, Pittsburgh Theological Monograph Series 30 (Pittsburgh: Pickwick Press, 1981), 110-15. The close connection between descriptive theology and "intratextual" biblical interpretation is evident in this quotation.

This descriptive task, embodied so well by Barth, was, for Frei, the aim of theology.

However, as Frei's comment about Barth makes clear, this descriptive aim does not mean that theology has nothing at all to do with philosophical concepts or methods. Because theology always and inevitably draws upon the philosophical conceptuality of the day in its descriptions, theology always to some degree has the more specific aim of faithful "redescription"; it is not simply the rote repetition of the language of the Bible. Rather, philosophical concepts have a necessary, though subordinate, role in theology.[58]

Frei's understanding of the relationship between philosophical concepts and descriptive, biblical theology is important. It is at this point that his interpretation and appropriation of Barth is especially significant.[59] Frei never rejected the use of philosophical concepts in theology.[60] In fact, even when he was at one of his most formal stages, Frei explicitly asserted that "we must approach the Gospels with some conceptual tool in hand, otherwise we understand nothing at all."[61] Frei consistently wrestled with "the necessity and yet the distortion of approaching the interpretation of the Bible with conceptual tools in hand."[62] Indeed, Frei himself employed the concepts of identity and presence in his Christological works. The critical issue for Frei was not the use of such concepts, which was inevitable, but the way in which these concepts were employed.[63]

58. The relationship between theology and philosophy was a lifelong concern of Frei's, from his doctoral study of Barth's use of different philosophical conceptualities in the first two editions of the *Epistle to the Romans* through Frei's final work, *Types of Christian Theology*, in which Frei explored this issue in relation to various theological positions. See also Frei, "Religion: Natural and Revealed," 314-17.

59. In his comments on Frei's "Theological Reflections" Daniel Day Williams stated that Frei "went beyond Barth" in using philosophical concepts in theology. Frei would have viewed this comment as completely off the mark; here is one place where he saw himself as carrying forward Barth's work. See Daniel Day Williams, "Comment," *The Christian Scholar* 49 (Winter 1966): 310.

60. Frei criticizes "Wittgensteinian fideism" in *Types of Christian Theology*; it is represented by "Type V," which Frei explicitly rejects. See *Types*, 46-55.

61. Frei, "Theological Reflections," 274; Frei, *Types*, 81, 85.

62. Frei, "Theological Reflections," 275.

63. In addition to *Types*, one of Frei's best discussions of this issue can be found in his essay, "Barth and Schleiermacher: Convergence and Divergence," in *Barth and Schleiermacher: Beyond the Impasse*, ed. James O. Duke and Robert F. Streetman (Philadelphia: Fortress Press, 1988).

Three points can be made in this regard. First, for Frei philosophical concepts, though essential, can only play a formal, descriptive, *ad hoc* role in theological redescription. Philosophical concepts remain subordinate to the logic of belief; they function descriptively, rather than in an explanatory fashion. The theologian, he writes, "wants to use philosophical concepts for relatively modest, descriptive purposes," not to provide a "metaphysical explanation."[64] When philosophy seeks to explain, it "takes over," with the result that the distinctiveness of Christian theology is lost within a larger, explanatory framework (the tendency of liberal theology). With respect to the gospel narratives, as Frei noted of Barth, all descriptive or redescriptive schemes remain subordinate to the logic of the biblical narrative; the story, not the redescription, identifies Jesus Christ. "The meaning of the doctrine is the story; not: the meaning of the story is the doctrine."[65]

Barth, again, is the primary influence on Frei at this point. As early as his dissertation Frei demonstrates how Barth employed varieties of different philosophical schemes and concepts at different points in his work, depending on his particular theological needs and concerns. In the process Barth sought to avoid subordinating Scripture to general philosophical theories and systems; he was never hesitant to throw out a philosophical conceptuality if it did not adequately serve the purpose of redescription, as his explicit rejection of the early existentialism of *Romans* demonstrated. Frei himself followed just this path in *The Identity of Jesus Christ*. When he thought the concept of "presence" threatened to overwhelm the logic of the narrative, he did not hesitate to drop it.[66] Frei's summary of Barth's use of philosophy could have been applied to himself:

In order not to become trapped by his philosophy, it is best for a theologian to be philosophically eclectic, in any given case employing

---

64. Frei, "Theological Reflections," 277; Frei, *Types*, 85-87.

65. Frei, *Types*, 90. William Placher has clarified this point nicely: ". . . the hermeneutical goal should not be to find a series of doctrinal propositions that constitute the 'real meaning' of the stories, such that we could then discard the stories themselves. Rather, conceptual formulations in the form of doctrines serve as heuristic aids that serve us best when they thrust readers back to the stories themselves with new understanding." William C. Placher, *Narratives of a Vulnerable God: Christ, Theology, and Scripture* (Louisville: Westminster/John Knox Press, 1994), 15.

66. Frei, *Identity*, vii-ix.

the particular "conceptuality" or conceptualities . . . that serve best to cast into relief the particular theological subject matter under consideration. The subject matter governs concepts as well as method, not vice versa.[67]

For Frei, then, the logic of the faith can be captured in different philosophical conceptualities, and the statement of belief can indeed change with the changing world. However, in the process philosophical categories remain subordinate to the logic of Christian belief embodied in the Scripture and tradition of the church. The aim is always the conceptual redescription of the logic and content of faith, not a general philosophical apologetic for its meaningfulness.[68]

Second, for Frei the relation between philosophical concepts and theological redescription is never theorized; it is always an *ad hoc practice.*[69] There is no general theoretical justification for the employment of philosophical conceptualities; nor are there general rules that can guide the practice, other than "be aware of what you are doing."[70] Philosophical concepts are simply used and critiqued within the ongoing practice of theological redescription in the "common community of interpretation," the church.[71] No conceptuality or interpretation is ever "the last word," because theological reflection is an eschatological enterprise; it is always fragmentary, more like entering into a mystery than like solving a problem.[72] Particular philosophical concepts, as well as specific redescriptions, are always open to criticism as to their faithfulness to Scripture. The theological dialogue in the church, with its various "voices," will sort out the faithful from the unfaithful.[73] Frei's understanding of the theological enterprise is fluid and communal.

67. Frei, "Busch's Biography," 115.

68. Obviously, this is an extremely difficult task. Frei sought to embody it in detail in *The Identity of Jesus Christ.* John Howard Yoder has examined the way the biblical writers themselves employed various "philosophical" conceptualities, but subordinated them to the logic of the gospel, which at times meant turning the philosophy on its head. See Yoder, "But We Do See Jesus." Yoder highlights within Scripture itself the process that Frei has in mind.

69. Frei, *Types,* 19, 41, 42-43; Frei, *Identity,* xv.

70. Frei, *Types,* 86.

71. Frei, *Types,* 57.

72. Frei, *Types,* 56, 90.

73. Frei, *Types,* 56-57; Hans W. Frei, "Response to 'Narrative Theology: An Evangelical Appraisal,'" *Trinity Journal* 8 (Spring 1987).

In *The Identity of Jesus Christ,* for example, Frei argues that his concept of identity, drawn primarily from Gilbert Ryle's philosophy of mind, is adequately formal and minimal so that it does not distort the ascriptive logic of the biblical message about the unique, unsubstitutable identity of Jesus Christ. In addition, he argues that his categories are more appropriate for identity description in "realistic narrative," which emphasizes the inseparable relation between character and incident, than are alternative descriptions focusing on substance, consciousness, or self-understanding.[74] However, Frei does not seek to develop a general theory for employing these particular descriptive categories. Rather, he tries to make his case for the value of these particular concepts by writing *The Identity of Jesus Christ,* by putting them into practice. Whether or not Frei's redescription is faithful to the logic of Christian belief will be decided not by external, neutral standards of truth, but by ongoing argument within the Christian community. The significant thing is that the actual practice of redescription should be the focus of the discussion.[75]

Third, in addition to their positive role in theological redescription, philosophical concepts can play a role in what Frei calls *ad hoc* apologetics.[76] In particular, Frei used philosophy in an unsystematic way to provide internal critiques of opposing positions, which not only served to demonstrate the partial inadequacy of those positions, but also to set into relief the distinctiveness of his own program.[77] In the

74. The category of "realistic narrative" itself is an "external" one, though Frei seeks to demonstrate its appropriateness to the way in which the gospel narratives have been read in the tradition of the church. In his later work, as I will demonstrate in Chapter Four, Frei critiques and qualifies his use of the category of "realistic narrative."

75. Frei, *Types,* 19. Unfortunately, the formal character of most of Frei's work belies his concern for the kind of practice he says we need. In the bulk of his work Frei primarily provided a second-order language for describing what Barth actually did. In fact, Frei seemed frustrated with himself at this point (Frei, *Types,* 19). Frei seemed on the right track with *Identity;* practice is the key, and more of it is needed. At this point Frei and the "Yale School" have not always been faithful to their Barthian roots, possibly because of their concern to justify theology's place in the academy.

76. Frei notes that Barth himself engaged in a similar kind of apologetics (Frei, "Busch's Biography," 14).

77. David Kelsey, "Biblical Narrative and Theological Anthropology," in *Scriptural Authority and Narrative Interpretation,* ed. Garrett Green (Philadelphia: Fortress Press, 1987), 123.

process, Frei sought to demonstrate that reliance on general philosophical frameworks is in fact detrimental to the task of theology and that his own Anselmian project can succeed on its on terms.[78] One of the best examples of this practice is Frei's use of Derrida and deconstruction in his critique of phenomenological hermeneutics in "The 'Literal Reading' of Biblical Narrative in the Christian Tradition: Does It Stretch or Will It Break?" His internal critique of liberal approaches to Christ's presence in *Identity* is another good example.[79] This kind of *ad hoc* apologetics has been described by Jeffrey Stout as "a form of intellectual guerilla warfare in which one attempts to inflict devastating polemical effects on the opposition without incurring the theoretical costs of systematic defense."[80] Frei was a master of it.

For Frei, then, the aim of theology is dogmatics, Christian self-description, not apologetics. However, this does not preclude the modest, eclectic use of philosophy in the development of theological descriptions or in the service of *ad hoc* apologetics. In fact, as "conceptual redescription," theology demands the careful use of philosophical concepts.

An Anselmian Method: Faith Seeking Understanding

The method appropriate to this dogmatic aim is not "correlation" — the attempt to defend the meaningfulness of Christian belief by relating it to general human experience — but rather an Anselmian method of "faith seeking understanding." "Even the meaningfulness, to say nothing of the truth of Christian statements, is a matter of faith seeking understanding rather than faith arising from the statement of general meaning."[81] This method is most apparent in what Frei does *not* do in *The Identity of Jesus Christ*. He does not provide a "foundational" epistemological theory of revelation. Nor does he seek to

---

78. Jeffrey Stout, "Hans Frei and Anselmian Theology" (paper presented at the annual meeting of the American Academy of Religion, Boston, 1987, TMs [photocopy]), 21. Stout agrees with Frei, noting that "it is precisely where its philosophical debts have been highest that modern theology has proved most susceptible to immanent criticism" (Stout, 22).

79. Frei, *Identity*, 83-87.

80. Stout, 8.

81. Frei, *Types*, 81.

justify the validity of the biblical narrative through some theory of inspiration. Nor does he begin with a general account of human existence that will make the Christian story meaningful. Rather, he simply begins with the Scripture that functions authoritatively within the community of faith, and he turns to that part — the gospel narratives — which has been central in the church's tradition of reading. Frei begins "nonfoundationally" within a particular community and tradition.

As Frei's starting point suggests, the "faith" that seeks understanding is not primarily an inner experience or relation or encounter; it is not a unique, privileged way of knowing. Rather, while faith is certainly "self-involving," embodied in worship and discipleship, it is also an acceptance of the *Credo* of the community; it is an assenting to and learning of the language of the community. Faith here is the "faith which is believed" as well as the "faith which believes"; it is faith with an inescapably cognitive dimension, which is first given to the believer in the language of the church's *Credo*.[82] Theology is not primarily concerned with individual, inner experience, but with the Scripture and language of the community. Theology is a linguistic skill.[83] Frei's method of faith seeking understanding is Anselmian; he has something quite different in mind from the existentialist understandings of faith that he saw all around him.

Karl Barth, in his book on Anselm, captured this Anselmian "manner of theology" remarkably well:

> In explaining Anselm's use of '*intelligere*' it is vitally important to remember the literal meaning of the word: *intus legere*. After all that we have said there can be no question but that the fundamental meaning of *intelligere* is *legere*: to reflect upon what has already been said in the *Credo*. . . .
>
> Anselm is distinguished from the 'liberal' theologians of his time in that his *intelligere* is really intended to be no more than a deepened

---

82. Frei, *Types*, 25-26. See Karl Barth, *Anselm: Fides Quaerens Intellectum,* trans. Ian W. Robertson, Pittsburgh Reprint Series (London: SCM Press, 1960), 15-25. Like Barth, Frei consistently sought to hold together these two forms of belief in his work. Part of his critique of Protestant relationalism focused on its loss of the "faith which is believed" dimension.

83. Frei, *Types,* 78.

form of *legere*. But — and this distinguishes him just as definitely from the 'positivists', the traditionalists of his day — it does involve a deepened *legere*, an *intus legere*, a reflecting upon.[84]

As Frei summarizes, what Anselm was about in the *Proslogion* was "reflection on the *grammar* of the word *God* as it is used in the Christian Church."[85]

Frei emphasized even more than Barth the fundamentally linguistic character of this theological method. Frei not only highlighted this characteristic of Barth's theology, affirming that Barth was ahead of his time, but consciously interpreted Barth in this direction. Commenting on the opening paragraph of Barth's *Church Dogmatics*, Frei wrote the following:[86]

Theology constitutes an inquiry into the specific language peculiar to, in fact constitutive of, the specific semiotic community called the Christian church or churches. . . .

Here I admit to doing a bit of finagling or making Barth say what I want him to say — the word for that is "interpretation" — the subject matter of theology (the very word itself involves it) is "God"; that is the "object" or "referent" of the language. When I say I am interpreting Barth, what I mean is that for Barth we have the reality only under the description, only linguistically, not independently of the concept as we use it in preaching and liturgy, in action in church and world, in prayer and praise. Barth doesn't always, but logically he *should*, make a distinction not between words and concepts but between "signifier" and "signified" (to use the terms that deconstructionists employ), between the sense of the words and their *semiotic referent*, and then he should say, "Don't get these distinctions, especially the last one between semiotic sense and semiotic referent, confused with the distinction between meaning (semiotic sense and referent) and truth or reality referent."[87]

84. Barth, *Anselm*, 40-41.
85. Frei, *Types*, 79.
86. Frei cites the 1936 edition: "As a theological discipline dogmatics is the scientific test to which the Christian church puts herself regarding the language about God which is peculiar to her." Karl Barth, *Church Dogmatics*, I, 1, trans. G. T. Thomson (Edinburgh: T & T Clark, 1936), 1.
87. Frei, *Types*, 78-79.

Influenced by Wittgenstein, Frei took the "postmodern," linguistic turn in his interpretation and appropriation of Barth's Anselmian theological method.[88]

The implications of Frei's theological method for his understanding of the role of narrative in Christian theology are particularly important. His Anselmian method distinguishes Frei's approach from most forms of narrative theology and narrative homiletics. In fact, as Stout has correctly pointed out, Frei's approach to narrative is a function of his Anselmian theology, and not vice versa. Christian theology, as Frei understood it, is not concerned with narrative *per se,* but rather seeks to discern and describe the structure and content of a particular narrative.

Several implications of Frei's method for his approach to biblical narrative are clear. To begin with, the gospel narratives have a cognitive *content* — the identity of Jesus of Nazareth as Redeemer — not just an experiential thrust.[89] Although the language and practices of the community are prior to both ideas and experience, and although practice is finally more important than cognition, Frei nevertheless highlights the cognitive aspect of the Christian faith and the biblical narrative. In addition, the gospel narratives have a distinctive *logic.* This logic may differ considerably from the canons of general philosophy, but it guides Christian thought, speech, and action.[90] Although he would not have

88. It is with regard to Frei's linguistic, Anselmian method and its descriptive goal that his work clearly belongs in the "postmodern" camp. However, Frei eschewed such general labels as "postmodern" and would have preferred to be understood in more specific terms. Frei's goal was to be a "full-blooded" Christian theologian, not a "postmodern" one. However Frei's theology, like that of Lindbeck, clearly meets the three "postmodern" criteria set forth by Nancey Murphy and James McClendon: holistic epistemology (including a recognition of the "traditioned" character of rationality); language as discourse and meaning as use; and a "corporate metaphysics" (i.e., an emphasis on the "organic community," rather than the individual). Murphy and McClendon set these over against modern views, which wavered between two poles in the areas of epistemology, language, and metaphysics: between foundationalism and skepticism in epistemology, representationalism and expressivism in language, individualism and collectivism in "metaphysics." See Nancey Murphy and James William McClendon, "Distinguishing Modern and Postmodern Theologies," *Modern Theology* 5 (April 1989): 191-214.

89. Frei, "Theological Reflections," 264, 300.

90. I discussed earlier the ascriptive logic of the gospel narratives in relation to Jesus of Nazareth. Another way this logic differs from that of philosophy and science is that it is "self-involving." Christian "facts" cannot simply be accepted in a neutral or objective fashion. Rather, they require discipleship. As Frei writes of the "fact" of the

generalized about narrative in the ways that Alasdair MacIntyre does, Frei would have at least agreed that there is a distinctive kind of rationality in the Christian narrative that is understood and lived in various Christian communities.[91] Finally, the New Testament narratives, with their peculiar ascriptive logic, have a specific *function,* which is to render the unique, unsubstitutable identity of Jesus Christ and to form the community of faith into a "distant" embodiment of that identity. As Frei's discussion of Christ figures suggests, most narratives, including those that seek to render a Christ figure, fail to capture this content, logic, and function of the gospel stories. "Mythical" narratives, which are accepted as true because of their resonance with "general human experience," come in for Frei's special criticism.[92]

For Frei, the key is not the genre of narrative, but the content, logic, and function of the particular narrative of the Christian community — the "world" of the Bible. Accordingly, for Frei the important thing is not simply to use a particular genre in Christian speech — for example, to tell stories because they have an inherent appropriateness or to employ some general narrative structure. On the contrary, Frei asserts, while the gospel narratives are always primary, various forms of speech can faithfully capture, though always in a fragmentary way, the content, logic, and function of the narratives. In fact, although few people seem to have noticed it, Frei does cite texts from the New Testament epistles, some of them examples of early Christian preaching, as instances in which the "grammar" of the gospel narratives is appropriately used.[93] In short, for

---

resurrection, "grateful discipleship and factual acknowledgement seem to have been — mysteriously — one and the same act" (Frei, *Identity,* 147).

91. See Alasdair MacIntyre, *Whose Justice? Which Rationality?* (Notre Dame, Indiana: Univ. of Notre Dame Press, 1988).

92. Frei, *Identity,* 54-84.

93. See Frei, *Identity,* 59, 104-5, 110, 128. Frei's work, in fact, suggests a way of linking the gospels and the epistles; he understands the epistles as commentaries on the story of Jesus, which do in fact capture its content, logic, and function. Indeed, there is evidence that Frei understood this relationship between the gospels and the epistles as part of his larger project. Discussing this project, he wrote the following in an early lecture: ". . . for a beginning let's start with the synoptic gospels, or at least one of them, because their peculiar nature as narratives, or at least partial narratives, makes some hermeneutical moves possible that we don't have available elsewhere in the New Testament. And having started there, I would propose to go on to say, let's see how much more of the New Testament can be coordinated by means of this series of hermeneutic moves." Hans W. Frei, "Remarks in Connection with a Theological Proposal," in Frei, *Theology and Narrative,* 32.

Frei a theory of narrative could no more become the dominant framework within which Christian belief must be interpreted than could any other general theory.

Not surprisingly, in some of his later writings Frei was critical of forms of "narrative theology" that begin with a general narrative anthropology rather than with the particulars of the biblical narrative. In fact, he can even place this kind of theology in the liberal camp because of its anthropological starting point.

> ... clearly it is a case of putting the cart before the horse — but this time the wagon is theological rather than literary — if one constructs a general and inalienable human quality called "narrative" or "narrativity," within which to interpret the Gospels and provide foundational warrant for the possibility of their existential and ontological meaningfulness. The notion that Christian theology is a member of a general class of "narrative theology" is no more than a minor will-o'-the-wisp.[94]

Indeed, Frei could say of Barth, in a statement that he would surely apply to himself, that he was a "narrative theologian" only to the extent that Jesus was what he did and underwent.[95] If, as Frei asserts, theology provides a normative description and critique of the use of Christian language in the church, then Frei's theology clearly challenges contemporary homiletics to think carefully about the role of narrative in the church's preaching.

Christological Content: The Unsubstitutable Identity of Jesus Christ

Simply to assert the Christological content of Frei's work is not very helpful. As Frei himself noted, much of the liberal theology of the nineteenth century was unquestionably Christocentric. Similarly, the more recent liberal theologies that Frei critiques have a Christological focus. However, Frei would argue, in most of these cases Jesus Christ becomes simply the form for a content developed through an independent analysis of human existence or human experience. As in the case of Tillich's sermon "You Are Accepted," Christology becomes a function of an understanding of salvation developed on other grounds.

94. Frei, "Literal Reading," 73.
95. Frei, "Barth and Schleiermacher," 72.

Frei's emphasis on Christological content is something decidedly different. For Frei the starting point is not human experience or existence, but rather the specific, unsubstitutable identity of Jesus Christ, which is rendered in the interplay of character and incident in the gospel narratives. Jesus Christ, as depicted in the gospels, rather than a general anthropology, is the key to the gospel's meaningfulness. Soteriology is a function of Christology.[96]

Obviously, Barth's influence is again of importance. However, the initial direction for Frei's approach to Christology came not from Barth, but, ironically, from H. Richard Niebuhr. Although Frei criticized the existentialist approach of *The Meaning of Revelation* for its tendency to reduce Jesus to his meaningfulness for the believer,[97] Frei found in Niebuhr's brief Christological discussion in *Christ and Culture* the seeds for his own approach to Christology.[98]

In one of his earliest essays Frei noted several aspects of Niebuhr's position that impressed him.[99] To begin with, Frei appreciated Niebuhr's respect for the ascriptive logic of the gospels. According to Frei, Niebuhr refuses to let the moral predicates applied to Jesus (love, faith, etc.) become dominant. Rather, these predicates are transformed as they are taken up into the subject Jesus of Nazareth; each one of them becomes "extreme and disproportionate" because Jesus practices them in obedience to God. There is no exaltation, for example, of love for love's sake.[100]

---

96. In other terms, one might say that the person and work of Jesus Christ are inseparably one. Indeed, in Frei's understanding, this inseparable relationship between person and work is the very point of realistic narrative: there is no hidden "person" lurking mysteriously behind the work (in Ryle's terms, no "ghost in the machine"), but rather "Jesus is what he does." When Jesus is reduced to his meaningfulness for the believer, then Christology is reduced to Jesus' work; the unique, unsubstitutable subject, Jesus of Nazareth, disappears. Hans W. Frei, "The Theology of H. Richard Niebuhr," in *Faith and Ethics: The Theology of H. Richard Niebuhr,* ed. Paul Ramsey (New York: Harper and Brothers, 1957), 107.

97. Frei, "Theology of H. Richard Niebuhr," 106-7.

98. H. Richard Niebuhr, *Christ and Culture* (New York: Harper and Row, 1951; Harper Colophon Edition, 1975), 11-29.

99. Frei, "Theology of H. Richard Niebuhr," 104-16. Frei continued to appreciate Niebuhr's work at this point, noting it again in *Types,* 143-46.

100. Frei, "Theology of H. Richard Niebuhr," 108-9. I think Frei gives Niebuhr too much credit at this point. In Niebuhr's presentation Jesus actually seems more like a good "radical monotheist." Radical monotheism, rather than Jesus himself, structures each of the virtues.

In addition, Frei highlights Niebuhr's focus on Jesus' "moral Sonship" as the best way to understand Jesus' unity with God. According to Niebuhr, Jesus' virtues all have a mediatorial quality between God and humanity. For example, because of Jesus' perfect, trusting love of the faithful God, Jesus also demonstrates perfect, faithful love of humanity. Herein lies the unity between Jesus and God — a unity not described in terms of "substance" or "consciousness," but rather a unity shaped by intentions and actions. "In sum," Frei writes, "it has to be said that the moral Sonship to God of Jesus Christ involves not two persons or beings but one."[101]

Finally, Frei particularly appreciated the way Niebuhr discerns the clue to Jesus' "moral Sonship," not through subjective or psychological understandings of personal identity, but in "the character of Jesus Christ as it is manifest in his teaching and acts, i.e., in the unity of his moral being."[102] This approach, Frei suggests, shifts "the emphasis, in understanding the person of Jesus Christ, away from psychological interpretation to a more concrete basis."[103] For Niebuhr,

> The being of the person Jesus Christ is not — as it is for the psychologizing school — an ineffable state of awareness behind act and teachings; nor is the full personal being inaccessible to us — as it is for the theologians influenced by form criticism. The unity of the person of Jesus Christ is embedded in and immediately present to his teaching and practice. It is the focus of unity in the teaching and acts of the Lord. In one sense, no series of acts or moral virtues in teaching and active exemplification exhausts the significance of a person's being. Nevertheless, one can say that the being does not stand ineffably behind the series or the essence behind the phenomena, distinguished from them and only inferentially to be interpreted: rather, the being is concretely exhibited, embodied in the series of phenomena. Hence, the teaching and the acts of Jesus Christ, his moral virtues, are themselves the direct clue to his being. In them one may find, by an historical and at the same time theological exegesis, in faith, hope, and love, the unique moral Sonship to God of one who is completely at one with men.[104]

101. Frei, "Theology of H. Richard Niebuhr," 110.
102. Frei, "Theology of H. Richard Niebuhr," 110.
103. Frei, "Theology of H. Richard Niebuhr," 114.
104. Frei, "Theology of H. Richard Niebuhr," 115.

At this point Frei had obviously not yet developed his approach to the gospels as realistic narratives. He is also still trapped in older formulations of the faith-and-history question. Nevertheless, the seeds of Frei's Christology are apparent in his interpretation of Niebuhr's work. Frei sensed that Niebuhr's Christology offered a way of moving beyond both "substance" and "consciousness" approaches to the unity and differentiation of Jesus and God, as well as beyond the epistemological agnosticism about Jesus of Nazareth characteristic of Bultmann and the early Barth.[105] One can almost feel Frei's excitement in this early essay; he is obviously ready to give Niebuhr's suggestion the close attention he thinks it merits.[106] Indeed, it is no surprise that in his next major essay, published nine years later, Frei began developing a Christology based on the interplay of character and incident in the gospels, rather than on Jesus' self-consciousness or anything else inferred "behind" the narrative.[107] The initial impetus for Frei's distinctive approach to Christology came from H. Richard Niebuhr.[108]

105. Frei, "Theology of H. Richard Niebuhr," 111-15.

106. Frei, "Theology of H. Richard Niebuhr," 116.

107. That essay was Frei's "Theological Reflections on the Gospel Accounts of Jesus' Death and Resurrection." During the nine years between the Niebuhr essays and this one, Frei published only one brief article: "Religion: Natural and Revealed."

108. The influence of H. Richard Niebuhr possibly helps to explain why Frei's own Christology has been criticized as too close to a Nestorian or "moral union" view of the relationship between Jesus and God. See Hunsinger, "Hans Frei as Theologian," 114-17. Going beyond this criticism, John Webster suggests that Frei's method itself leads necessarily to a "low Christology" (John Webster, "Response to George Hunsinger," *Modern Theology* 8 [April 1992]).

Despite these criticisms, Frei does carefully defend Jesus' union with God. The gospel narratives, Frei argues, depict the simultaneous distinction and union of Jesus and God. Frei develops this complex unity not through the traditional categories of substance, nature, or being, but rather through the narrative logic of Jesus' intentionally enacted identity. In the gospel narratives, Jesus obediently enacts the intention of God for the good of humanity. In the course of the narrative, the agent of this enactment — Jesus and/or God — becomes increasingly complex. As Jesus undergoes a transition from power to powerlessness in his passion, God's activity increasingly supplants, but nevertheless remains identified with, that of Jesus. In the resurrection this complex unity reaches its climax. At this point in the narrative God is the sole agent (Jesus cannot raise himself), but Jesus alone appears. At the very moment where God's supplantation of Jesus as agent is complete, Jesus alone is present. In the resurrection Jesus' unique identity is most fully manifested; he alone marks the presence and action of God. Unquestionably for Frei, Jesus and God are one in a unity that is narratively rendered

The final result of Frei's Christology is, as Hunsinger points out, an "objectivist soteriology."[109] That is, Jesus' concrete enactment of salvation for the world, rendered in the gospel narratives, is logically prior to and distinguishable from the relationship of faith (just as Jesus' identity is logically prior to and distinguishable from his presence). In Frei's words, "the story of salvation is completely and exclusively that of the savior Jesus from Nazareth in Galilee."[110] Rather than an independent analysis of human experience defining salvation, the story of Jesus does. Consequently, the crucial issue is how contemporary persons enter into the particular salvation accomplished by Jesus Christ, rather than how we correlate him with a salvation that we consider meaningful. In direct opposition to liberal theology, Frei seeks to move from the sense of the story to its contemporary meaningfulness, from Christology to soteriology, rather than vice versa.

It is thus not surprising that Frei concludes *The Identity of Jesus Christ* with a discussion of the church.[111] For Frei the salvific meaning-

---

and indissolubly complex (*Identity*, 116-25). Nevertheless, it is important to remember, whether one finds Frei's Christology satisfactory or not, that Frei was emphasizing a general orientation, a way of approaching Christology; he was not setting up his specific position as the final word.

109. Hunsinger, "Hans Frei as Theologian," 119. Hunsinger's terminology is somewhat problematic at this point. Not only does "objectivist soteriology" sound rather static, but the term "objectivist" brings a lot of baggage and possible confusion with it. Frei himself made essentially the same point, highlighting the *logic* of the gospel in a more dynamic way: "Not only the *possibility* and the *actuality*, but also the *need* for incarnate reconciliation is simply to be affirmed as a reflexive consideration of the fact that it was actually so. For what do we really know of that need apart from or logically prior to that fact" (Frei, "Karl Barth: Theologian," 8).

110. Frei, "Theological Reflections," 263. This story of salvation enacted by Jesus is, for Frei, characterized primarily by a "pattern of exchange" (*Identity*, 64-65). Drawing on Isaiah 53, Frei develops a fairly traditional vicarious theory of the atonement. In his perfect obedience to God, Jesus vicariously assumes the guilt and literally assumes the powerlessness of humanity on the cross. So thoroughly does Jesus identify with humanity that he himself must be redeemed in the resurrection. However, in his very powerlessness, Jesus is the power of salvation; through his identification with humanity, he exchanges his own moral purity for humanity's sinfulness. As the Savior, Jesus is simultaneously in need of redemption, redeemed, and redeeming (*Identity*, 122). Unfortunately, Frei never develops in detail the nature of human sin or the specific character of salvation, though his twofold emphasis on guilt and powerlessness is suggestive. Neither does Frei clarify exactly how Jesus' purity is transferred to humanity (Hunsinger, "Hans Frei as Theologian," 115). Ultimately, Frei leaves this exchange as a mystery (*Identity*, 65).

111. Frei, *Identity*, 154-65.

fulness of Jesus Christ becomes a contemporary reality not by being correlated with human experience, but through the mysterious, eschatological work of the Holy Spirit in the church.[112] Specifically, Christ's saving "presence" becomes real and effective through the practices of the church, particularly Word, sacrament, and discipleship. The story of Jesus becomes salvifically meaningful as the church is formed by the particular identity of Jesus Christ, rather than as Jesus is correlated in meaningful ways with contemporary experience.[113]

> Ultimately therefore [the story's] capacity to be reenacted in your sensibility and your imagination cannot be the criterion of its significance for you. And surely, the followers of Jesus Christ have recognized this from the very beginning. For whomever it becomes the truth it does so not by imaginative obliteration of time but by hammering out a shape of life patterned after its own shape. That does not mean that we repeat the original events literally in our lives, and certainly not completely, but it means that our lives reflect the story as in a glass darkly. The shape of the story being mirrored in the shape of our life is the condition of its being meaningful for us.[114]

In short, Jesus' meaningfulness depends not on his relevance for us, but on our faithfulness to him, on our becoming a faithful community shaped by his identity.

Frei's Christology leads, in circular fashion, directly and necessarily back to the church, with whose language and practices it began. Theology, worship, and ethics (doctrine, liturgy, and life) are inseparably linked for Frei in the life of the church; for the "factual affirmation" of Jesus as Redeemer is never simply an intellectual matter, but is knowledge that must be practiced in worship and discipleship; it is truth that is done.[115]

---

112. See Hunsinger's excellent discussion in "Hans Frei as Theologian," 121-22; also Frei, *Identity,* 154-65. For Frei the Spirit is the "indirect" presence of Christ and the God who is one with him in the church. Although Christocentric, Frei was clearly Trinitarian.

113. Frei, *Types,* 87-89.

114. Frei, *Identity,* 170-71.

115. Frei, *Identity,* 157. This includes, for Frei, the church's activism and mission in and for the world. The church is not isolated from the world. Rather, word and sacrament, which constitute the church as the spatial and temporal locus of Christ's presence in the world, are inseparable from activism and mission in and for the world:

Although Frei offers no complete doctrine of the church, its importance is evident throughout his work and becomes even more explicit as he turns to a cultural-linguistic model of religion in his later writings. The "problem" of the meaningfulness of Jesus Christ is "solved" in the concrete worship and discipleship of the Christian community in and for the world, not by means of a general anthropology or philosophy. It is thus not surprising that Frei's sermon at the end of *Identity* invites us not to "accept the fact that we are accepted," but to be properly disposed to the story of Jesus through ritual recital and reenactment and through faithful discipleship:

> . . . the embodiment of the Easter story's pattern in our lives means no mysterious archetypal consciousness of it, but a new way of governing our bodies. That is how we are in touch with the story. A little humdrum perhaps, considering the dramatic quality of what happened at Easter. But the point is clear . . . : To know this story is to adopt a way of life consequent upon hearing it, and shaped by it. That is how we are to be disposed toward it.[116]

John Howard Yoder said it in other words: "The real issue is not whether Jesus can make sense in a world far from Galilee, but whether — when he meets us in our world, as he does in fact — we want to follow him."[117] Here is the ultimate meaning of Frei's distinctive approach to Christology and the final goal of Frei's descriptive, Anselmian, Christocentric theology: the faithfulness of the church to Jesus Christ. It is within this context that Frei's understanding of biblical narrative needs to be examined.

"It is only by reference to the Spirit, i.e., to the complete unity of Jesus Christ's identity and presence given to us now indirectly, that Word and Sacrament cohere with passionate Christian concern for the world in its mysterious passage from event to event" (Frei, *Identity*, 157-59).

116. Frei, *Identity*, 171, 168.

117. Yoder, 62. The affinities between Yoder and Frei are not coincidental. Yoder, too, was a serious and profound student of Barth.

Chapter Three

Continuation and Revision
in Frei's Later Work:
The Cultural-Linguistic Turn

U p until now most of the scholarly discussion and critique of Frei's
work has focused on his two major publications of the seventies,
The Eclipse of Biblical Narrative and *The Identity of Jesus Christ*.[1] However, in light of Frei's later work, these two books cannot be viewed as
the final word on Frei's approach to biblical narrative.[2] As Frei himself
notes, his later work represents both a continuation and a revision of
his earlier position.[3] Indeed, in one of his later essays Frei himself
provides his own perceptive critique of his earlier position, particularly
its similarity to Anglo-American New Criticism.[4]

1. The main exceptions are the collection of essays in Garrett Green, ed., *Scriptural Authority and Narrative Interpretation* (Philadelphia: Fortress Press, 1987), and the essays in *Modern Theology* 8 (April 1992).

2. By "later work" I mean Frei's work during the 1980s, beginning with his lecture "Theology and the Interpretation of Narrative: Some Hermeneutical Considerations," presented at Haverford College, Haverford, Pennsylvania in 1982. This essay has been published in Hans W. Frei, *Theology and Narrative: Selected Essays*, ed. George Hunsinger and William C. Placher (New York: Oxford Univ. Press, 1993), 94-116. Frei's two most important later works are "The 'Literal Reading' of the Biblical Narrative in the Christian Tradition: Does It Stretch or Will It Break?" in *The Bible and the Narrative Tradition*, ed. Frank McConnell (New York: Oxford Univ. Press, 1986) and *Types of Christian Theology*, ed. George Hunsinger and William C. Placher (New Haven: Yale Univ. Press, 1992).

3. Frei, *Types*, 6.

4. See Frei, "Literal Reading," 62-67. Despite Frei's dependence on the work of

In this chapter and the one that follows I will examine Frei's later work and consider his approach to biblical narrative in light of it. I will demonstrate that Frei's earlier "narrative hermeneutic" becomes embedded in a particular "communal hermeneutic" and that this development does in fact represent a continuation as well as a revision of Frei's earlier position. In this chapter I will examine Frei's turn to a "cultural-linguistic" model of Christianity, according to which the Christian religion is viewed as a social phenomenon, constituted by the language and practices of Christian communities.[5] In Chapter Four I will examine the way in which Frei's cultural-linguistic model of Christianity leads him to a much stronger emphasis on the reading community — the "community of interpretation."[6] Consistent with this turn to the community of interpretation, Frei's basic category for approaching biblical narrative becomes the "literal sense," or *sensus literalis*, of Scripture, rather than "realistic narrative." In addition, this turn to the community coincides with Frei's growing appreciation for variety in

---

Erich Auerbach and his focus on narrative rather than poetry, certain aspects of Frei's early work (e.g., his rejection of the intentional and affective fallacies; his apparent defense of an autonomous text and a disinterested interpreter; his focus on the formal aspects of the text) have led to his being lumped together with the Anglo-American New Critics — and criticized accordingly. The most extended criticism of Frei in this regard has come from Lynn M. Poland, *Literary Criticism and Biblical Hermeneutics: A Critique of Formalist Approaches,* American Academy of Religion Series, no. 48, ed. Carl A. Raschke (Chico, California: Scholars Press, 1985), 120-37. See also Lynn M. Poland, "The New Criticism, Neoorthodoxy, and the New Testament," *Journal of Religion* 65 (1985): 459-77. For another critique see Stephen D. Moore, "Are the Gospels Unified Narratives?" *Society of Biblical Literature Seminar Papers 1987* (Atlanta: Scholars Press, 1987), 443-58. One recent writer has praised Frei for his affinities with New Criticism: Mark Ellingsen, *The Integrity of Biblical Narrative: Story in Theology and Proclamation* (Minneapolis: Fortress Press, 1990). While I do not want to deny that Frei was influenced by Anglo-American New Criticism (which enjoyed its heyday at Yale while Frei was a student there), even Frei's early work cannot be simplistically lumped with New Criticism. Moreover, Frei's later work, with its turn to a communal hermeneutic, makes the criticisms of Frei in this regard virtually irrelevant.

5. Unlike Lindbeck and Frei, I will speak only of a cultural-linguistic model of Christianity, rather than a cultural-linguistic theory of religion. I am suspicious of any general theory of religion, even one as purportedly "low level" as the cultural-linguistic one. I do, however, think that the cultural-linguistic model is appropriate for examining Christianity, which is socially embodied in particular communities, even if the model is questionable as a general theory of religion.

6. Frei, *Types,* 56-57.

interpretive practice — for the polyphonous, at times cacophonous character of biblical interpretation within the dialogical community of believers. In the process of examining these developments in Frei's thought, I will also highlight the significant areas of continuity that exist in his work and the important places where further development is needed.

The material in these chapters has important implications for contemporary homiletics, which I will explore later in this book. Just as Frei comes out of a different theological framework from most contemporary homileticians who appropriate narrative, so his approach to biblical narrative reflects a different hermeneutic from that of most homileticians. Frei's cultural-linguistic turn, which focuses on the distinctive language and practices of the Christian community and stresses the ecclesial context of biblical interpretation, represents both a hermeneutical and theological challenge to contemporary homileticians, who have generally appropriated narrative within a very different framework.

A Cultural-Linguistic Model of Christianity

In 1984 George Lindbeck published his groundbreaking work, *The Nature of Doctrine: Religion and Theology in a Postliberal Age.* In this book Lindbeck develops a cultural-linguistic theory of religion and suggests some of its implications for ecumenism, interreligious dialogue, doctrine, and theology. According to Lindbeck, religions are best understood as "cultures" or "languages," rather than as sets of cognitive propositions or as particular expressions of some general, "prelinguistic" human experience.[7] Religions are not primarily cognitive or experiential phenomena, though these elements are undoubtedly present. Rather, religions are social phenomena. Consisting of a particular language and specific practices, religions are like cultural-linguistic "mediums" that shape all of life and thought;[8] they are "comprehensive interpretive schemes, usually embodied in myths or narratives and heavily ritualized,

7. Lindbeck distinguishes his cultural-linguistic model from what he calls "cognitive-propositional" and "experiential-expressivist" models. George Lindbeck, *The Nature of Doctrine: Religion and Theology in a Postliberal Age* (Philadelphia: Westminster Press, 1984).

8. Lindbeck, 33.

which structure human experience and understanding of self and world."[9] As Lindbeck summarizes, a religion

> is not primarily an array of beliefs about the true and the good (though it may involve these), or a symbolism expressive of basic attitudes, feelings, or sentiments (though these will be generated). Rather, it is similar to an idiom that makes possible the description of realities, the formulation of beliefs, and the experiencing of inner attitudes, feelings, and sentiments. Like a culture or language, it is a communal phenomenon that shapes the subjectivities of individuals rather than being primarily a manifestation of those subjectivities. It comprises a vocabulary of discursive and nondiscursive symbols together with a distinctive logic or grammar in terms of which this vocabulary can be meaningfully deployed. Lastly, just as a language (or 'language game,' to use Wittgenstein's phrase) is correlated with a form of life, and just as a culture has both cognitive and behavioral dimensions, so it is also in the case of a religious tradition. Its doctrines, cosmic stories, or myths, and ethical directives are integrally related to the rituals it practices, the sentiments or experiences it evokes, the actions it recommends, and the institutional forms it develops.[10]

In short, through their specific languages and practices religions identify and describe "what is more important than anything else in the world" and organize all of life in relation to this.[11]

Lindbeck specifically notes the differences between this cultural-

---

9. Lindbeck, 32.

10. Lindbeck, 33. Lindbeck's work is heavily influenced by that of the anthropologist Clifford Geertz. See, in particular, Clifford Geertz, *The Interpretation of Cultures* (New York: Basic Books, 1973). As the above quotation indicates, Lindbeck, like Frei, has also been influenced by the linguistic philosophy of the later Wittgenstein, though he has appropriated Wittgenstein rather loosely. For example, several people have recently argued persuasively that a "religion" is far too large to qualify as a Wittgensteinian "language game" or "form of life." See Nicholas Lash, "How Large Is a Language Game?" *Theology* 87 (1984): 19-28; also Fergus Kerr, *Theology after Wittgenstein* (Oxford: Basil Blackwell, 1986; paperback ed., 1988), 30-31. In addition, Wittgenstein retained an understanding of the "natural" that can lead to a more experiential-expressivist view of religion, as in the case of Kerr's work (Kerr, 162-63). Indeed, Frei himself criticized the "experiential-expressivist" direction toward which Kerr's appropriation of Wittgenstein tended (Frei, *Types*, 93-94).

11. Lindbeck, 32-33.

linguistic approach and the dominant, "experiential-expressivist" approach in American theology, according to which "religion" is fundamentally an expression of general human experience or consciousness. With regard to experience, Lindbeck argues that in the cultural-linguistic model the relationship between "inner" and "outer" is reversed from that in experiential-expressivist approaches: ". . . in the interplay between 'inner' experience and 'external' religious and cultural factors, the latter can be viewed as the leading partners, and it is this option which the cultural and/or linguistic analyst favors."[12] That is, the religion is not a particular expression of some common human experience, but rather the particular language and practices of a given religion shape experience in particular ways.[13]

Within this framework, becoming a Christian is like learning a set of cultural and linguistic skills; it is like learning a language. As Lindbeck writes,

> to become religious — no less than to become culturally or linguistically competent — is to interiorize a set of skills by practice and training. One learns how to feel, act, and think in conformity with a religious tradition that is, in its inner structure, far richer and more subtle than can be explicitly articulated. The primary knowledge is not *about* the religion, nor *that* the religion teaches such and such, but rather *how* to be religious in such and such ways. Sometimes explicitly formulated statements of the beliefs or behavioral norms of a religion may be helpful in the learning process, but by no means always. Ritual, prayer, and example are normally much more important.[14]

Becoming a Christian is a process of socialization or enculturation within a particular cultural-linguistic community. It is a matter of ac-

---

12. Lindbeck, 33-34; 36. Lindbeck here does not deny a reciprocal, "dialectical" relation between the language and practices of a religion and various human experiences, but he gives the primary role to the former.

13. For Lindbeck, as for Frei, there are no "prelinguistic" experiences. Experience is not a "natural" phenomenon, but is both expressed within and formed by some particular language and practices. Lindbeck cites Wittgenstein's argument against "private languages" to support his position (Lindbeck, 38-39; see also Frei, *Types*, 74).

14. Lindbeck, 35.

quiring competence in the language and practices of the Christian community, which come to shape one's experience, understanding, and life.

Even before Lindbeck had published *The Nature of Doctrine*, Hans Frei had signaled his own movement in this cultural-linguistic direction in a lecture given at Haverford College.[15] Over the final years of Frei's life, this approach became increasingly important in his work. Unfortunately, this particular aspect of Frei's thought has not yet been fully examined or appreciated, largely because much of his later work has only recently been published. However, it is difficult to overestimate the significance of this cultural-linguistic turn for Frei's approach to biblical narrative.

In the Haverford lecture Frei emphasizes the public, social character of Christianity. Sounding very much like his friend and colleague Lindbeck, Frei writes that

> Christianity is a religion, a social organism. Its self-description marks it typically as a religion in ways similar to those given by sociologists of religion or cultural anthropologists. It is a community held together by constantly changing, yet enduring structures, practices, and institutions — the way religious communities are, e.g., a sacred text, regulated relations between an elite (overlapping but not identical with a professional group) and a more general body of adherents, and by a set of rituals — preaching, baptism, the celebration of communion, common beliefs and attitudes, all of these linked — again typical of a religion — with a set of narratives connected with each other in the sacred text and its interpretive tradition. All of these are, for social scientist and theologian (qua adherent or agent of the self-description of the religion) not the *signs* or *manifestations* of the religion, rather they *constitute* it, in complex and changing coherence.[16]

In addition to the Haverford lecture, the two major works of Frei's later period are likewise shaped by this cultural-linguistic model of Christianity. In *Types of Christian Theology*, for example, Frei understands Christianity as a "semiotically coherent cultural system."[17] Indeed, he repeats almost verbatim the definition he gave in the Haver-

---

15. Frei, "Theology and Interpretation of Narrative."
16. Frei, "Theology and Interpretation of Narrative," 96-97.
17. Frei, *Types*, 7.

ford lecture, which I just quoted.[18] Similarly, in "Literal Reading" Frei emphasizes the cultural-linguistic character of Christianity. This understanding of Christianity is spelled out in relation to the *sensus literalis* of Scripture:

> The descriptive context, then, for the *sensus literalis* is the religion of which it is a part, understood at once as a determinate code in which beliefs, ritual, and behavior patterns, ethos as well as narrative, come together as a common semiotic system, and also as the community which is that system in use — apart from which the very term ("semiotic system") is in this case no more than a misplaced metaphor.[19]

Like Lindbeck, Frei also sets this position over against understandings of Christian faith that focus on "consciousness" or "experience." For Frei, experience is secondary to and shaped by the particular sociolinguistic community. The "outer" is prior to the "inner," though Frei would certainly not have used these metaphors because of his suspicion of any "ghost-in-the-machine" anthropology. The language and practices of Christianity are not simply particular expressions or manifestations of some common human experience. Rather, the "social organism" of the Christian community actually *constitutes* Christianity and forms particular experiences.[20] Correlatively, coming to be a Christian is not primarily associated with having some "religious experience," but rather with learning a particular language and set of practices; it is the acquisition of particular skills, which are behavioral and dispositional as well as linguistic and conceptual.[21] Becoming a Christian is a communal journey, rather than an individual, experiential event. As Frei writes, "To learn the language of the Christian community is not to undergo a profound 'experience' of a privileged sort, but to learn to make that language one's own, in faith, hope, and love."[22]

This cultural-linguistic understanding of Christianity permeates Frei's mature theological position. As was already apparent in the previous chapter, Frei's cultural-linguistic turn is evident in his understand-

---

18. Frei, *Types*, 22.
19. Frei, "Literal Reading," 70-71. In Chapter Four I will examine more fully Frei's understanding of the *sensus literalis*.
20. Frei, *Types*, 22, 54.
21. Frei, *Types*, 4.
22. Frei, *Types*, 54.

ing of theology itself, which he comes to view as the normative self-description of the language and practices of the Christian community. The cognate discipline of theology, he argues, is not philosophy, but the interpretive social sciences.[23] As Frei writes in "Theology and the Interpretation of Narrative,"

> . . . Christianity, precisely as a community, is language forming, not purely, of course, but sufficiently so that that language as embodied in its institutions, practices, doctrines, and so on, is a distinctive and irreducible social fact. The language is religion-specific, and theology is the constant testing of the way it is used in a given era, against a norm that consists of *some* ordering of the paradigmatic instances of the language (such as the sacred text), but also the cumulative tradition and the most supple and sensitive minds and consciences in the community past and present. No theologian here speaks for himself without first speaking for the community, and his first task is therefore to give a normative description rather than positioning himself to set forth or even argue the status of truth claims.[24]

In short, as Frei writes in *Types of Christian Theology,* "the social, linguistic community is the necessary condition or context for having a common self-description"; that is, the cultural-linguistic community is the necessary condition for theology.[25]

Other dimensions of Frei's understanding of theology also reveal his strong cultural-linguistic turn. For example, in his later work Frei emphasizes the practical character of theology, which is to be in the service of the Christian community.[26]

> Theology . . . is a practical discipline; it is in effect part of learning the grammar of a linguistic symbol system; it is Christian self-description under some norm for its specific language use. No matter what it may entail logically in matters of theory, it is part of the praxis, the ruled practice of culture. . . .[27]

23. Frei, *Types,* 2.
24. Frei, "Theology and Interpretation of Narrative," 100.
25. Frei, *Types,* 33; also 112-13.
26. Frei, *Types,* 25, 126.
27. Frei, *Types,* 126.

Consistent with this approach, Frei explicitly locates the work of the theologian within the practices of the Christian community. The theologian is a functionary of the community and is to be trained for that purpose. Theology is "part of social tradition enacted by a participant, an agent who knows how to use the language in its appropriate context."[28] Although Frei does defend a place for theology in the academy, he increasingly emphasizes practical theology, "the nurture of leaders in the Christian community."[29]

In addition, Frei's cultural-linguistic turn is evident in his appreciation for the regulative function of doctrine, an important dimension of the cultural-linguistic model in Lindbeck's work.[30] For Frei, as for Lindbeck, Christian doctrines, in their second-order function, are not primarily expressions of experience or statements of timeless propositional truths, but rather "communally authoritative rules of discourse, attitude, and action."[31] Although incomplete and inadequate in themselves, Christian doctrines instantiate important rules for Christian discourse and biblical interpretation.[32] As Frei writes, "Christian doctrinal

28. Frei, *Types*, 126.
29. Frei, *Types*, 116.
30. Lindbeck speaks of this as a "rule theory" of doctrine (Lindbeck, 4-5, 18, 81).
31. Lindbeck, 18. Lindbeck suggests that this regulative understanding of doctrine is reflected in the ancient notion of *regula fidei*. Lindbeck's emphasis on the use or function of doctrines is important at this point. Doctrines can in fact be used in different ways in various contexts. For example, in worship the Nicene Creed functions differently than it does as doctrine qua doctrine. In discussing the regulative character of doctrines, Lindbeck highlights one specific function of doctrines, though in the cultural-linguistic model, this is the central function (Lindbeck, 19, 80). Although Lindbeck's work is helpful for clarifying the function of doctrines as rules, one should not simply lump Frei and Lindbeck together at this point. Frei is not concerned to develop a "theory of doctrine." He simply seeks to describe the ways doctrines function regulatively in Christianity.
32. Frei, *Types*, 124-28. Doctrines, Lindbeck and Frei both assert, don't usually state the "grammar" or logic of Christian discourse directly, but rather embody and illustrate it. As Lindbeck writes, "Some doctrines, such as the *sola gratia* or the *sola fide* in Christianity, are explicit statements of general regulative principles, but most doctrines illustrate correct usage rather than define it. They are exemplary instantiations or paradigms of the application of rules. Faithfulness to such doctrines does not necessarily mean repeating them; rather, it requires, in the making of any new formulations, adherence to the same directives that were involved in their first formulation" (Lindbeck, 81). Lindbeck's generalizations get him into trouble at this point; "doctrinal regulation" is a messier business than Lindbeck suggests. For example, Lindbeck gives away his own particular tradition — Lutheran — by highlighting *sola gratia* and *sola fide* as regulative

statements are understood to have a status similar to that of grammatical rules implicit in discourse. . . ."[33]

An equally significant indication of Frei's cultural-linguistic turn can be seen in the shape of Frei's late work, *Types of Christian Theology*. Although the work is in some ways a typology similar to others developed by scholars at Yale, there are dimensions to the work that reflect Frei's appreciation for the cultural and institutional factors that shape theology. Most significant in this regard is the way in which Frei locates the development of liberal theology in the formation of the Berlin Academy in the nineteenth century. Frei's "types" are not mere abstractions, but are located in historical developments growing out of the specific cultural and institutional pressures surrounding the struggle of theology with *Wissenschaft* in the formation of the Berlin Academy. Indeed, in Appendix A in *Types* Frei provides an analysis of the cultural, political, and institutional factors that contributed to the development of the academy and the consequent shaping of academic theology.[34] Here Frei indicates his growing appreciation for the social and cultural factors that produce and reproduce various types of theology.

In these various ways, then, Frei's theological position, discussed

---

principles. These might not be central regulative principles in every Christian tradition, nor might they have the same function and force in traditions where they nevertheless remain central. That is, they might be related to other doctrines by a somewhat different "grammar," and they might even have different nuances of meaning — a different semantic force. For example what is the *fide* that is *sola*? This *fide* might have a very different grammar and meaning in the Lutheran, Reformed, Orthodox, and Anabaptist traditions. Neither Lindbeck nor Frei has taken these differences seriously enough, though there is nothing in their positions to prevent them from doing so. See Frei, *Types*, 13-14, 127-28; Lindbeck, 80.

33. Frei, *Types*, 4; also 90. Kerr's discussion of "theology as grammar" is helpful at this point and once again suggests the importance of Wittgenstein: "Theology as grammar is, then, the patient and painstaking description of how, when we have to, we speak of God." ". . . by remarking that theology is grammar, [Wittgenstein] is reminding us that it is only by listening to what we say about God (what has been said for many generations), and to how what is said about God ties in with what we say and do in innumerable other connections, that we have any chance of understanding what we mean when we speak of God" (Kerr, 147-48). This understanding of theology, however, does not mean that God is limited to human language; that very language may, as the Christian language does in fact, include a recognition of the limits of language and the transcendence of God.

34. Frei, *Types*, 95-132.

in the preceding two chapters, is informed in his later work by his cultural-linguistic model of Christianity. However, this development does not represent a radical shift in Frei's work, but rather a continuation as well as a revision. As early as the "Theological Reflections" essay Frei was emphasizing the descriptive, rather than explanatory, character of theology.[35] In his turn to the cultural-linguistic model Frei simply spells out more fully the communal context within which descriptive theology is located. He focuses more attention on the communal language and practices on which theology depends as a second-order discipline. As George Hunsinger has written, in his later work Frei's theology is "located in a much wider and more abundant context than before."[36]

Similarly, this turn to a cultural-linguistic model is consistent with Frei's Anselmian approach to theology, which, as I noted earlier, was already central in *Identity*. Anselmian theology, as Frei appropriated it through Barth, begins with the specific language of the Christian community — the *Credo*, in Barth's terms.[37] Consequently, it is not surprising that Frei suggests in his later work that Anselm's *Proslogion* was in fact an exercise in "reflection on the *grammar* of the word *God* as it is used in the Christian church."[38] Frei's cultural-linguistic model of Christianity is in fact nothing more than the appropriation of sociological and anthropological categories to help flesh out the communal context of a particularistic, Anselmian theology. Frei's theological concerns shaped his turn to the cultural-linguistic model, rather than vice versa. Frei's particularistic theology leads him to an appreciation for Christianity as a cultural-linguistic community, which in turn leads him, as I will discuss later, to a particularistic communal hermeneutic.

Frei's turn to the cultural-linguistic model of Christianity also reflects a continuation as well as a revision of other aspects of his earlier position. For example, in his earlier work Frei emphasized the public character of Jesus' identity and, derivatively, of Christian identity itself. Based on his reading of the gospels as realistic narratives, which cumu-

35. Frei, "Theological Reflections," 277.
36. George Hunsinger, "Hans Frei As Theologian: The Quest for a Generous Orthodoxy," *Modern Theology* 8 (April 1992): 128.
37. Frei, *Types*, 78-79.
38. Frei, *Types*, 79.

latively depict Jesus' identity through the interplay of character and circumstance, Frei critiqued understandings of Jesus that focused on his consciousness. Implicit in this critique was not only a criticism of "liberal" understandings of religions as expressions of experience or consciousness, but also a challenge to the mind-body dualism implicit in "individualistic-mentalistic" (i.e., Cartesian) views of the self. In this area, too, Frei's turn to a cultural-linguistic model of Christianity is consistent with, as well as an enrichment of, his earlier work. The cultural-linguistic turn represents an even more thorough rejection of theological liberalism, with its focus on human experience or consciousness. Through this cultural-linguistic model Frei affirms the public, social character of Christian identity, enriching his earlier intention-action emphasis with an explicit social and communal dimension.

In fact, Frei signals this later move in the preface to *Identity,* which was written after the body of the work was completed. In the preface Frei expresses his dissatisfaction with the category of "self-manifestation," which had supplemented that of intention-action in his description of Jesus' identity. This category, Frei notes, is too deeply rooted in "Idealist subjectivity or romantic consciousness."[39] He then asserts that he wants to supplement his future work "by exploring the formal analytical devices which sociologists of knowledge and Marxist literary critics use to identify the relation between individual personhood and the contextual social structures."[40] It is thus not surprising when in *Types of Christian Theology* Frei writes the following about human actions:

39. Hans W. Frei, *The Identity of Jesus Christ: The Hermeneutical Bases of Dogmatic Theology* (Philadelphia: Fortress Press, 1975), viii-x. Here again, Wittgenstein is an important influence. For a discussion of Wittgenstein's challenge to Cartesian understandings of the self, see Kerr, 4-5, 14, 19, passim. In the meditation at the end of *Identity* Frei emphasizes in good Wittgensteinian fashion that we dispose ourselves toward the story of Jesus Christ through our *bodies* (Frei, *Identity,* 171). For Wittgenstein on the body, see Kerr, 27, 139-40.

40. Frei, *Identity,* x. The influence of Marxist thought on Frei's work is evident at several points. In his early, major works, *Eclipse* and *Identity,* there are significant reflections on Marx and Marxist criticism (Hans W. Frei, *The Eclipse of Biblical Narrative: A Study in Eighteenth and Nineteenth Century Hermeneutics* [New Haven: Yale Univ. Press, 1974], 217, 224-27, 230-32; Frei, *Identity,* x, 164). Similarly, in his essay, "Feuerbach and Theology," written at about the same time, Frei writes positively about the contribution of Marxist thought: "Marx understood far more clearly than Feuerbach that man (including his thinking) exists both as the moving, dialectical relation of individual and society and as the conjunction of culture with material nature. He offered to Christian theologi-

... to say that action is a text is to accent not only its location in the public domain but that, more than oral communication, it is fixed, at least long enough to be read, and fixed because of its communal dimension, the antecedent conventions that enter into it. To be meaningful, any action must be both conceptually informed, on the one hand, and in accordance with the structures that are its condition, on the other. While we might be tempted to give precedence to the second criterion, we do so at the risk of reifying it; we might be tempted to give precedence to the first, but in that case we not only atomize actions but tend to mentalize them. When we use terms like culture, symbol system or, in our case, a religion as a symbol system, we had best think of both together, *intentional action* and *social structure*.[41]

What is fascinating about this passage is the way in which "social structure" has replaced "self-manifestation" as the key category alongside intentional action, a change reflecting the growing importance of the cultural-linguistic model in Frei's later work.

Frei's turn to this model is also continuous with his appreciation for realistic narrative, the understanding of which he appropriated primarily from Erich Auerbach's *Mimesis*. Auerbach's work not only emphasizes the interplay of character and circumstance in realistic narrative, but also highlights the importance of historical forces and social structures in the depiction of characters.[42] This aspect of Auerbach's influence on Frei usually goes unnoticed, though Frei himself was well aware of this dimension of Auerbach's work.[43] As Frei discerned, Auerbach's understanding of realistic narrative — that is, his understanding

---

ans the greater challenges and perhaps also the more powerful — albeit in part antagonistic — kinship." Hans W. Frei, "Feuerbach and Theology," *Journal of the American Academy of Religion* 35 (1967): 256. In addition, Frei was familiar with the work done on realistic narrative by the Marxist critic George Lukacs (Frei, *Eclipse*, 325, n. 7; 335, n. 23). The increasing influence of Wayne Meeks on Frei is also significant at this point. Meeks himself has clearly been influenced by Marxist thought, specifically by the work of the Russian philosopher and literary critic Mikhail Bakhtin. See, for example, Wayne Meeks, "The Polyphonic Ethics of the Apostle Paul," in *The Annual of the Society of Christian Ethics, 1988*, ed. D. M. Yeager (Washington, D.C.: Georgetown Univ. Press, 1988), 17-29.

41. Frei, *Types*, 128; italics mine.

42. Erich Auerbach, *Mimesis: The Representation of Reality in Western Literature*, trans. Willard R. Trask (Princeton, New Jersey: Princeton Univ. Press, 1953; Princeton Paperback Edition, 1974), 31-33, 454-524, passim.

43. Frei, *Eclipse*, 13, 147.

of what counts as an adequate representation of "reality" — is intimately
related to his view of the way historical and social forces shape character
and action. Indeed, it is not surprising that the preeminent American
Marxist literary critic, Fredric Jameson, studied under Auerbach.[44]

Even more explicitly, the early work of the Marxist critic George
Lukacs, with which Frei was familiar, emphasizes the individual-social
dynamic as *the* distinguishing characteristic of realistic narrative. In his
Studies in European Realism Lukacs highlights the "inner dialectic" between social and individual existence at the heart of realistic literature.[45]
"The point in question," he writes, "is the organic, indissoluble connection between man as a private individual and man as a social being, as
a member of a community."[46]

The views of Auerbach and Lukacs on "realistic narrative" are
consistent with Frei's later turn to a cultural-linguistic model of Christianity. In *Eclipse* Frei notes this connection:

> Once consciousness becomes the basic element characterizing human
> being, the bond between society and individual being loosened, the
> mutual fitness of character with the suffering or doing of significant
> action or incident likewise becoming increasingly tenuous, the signif-
> icance of narrative . . . is bound to be minimal.[47]

Frei's "realistic" reading of the biblical narrative alerted him to the
socio-cultural character of human identity in a way that foreshadowed
his later turn to a cultural-linguistic model of Christianity.

However, although Frei's understanding of realistic narrative was
consistent with the direction of his later work, the most significant
dimension of Frei's cultural-linguistic turn appears, ironically, in his
movement away from the general category of "realistic narrative" in his
approach to Scripture. In his interpretation of biblical narrative, Frei

---

44. I am indebted to Kenneth Surin for this information.

45. George Lukacs, *Studies in European Realism,* trans. Edith Bone (London:
Hillway Publishing Co., 1950), 11.

46. Lukacs, 8. Lukacs goes beyond Frei in taking seriously the social location of
the writer and the social function of literature (Lukacs, 11-18). However, as I will note
below, there is evidence that Frei himself was prepared to take more seriously the social
context and function of biblical literature. For Frei's brief critique of Marxist interpretation for the overly systematic character of its dialectical explanation, see *Eclipse,* 321.

47. Frei, *Eclipse,* 313.

turns from a general, literary approach based on the genre of realistic narrative to a particular "communal hermeneutic" focused on the church's tradition of literal reading. His key categories become not text and interpreter, but Scripture and community. Frei increasingly views the biblical text not as an autonomous object to be interpreted in a formal, disinterested way, but rather as Scripture, which, by definition, must be considered from within the cultural-linguistic community for which it functions as the sacred text.[48]

Although I will examine Frei's mature approach to biblical narrative more fully in the following chapter, at this point I will simply note how far Frei was moving in the cultural-linguistic direction before his death. Frei not only increasingly emphasizes the function of Scripture within the Christian community, but even suggests, albeit rather cryptically, that a literary approach to Scripture might need to be supplemented by an examination of the function of Scripture within the earliest Christian communities:

> . . . the Babel of contemporary literary theory is such that it is too early to tell whether literary inquiry into the New Testament narratives will prove a bane, blessing, or neither to the literal tradition. It is possible that the latter may have to find hermeneutical aid and analogies elsewhere, for example, among those who try to understand the language of the New Testament by correlating its varieties, including its various belief statements, with the social matrices in which they functioned but *without* strong causal explanation for that correlation and thus without recourse to a theory of referential meaning for that language as a symbol system.[49]

48. I will discuss this important dimension of Frei's work in detail in Chapter Four.
49. Hans Frei, "Narrative in Christian and Modern Interpretation," in *Theology and Dialogue,* ed. Bruce Marshall (Notre Dame, Indiana: Univ. of Notre Dame Press, 1990), 154. Here Frei not only reveals his engagement with contemporary literary theory, but also the increasing influence of Wayne Meeks. What Frei describes is Meeks's project. Indeed, Frei cites chapter 6 of Meeks's book, *The First Urban Christians,* as an example. In that chapter Meeks explores the ways various Christian beliefs functioned in the Pauline communities. He concludes: "The force of a belief statement is determined by the whole matrix of social patterns within which it is uttered. The matrix includes conventions of language, but is not limited to them. Abstracted from that setting or placed in a different one, the stated belief is liable to mean something quite different. . . ." Wayne A. Meeks, *The First Urban Christians: The Social World of the Apostle Paul* (New Haven: Yale Univ. Press, 1983), 164. Incidentally, Meeks dedicated the book to Frei.

This is quite an admission for one of the early champions of a "formal" literary interpretation of Scripture. What is important, Frei suggests, is the function of Scripture within a particular cultural-linguistic community — the church — both past and present. Frei's colleague, Wayne Meeks, has summarized this approach:

> On this [cultural-linguistic] model the "pre-understanding" is not defined by the supposedly universal structures of individual human existence, but by the whole range of passive as well as active learning which members of a given culture and of particular subcultures within it have absorbed. What the first hearers knew by simply being where they were, it is the task of the historical critic to reconstruct by prodigious effort. On the other end, what the text means, by the same model, entails the competence to act, to use, to embody, and this capacity is also realized only in some particular social setting.
>
> If that is the case, then the interpreter may be obliged to find or to try to help create a community competent to understand, and that means a community whose ethos, worldview, and sacred symbols (to use Clifford Geertz's famous trilogy) can be tuned to the way in which that text worked in time past. . . . The goal of a theological hermeneutics on the cultural-linguistic model is not belief in objectively true propositions taught by the text nor the adoption by individuals of an authentic self-understanding evoked by the text's symbols, but the formation of a community whose forms of life correspond to the symbolic universe rendered or signaled by the text.[50]

Although Meeks's discussion is located within a "meant-means" framework, which Frei never adopts, his emphasis on the social context of interpretation and the importance of the cultural-linguistic "community of interpretation" reflects clearly the direction of Frei's work. This communal context becomes so important for Frei that he too not only comes to emphasize the need to "find or try to help create a community competent to understand," but even hints at the necessity of the social-historical-critical work that Meeks proposes. Frei's appreciation for Meeks's project demonstrates the significance of the cultural-linguistic model of Christianity in his later work.

---

50. Wayne Meeks, "A Hermeneutics of Social Embodiment," *Harvard Theological Review* 79 (January, April, July, 1986): 180-81.

A final, related indication of the extent to which Frei's cultural-linguistic model influences his later thought can be seen in his understanding of "text." In his later work Frei speaks not just of the text of Scripture, but also of the "acted text" of tradition, found in the community's performative language and practices.[51] The "text" is not only the written Scripture, but also the "enacted text" of the "culture" within which Scripture functions.[52] In Meeks's words, "text" becomes "a metaphor for the entire cultural system of the religious community," of which Scripture is only a part, even if the paradigmatic part.[53]

The importance of this broader understanding of "text" can be seen in its implications for the concept of "intratextuality." Intratextuality, as I noted earlier, refers to the process of interpretation in which reality is redescribed within the Scriptural framework rather than Scripture being translated into "extrascriptural" categories. "The direction in the flow of intratextual interpretation is that of absorbing the extratextual universe into the text, rather than the reverse (extratextual) direction."[54]

In light of Frei's broader understanding of "text," the concept of intratextuality in his later work must remain metaphorical, embracing the language and practices of the community of interpretation, rather than being applied literally to the structure of an autonomous biblical text. Indeed, Meeks rightly criticizes Lindbeck for presenting intratextuality in this narrowly "literal" sense.[55] Frei's later work, with its broad understanding of "text," offers the possibility for such a metaphorical understanding of intratextuality, which is more defensible than one focusing on the literary structure of Scripture apart from the community of interpretation.

---

51. Frei, *Types*, 113, 115. "Tradition" in Frei's later work is not simply a body of doctrines or specific interpretations, which it seemed to be in *Eclipse* (pp. 3-5). Rather, tradition is more like the "tacit" work of the Spirit in the church's language and practices, an understanding of tradition developed by Andrew Louth in *Discerning the Mystery: An Essay on the Nature of Theology* (Oxford: Clarendon Press, 1983), 73-95.

52. Frei, *Types*, 117. The religion itself, Frei writes, is understood as "both a written and an enacted text" (*Types*, 131).

53. Meeks, "Social Embodiment," 179.

54. Frei, "Literal Reading," 72. See also Lindbeck, 118. This exercise is an eschatological one, never fully accomplished, but only at best asymptotically approached in human history.

55. Meeks, "Social Embodiment," 179-80.

In his later work, then, Frei does not approach Scripture as an autonomous object to be interpreted by disinterested readers. Rather, the interpretation of Scripture is inseparable from the particular language and practices embodied in the life of Christian communities. With his cultural-linguistic turn, Frei moves away from any general hermeneutical theory, even one governed by the literary category of realistic narrative, to an emphasis on the concrete interpretive practices of the Christian community as it uses Scripture in its own life and work. As I will demonstrate in what follows, the implications of this cultural-linguistic turn are significant for Frei's approach to biblical narrative. However, before examining this matter I need to suggest one way in which Frei's cultural-linguistic model requires further development.

Critique and Development

Despite the care with which Frei developed his position, his cultural-linguistic model of Christianity remains too idealistic. Frei, like Lindbeck, does not take sufficiently seriously the social, historical, and material dimensions of culture. At this point the work of Raymond Williams is instructive. Toward the end of his important book *The Sociology of Culture,* Williams argues that understandings of culture based on anthropology tend to be too monolithic.[56] Focusing on culture as a "whole way of life," anthropological approaches tend to downplay or ignore some of the complex material and social relations that are a critical part of culture and contribute to its internal dynamic.

Williams's critique clearly applies to the view of culture present in Lindbeck, and, to a somewhat lesser extent, in Frei, both of whom depend primarily on the work of the anthropologist Clifford Geertz. Although Frei, because of the Marxist influence, takes the social, historical, and material dimensions of culture more seriously than Lindbeck, he nevertheless does present culture in rather monolithic terms as a "whole way of life," a semiotic system that shapes the entirety of human thought and action. In contrast, Williams's more nuanced understanding of culture brings more prominently into view the social,

56. Raymond Williams, *The Sociology of Culture* (New York: Schocken Books, 1982), 209-10.

historical, and material dimensions that are so important to the dynamics of culture.

Williams, for example, highlights three definitions of culture which have been significant at different points in history: (1) culture as a noun of process (e.g., the culture of animals; agriculture); (2) culture as a "whole way of life"; and (3) culture as "the arts."[57] This historical exploration of various understandings of culture is significant for Williams's work. In fact, in *The Sociology of Culture* Williams simply seeks an understanding of culture that will incorporate the internal relations among the aspects of culture highlighted by each of these three definitions. In the first place, Williams affirms that culture is a "realized signifying system" through which the social order is communicated, reproduced, experienced, and explored.[58] This dimension of Williams's thought comes close to the view of culture as a "whole way of life" (Williams's second definition).

Second, Williams emphasizes the central place of production and reproduction in cultures, including the social relations of cultural producers (both institutional and formational), the material means of production, and the processes of cultural reproduction themselves.[59] Here Williams draws on the first definition of culture as a noun of process — the culture of cultures, if you will excuse the pun. Williams highlights the important social relations and organizations, including the economic and political, which play an important role in the production and reproduction of culture. His important concept of dominant, residual, and emergent forms of culture provides a helpful conceptual tool for exploring the dynamics of cultural change.[60]

Finally, Williams highlights the aspect of culture as "the arts" (defined very broadly by Williams to include journalism, advertising, fashion, etc.).[61] This aspect of culture can be seen in the *forms* of culture. These variable forms serve as "manifest signal systems" that reveal the underlying "realized signifying system" in special ways at particular socially defined locations. These "manifest signal systems" are integrally and dynamically related to other social activities in various "solutions,"

57. Williams, 10-14.
58. Williams, 207.
59. Williams, 87-118; 181-205.
60. Williams, 203-5.
61. Williams, 119-80.

depending on whether these activities more or less clearly and autono-
mously make manifest the underlying signifying system.[62]

By viewing culture historically, Williams develops a carefully
nuanced understanding of its various dimensions and processes. While
he can take seriously the aspect of culture highlighted by Lindbeck and
Frei, Williams's approach does not become too monolithic or static. The
historical, social, and material factors that contribute to the production
and reproduction of culture are taken seriously and related in extraordinarily complex and dynamic ways. For example, if Williams were to
view the Christian religion as a culture, he would not only examine its
"interpretive framework," or "symbol system," but also its social organization, its "manifest signal system" (which would surely include preaching), its means of production and reproduction (again, the practice of
preaching would be important), and its relation to the non-Christian
culture around it. And Williams would do all of this in a way that takes
particular historical developments and changes seriously.

Williams's work thus suggests some helpful ways for fleshing out
Frei's understanding of Christianity as a culture and for thinking more
concretely about the practices that are part of the production and reproduction of that culture in particular contexts. Frei's work, like Lindbeck's, would be enriched by a more dynamic and nuanced understanding of culture such as that provided by Williams, as long as the
sociological and anthropological concepts do not become dominant,
but simply serve the fuller self-description of the Christian community.
Such an enrichment will be important for any discussion of the practice
of preaching within a cultural-linguistic model. Nevertheless, even Frei's
rather general model has important implications for his approach to
biblical narrative, which can now be examined in more detail.

62. Williams, 208-10.

Chapter Four

Scripture and Community

I n an essay about *The Eclipse of Biblical Narrative*, George Schner offers the following critique:

> Essential to the retrieval and refusal which *Eclipse* launches is the recovery of something more than a lost 'analytic procedure.' Recovering the traditioning of interpretation, the community within which interpretation takes place, and the liturgical and spiritual life forms which embody the vitality of realistic narrative are equally important procedures.[1]

This criticism is an important one. Schner not only highlights the integral relationship between the Bible and the community in which it functions as sacred Scripture, but also lifts up the central role of the interpretive community in the reading of any text, especially that of the Bible.[2] Schner rightly argues that the distinctive language and practices of the Christian community play a central and necessary role in the faithful interpretation of Scripture. Unquestionably, Frei gave too little attention to these matters in his early work. All too often in *Eclipse*, Schner accurately writes, "it would seem that realistic narrative must be

---

1. George P. Schner, "*The Eclipse of Biblical Narrative:* Analysis and Critique," *Modern Theology* 8 (April 1992): 170.

2. I have borrowed the term "interpretive community" from Stanley Fish, *Is There a Text in This Class? The Authority of Interpretive Communities* (Cambridge, Massachusetts: Harvard Univ. Press, 1980). Frei uses the phrase "community of interpretation."

somehow independent of liturgical enactment and the community of interpretation. . . ."[3]

In his critique, however, Schner actually points to the very dimensions of interpretation that Frei himself emphasizes in his later work. In fact, one could not ask for a better description of the key elements in Frei's later position: the traditioning of interpretation, the community of interpretation, and the liturgical and life forms that embody the vitality of Scripture. These are the very elements that become critical in Frei's later work, moving him beyond a narrow focus on a mere "analytic procedure."

The Community of Interpretation

The interpretive community, the church, occupies a central place in Frei's mature hermeneutical thought. Within his cultural-linguistic model, Frei does not view Scripture as an autonomous text, but approaches it within the context of the rules and conventions of the community within which it functions as the sacred text.[4] Christians learn to interpret Scripture not by learning general hermeneutical or literary theories, but by being trained to apply the informal rules and conventions for the use of Scripture that are embodied in the language and practices of the Christian community.[5] It is the "common community of interpretation" that provides the conventions and sets the "reasonable bounds" for the faithful interpretation of Scripture.

> . . . if there *is* a community of interpretation, a tradition for which this is the sacred text, its analogue might be one school of British

---

3. Schner, 170.

4. Hans W. Frei, *Types of Christian Theology,* ed. George Hunsinger and William C. Placher (New Haven: Yale Univ. Press, 1992), 13-14. In an implicit criticism of his earlier work, Frei writes, "it is similarly artificial and dubious to claim a purely external relation of text and reading, which in effect sets aside the mutual implication of interpretation and textual meaning (in the words of hermeneutical theory) or of reading and the textuality of the text (in terms of deconstruction)." Hans W. Frei, "The 'Literal Reading' of the Biblical Narrative in the Christian Tradition: Does It Stretch or Will It Break?" in *The Bible and the Narrative Tradition,* ed. Frank McConnell (New York: Oxford Univ. Press, 1986), 64.

5. Frei, *Types,* 14.

moralists in the eighteenth century: right exegesis, like right moral sentiment and action, is what sane, judicious, and fair-minded judges declare it to be. I do not mean to subvert hideously difficult questions about the meaning of the text and how one can get at it, but I do think that if, within a community and also without, later judges say that a certain form of combination — say, a very vivid allegorical reading; or a particular figural interpretation of the Old Testament within the New, undertaken as part of the later interpretive tradition — if this finally stretches the imagination to the breaking point, as the Antiochene theologians said about the school of Origen, then the assessment probably sets reasonable bounds to what can and cannot be done. Even then, the existence of limits does not mean that one cannot exceed them as a private scholar, but only that as an adherent who speaks for the common community of interpretation, one has probably at that point gone too far, even if that is a judgment that ought always to be made provisionally and had best be made in retrospect, except where the love of God and neighbor — those ultimate norms of Christian life and thought — are immediately at stake.[6]

In Frei's later work it is the dynamic, ongoing conversation of the Christian community, not a formalist, literary analysis, that provides the key context for the faithful interpretation of Scripture. Frei's approach to interpretation has become "community centered."[7]

---

6. Frei, *Types*, 57. This emphasis on the interpretive community does not mean that the biblical text exerts no pressure on the readers. Within the community of interpretation, which recognizes the authority of Scripture and seeks to conform its life to Scripture, the Bible does exert pressure, though not as an autonomous text. Even Stanley Fish, who emphasizes in a radical way the centrality of "interpretive communities" in interpretation, makes this point: "The fact that the objects we have are all objects that appear to us in the context of some practice, of work done by some interpretive community, doesn't mean that they are not objects or that we don't have them or that they exert no pressure on us." Stanley Fish, *Doing What Comes Naturally: Change, Rhetoric, and the Practice of Theory in Literary and Legal Studies* (Durham, North Carolina: Duke Univ. Press, 1989), 153. For another perspective on the constraints that social practices and linguistic usage place on interpretation, see Terry Eagleton, *Literary Theory: An Introduction* (Minneapolis: Univ. of Minnesota Press, 1983), 87-88. For a discussion of the moral constraints, such as "love of God and neighbor," that communities place on the use of texts, see Jeffrey Stout, "What Is the Meaning of a Text?" *New Literary History* 14 (Autumn 1982): 8.

7. The term "community centered" comes from Wayne A. Meeks, "On Trusting an

Frei's emphasis on the communal context of biblical interpretation surfaces most clearly and explicitly in his turn from a focus on "realistic narrative" to an emphasis on the "literal sense" of Scripture, a move that requires detailed examination. Frei notes this shift quite clearly in the opening paragraph of his essay, "The Literal Reading":

> An outsider to the lively, cacophonous discussion among contemporary theorists of literature is bound to wonder whether the very term "narrative tradition" isn't one more among the hypostatized constants, like the "canon" of literature or the notion of "literariness," which some of the discussants want to consign to dissolution. As a Christian theologian rather than a literary or biblical scholar, I shall not try to position the Bible in relation to this putative tradition; instead, I will comment on what I perceive to be a wide, though of course not unanimous, traditional consensus among Christians in the West on the primacy of the literal reading of the Bible, on its connection with narrative, on its present status and future outlook.[8]

Unpredictable God," in *Faith and History: Essays in Honor of Paul Meyer,* ed. John T. Carroll, Charles H. Cosgrove, and E. Elizabeth Johnson (Atlanta: Scholars Press, 1990), 121.

Frei's turn to the community of interpretation is *not* a "turn to the subject." It is not an affirmation of the role of the historically self-conscious, subjective "stance" of the interpreter in interpretation. As in his earlier work, Frei challenges the place of individual subjectivity in interpretation; he has little patience for interpretation that highlights Scripture's "inner connection with me" (Hans W. Frei, "Remarks in Connection with a Theological Proposal," in *Theology and Narrative: Selected Essays,* ed. George Hunsinger and William C. Placher [New York: Oxford Univ. Press, 1993], 20). Frei thus rejects *both* an autonomous text and subjective interpretation (*Types,* 85-87). The rules of the community, rather than an autonomous text, provide the check to subjectivism. To put it another way, the rules of the community enable Christians to read faithfully so that the text may exert its pressure. Stanley Fish has similarly argued that interpretive communities prevent both subjectivism and nihilism in interpretation by causing the meaning of the text to be quite determinate (Fish, *Doing What Comes Naturally,* 138).

8. Frei, "Literal Reading," 36. The importance of Frei's turn to the literal sense cannot be overestimated. In "Literal Reading," Frei critiques phenomenological hermeneutics, particularly the work of Paul Ricoeur, for its inability to "stretch" the literal reading "across the critical abyss" into the postcritical period; in the hands of the phenomenologists the literal reading does not stretch, but "breaks." Frei's turn to the reading community and the literal sense is not a retrenchment, but a coherent postcritical option. For a helpful discussion of these aspects of Frei's later work, see Paul Schwartzentruber, "The Modesty of Hermeneutics: The Theological Reserves of Hans Frei," *Modern Theology* 8 (April 1992): 190-91.

Consistent with his turn to a cultural-linguistic understanding of Christianity, Frei here notes his turn away from a general narrative tradition to an examination of the *sensus literalis* of Scripture, which "is deeply embedded in the Christian interpretive tradition of its sacred text, and in that way embedded in the self-description of the Christian religion as a social complex. . . ."[9] Frei thus takes his descriptive categories not from a general literary tradition, but rather from the tradition of the church's use of Scripture.

Just as important as this turn to the "literal sense" is Frei's understanding of the *sensus literalis* in the Christian tradition. Frei recognizes that the *sensus literalis* does not mean one thing; no single definition is adequate.[10] Instead of seeking such a definition, Frei notes some "rough rules" that have governed the literal reading in the Christian tradition.[11]

The first rule, which explicitly affirms the communal context within which the literal sense must be understood, is ultimately the most important one and provides the framework within which the other rules must be explicated. According to this rule, the literal sense is fundamentally the consensus reading of the Christian community.

> . . . the literal meaning of the text is precisely that meaning which finds the greatest degree of agreement in the use of the text in the religious community. If there is agreement in that use, then take that to be the literal sense. . . . So the first sense of the literal reading stems from the use of the text in the Church.[12]

9. Hans W. Frei, "Theology and the Interpretation of Narrative: Some Hermeneutical Considerations," in *Theology and Narrative*, 110. Frei's turn to the literal sense is initially signaled in this lecture, given at Haverford College in 1982.

10. Frei, *Types*, 14-15. For a discussion of some of the ways the literal sense has been understood, see *Types*, 138-39; also Brevard Childs, "The Sensus Literalis of Scripture: An Ancient and Modern Problem," in *Beitraege Zur Alttestamentlichen Theologie*, ed. Herbert Danner, Robert Hanhart, and Rudolf Smend (Göttingen: Vandenhoeck and Ruprecht, 1977), 80-95.

11. Frei discusses these "rough rules" in both "Theology and Interpretation of Narrative" and *Types*, though he only refers to them as "rules" in the later work, indicating his increasing emphasis on the communally rule-governed activity of biblical interpretation. My discussion draws primarily on *Types*, which reflects Frei's more mature thought on this topic. For another, brief discussion of this matter see Frei, "Literal Reading," 68-69.

12. Frei, *Types*, 15. A word of clarification about Frei's terminology is important.

The literal sense is, in short, "the sense of the text in its sociolinguistic context — liturgical, pedagogical, polemical, and so on."[13]

In his treatment of this dimension of the literal sense, Frei draws heavily on Raphael Loewe's essay on early Jewish exegesis.[14] Loewe argues persuasively that the "plain sense" of Scripture was a matter of communal consensus, rather than mere grammatical correctness, in early Jewish exegesis. Noting numerous instances where the "plain sense" of a passage was actually quite different from any simple reading of the "grammatical sense," Loewe concludes about early Jewish exegesis:

Frei actually uses the term "literal sense" in two different ways. First, and most basically, the term refers to the communal consensus, which has been noted here. At points, following the usage of Raphael Loewe, Frei refers to this consensus as the "plain sense" in distinction from the "literal sense" (*Types*, 87, 141). The second meaning of "literal sense" is the more common one; it is the sense traditionally distinguished from the allegorical, tropological, and anagogical senses. For Frei, this aspect of the literal sense has two dimensions: the grammatical/syntactical sense and, more importantly, the "literary literal" sense, which Frei spells out very carefully. Basically, what Frei argues is that in relation to the stories about Jesus of Nazareth the "literal sense" (the communal consensus) has been that of a "literal reading" (grammatical/syntactical and literary). I will follow Frei's dual usage of "literal sense" in my discussion, though I will try to be clear about how the term is functioning. By emphasizing the communal consensus Frei highly qualifies, and perhaps ultimately deconstructs, understandings of an "objective" literal sense inherent in the text.

13. Frei, "Theology and Interpretation of Narrative," 104. Despite Frei's emphasis on consensus, the literal sense should not be considered as simply the "majority opinion" of a particular group at a particular point in history. The consensus has a qualitative and traditional dimension as well as a quantitative one. Aristotle's examination of *endoxa*, or "common sense," on which rhetorical argument is based, is helpful at this point. As Aristotle notes, the number of persons who hold an opinion, the length of time an opinion has been held, and the wisdom and goodness of the persons who hold it are all important considerations (Aristotle, *Rhetoric*, 1098b18-24). Thus, "classic," precritical ways of reading Scripture, which shaped the formation of the Christian canon itself, are important. Indeed, it is this broad, traditional consensus that Frei defends. Lindbeck refers to the *sensus fidelium* and argues that this "classic" approach involves reading Scripture as a "Christ-centered, narrationally and typologically unified whole in conformity to a trinitarian rule of faith." George Lindbeck, "Scripture, Consensus, and Community," *This World* 23 (Fall 1988): 7.

14. Raphael Loewe, "The 'Plain Meaning' of Scripture in Early Jewish Exegesis," *Papers of the Institute of Jewish Studies in London* I (Jerusalem, 1964), 140-85; cited in Frei, "Theology and Interpretation of Narrative," 104-5; Frei, "Literal Reading," 74; Frei, *Types*, 15.

. . . what is understood as *peshat* ["plain sense"] was not necessarily the natural meaning of the biblical text [i.e. the grammatical meaning], but rather the meaning traditionally accepted as authoritative or at any rate familiar, however far from the primary sense of the words it might be.[15]

Despite its seemingly conservative tendencies, this understanding of the plain sense does not imply a static tradition. In fact, just the opposite is the case. According to Loewe, when an "experimental" reading *(derash)* is "popularly received and transmitted into the body of conventional or 'orthodox' opinion, it crystalizes into *peshat*."[16] A similar process certainly takes place in the Christian tradition. Through compelling interpretations of Scripture within the community of faith, the sacred text continues dynamically to assert its authority within and over the community. For example, Scripture exerted its authority during the Reformation not as some text qua text, but through the powerful and persuasive — at times "experimental" and "creative" — interpretations of the Reformers. Within particular traditions, these persuasive interpretations were "popularly received and transmitted into the body of conventional or 'orthodox' opinion." A similar process is taking place today as women, too long silenced in the church, offer persuasive interpretations of Scripture that challenge traditional, "consensus" readings of certain texts.[17] The "literal sense" is thus not a static, closed, rigid thing, but is rather embedded in the dynamic, dialogical life of the community of interpretation, which not only sets the boundaries of acceptable usage and interpretation, but also receives and incorporates new and creative readings into the consensus — a process that is evident in the Bible itself.[18] At the heart of this process

15. Loewe, "Plain Meaning," 167.

16. Loewe, 183. "Experimental exegesis" is that which is "concerned constantly to enlarge the significance of a given text by relating it to new ideas, conditions, or associations. . . ."

17. As will become clear, Frei's understanding of the consensus does not focus narrowly on the interpretation of individual passages of Scripture, but primarily on the ascriptive logic of the gospel narratives.

18. Wayne Meeks, in "On Trusting an Unpredictable God," has examined Paul's creative "misreadings" of Scripture (i.e., the Old Testament), which have now become canonical. Frei's student, Kathryn Tanner, has persuasively demonstrated how the church's understanding of the plain sense actually places Scripture over against all

is a community actively engaged with Scripture, faithfully trusting not simply "grammatical correctness," or "disinterested objectivity," but the promises of God.[19]

In his later work, then, Frei's understanding of the "literal sense" is inseparably related to the consensus reading of the Christian community. The *sensus literalis* is not some objective, disinterested reading of the text apart from the use of Scripture in the church, but is rather the dynamic, ruled consensus of the Christian community as it has wrestled with Scripture through the years and continues to wrestle with Scripture today.[20] For Frei, the *sensus literalis* is intimately bound to the cultural-linguistic community in which the Bible functions authoritatively as Scripture.

The second rule, which is part of this communal consensus, affirms that the literal sense is the "fit enactment of the intention to say what comes to be in the text."[21]

> This understanding of the literal sense does not say that the text wrote itself, and that therefore you can take it simply as it is — no, there's an admission by and large that texts are written by authors, human, or divine, for that matter. But what is interesting is that the intention and its enactment are thought of as one continuous process — one intelligent activity, not two — so that you cannot for this purpose go behind the written text to ask separately about what the author meant or what he or she was really trying to say. You had better take it that the author said what he or she was trying to say.[22]

The intention of the author — whether the historical human author or the divine author — has been fitly enacted in Scripture. Consequently, Scripture itself and not something "behind" it is the focus of interpretation.[23]

---

interpretations and encourages not only ongoing interpretation but in fact a plurality of interpretations. See Kathryn E. Tanner, "Theology and the Plain Sense," in *Scriptural Authority and Narrative Interpretation,* ed. Garrett Green (Philadelphia: Fortress Press, 1987), 59-78.

19. Meeks, "Unpredictable God," 119, 122-24.

20. See George Hunsinger, "Hans Frei As Theologian: The Quest for a Generous Orthodoxy," *Modern Theology* 8 (April 1992): 128; Frei, "Literal Reading," 36-43, 67-71.

21. Frei, *Types,* 15.

22. Frei, *Types,* 15-16.

23. Frei's understanding of authorial intention is different from that of New

The third general rule involves "the descriptive fit between the words [of Scripture] and the subject matter. . . ."[24]

> The literal sense, in my mind, is one that asserts not only the coincidence between sense and subject matter, but may even, as a matter of hermeneutical principle, go further and suggest that we may be asking a misplaced question when we make a sharp distinction between sense and subject matter.[25]

With regard to the gospel narratives, Frei would say that they render or constitute the reality they narrate; there is no "gap" between the narrative and its subject matter. The biblical narrative does not refer beyond itself for its meaning. This rule captures what Frei calls the "literary" character of the literal sense in the church's consensus reading of Scripture.[26]

Implicit in this rule is the crucial affirmation that the biblical stories, particularly the stories about Jesus of Nazareth, are unique and indispensable to the church.[27] The stories do not point to some general subject matter that is separable from the narratives themselves; they do not point to some "external" truth or experience that, when arrived at, permits the church to leave the story behind. Rather, as Frei repeatedly argues, the narratives about Jesus *constitute* the subject matter, rather

---

Criticism. Frei does not argue on the basis of the "intentional fallacy." Rather, Frei draws on Ryle's intention-action model to describe this dimension of the literal sense. The intention of the author is fitly enacted in the text; there is no "ghost" behind the text. In this way, Frei affirms the importance of authorial intention, but rejects it as something "behind" or "in addition to" the text itself. See Hans W. Frei, *The Eclipse of Biblical Narrative: A Study in Eighteenth and Nineteenth Century Hermeneutics* (New Haven: Yale Univ. Press, 1974), viii. Ryle's categories should be understood simply as heuristic devices for describing the way in which the Christian community has actually read Scripture. That is, Frei is not arguing for a general theory about authorial intention and textual enactment, but is rather arguing that the Christian tradition has read Scripture as the fit enactment of authorial intent. That is, the community has generally read the "surface" of the story, rather than seeking its real meaning "behind" it.

24. Frei, *Types,* 16; see also Frei, "Theology and Interpretation of Narrative," 103.

25. Frei, *Types,* 16. "Thereby," Frei notes, "hangs a very, very long story," which, of course, is the story he told in *Eclipse.* Again, it is important to note that Frei is not presenting this rule as a general hermeneutical principle. Rather, he is simply trying to describe the way Scripture has been read in the Christian tradition.

26. Frei, "Theology and Interpretation of Narrative," 112.

27. Frei, *Types,* 63-64.

than simply *referring* to it.[28] In short, the Christian community cannot
do without these stories or substitute something else for them, but must
repeatedly return to them to be formed and reformed as the church.

Frei thus suggests three rough rules that guide the literal reading
of Scripture in the Christian tradition. Within the framework of these
general rules, Frei spells out the literal sense more specifically in
relation to the stories about Jesus of Nazareth. Frei argues that the
literal sense pertains primarily, if not exclusively, to these stories; at
the heart of the consensus about the literal reading are "the texts
concerning Jesus of Nazareth. . . ."[29] The consensual guidelines,
embedded in the language and practices, doctrine and liturgy of the
church, focus on the person of Jesus as he is rendered in the gospel
narratives. As simple as it may sound, the consensus finally comes
down to this: these stories are about the unique, unsubstitutable
person, Jesus of Nazareth.

> The consensus that I think I see, tenuous and yet constantly
> reemerging from the earliest days through the Enlightenment period
> into the twentieth century, East and West, North and South, is that
> of the priority of the literal sense in regard to the texts concerning
> Jesus of Nazareth, chiefly the descriptions in the Gospels, but to some
> extent also in the rest of the New Testament. It is a very simple
> consensus: that the story of Jesus is about him, not about someone
> else or about nobody in particular or about all of us; that it is not
> two stories . . . or no story and so on and on. This does not mean
> that there are not other legitimate readings also: for example, readings
> in which we the readers are included in the text, or readings in which
> Jesus shares the spotlight with the Kingdom of God or with universal
> religious experience or with some specific quality which he embodied,
> such as love or moral reason or faith. But the general consensus has
> been that Jesus has primacy in these stories.[30]

28. At this point Frei discerns a connection between precritical and postcritical
reading. Both approaches have "reality" only under a description, only through a linguistic, narrative rendering. There is for neither the precritical nor the postcritical
approach a modern, neutral, objective stance over against "reality." Frei, *Eclipse*, 25, 36.

29. Frei, *Types*, 140. Frei, for example, notes that Jesus himself has not been
allegorized in the consensus reading of the church (Frei, *Eclipse*, 29-30; Frei, *Types*, 142).

30. Frei, *Types*, 140.

In short, at the heart of Scripture, in the stories about Jesus of Nazareth, the Bible, as it has been read in the Christian community, is not primarily an expression of some universal religious experience or general human consciousness; it is not a symbolic or mythical or allegorical story revealing an ideal truth or expressing "authentic human existence." Rather, the story is about the unsubstitutable person, Jesus of Nazareth, whose identity is rendered in the narrative. And it is from this center that the interpretation of the rest of Scripture radiates.

The literal reading, in this sense, is not simply a grammatical/syntactical matter, but involves primarily a "literary literal" reading, which focuses on the "surface description and plot" of the story about Jesus.[31] Specifically, the literal sense focuses on Jesus "as the specific, unsubstitutable personal subject of the stories."[32]

> For the *sensus literalis* . . . the *descriptive* function of language and its conceptual adequacy are shown forth precisely in the kind of story that does not refer beyond itself for its meaning, as allegory does, the kind of story in which the "signified," the identity of the protagonist, is enacted by the signifier, the narrative sequence itself. It is an instance of literary literal sense.
>
> The meaning of the gospel story for the *sensus literalis* is, then, that it is *this* story about *this* person as agent and patient, about its surface description and plot.[33]

Another way of putting this point is that the Christian community has read the gospel stories according to an ascriptive logic; the consensus reading has been a "literal-ascriptive-subject" reading. According to this reading, Jesus' identity is not merely illustrated, but constituted by what he says, does, and undergoes in the stories.

> [Jesus] is the subject of his personal predicates and his doings and sufferings, and holds them together, essentially, rather than they him; he is the subject to whom descriptions are ascribed. Predicates are general, subjects particular. By contrast, in allegorical reading as it was revived in the eighteenth century, predicates or general characteristics have priority over particular subjects — the particulars are illustrations

---

31. Frei, "Theology and Interpretation of Narrative," 112.
32. Frei, *Types*, 141.
33. Frei, "Theology and Interpretation of Narrative," 112.

of a general "meaning." In literal reading, as in a realistic novel, the general is contained in the particular. It is that contrast which makes it so difficult to coordinate systematically and on even terms a literal-ascriptive-subject reading of the Gospels and a reading that has some other, general meaning for its semiotic referent — a goal that a number of liberal theolograms [sic] would like to accomplish.[34]

This ascriptive logic provides a key link between Scripture and the regulative function of doctrine in the Christian tradition. For example, it is this logic that Frei discerns in the Chalcedonian formula, which has been authoritative within both Catholic and Protestant churches:

> The logic, I suggest, of the formula is that of a subject-predicate description, rather than that of substance-accident description. . . . The "grammar" of the formula, I suggest, is that the subject to whom predicates are to be ascribed, the unitary ascriptive subject, has a certain priority over the descriptive characteristics that he embodies. They are *his;* he holds them and is himself as each of them singly and both together. I shall return to this theme, for it suggests what I take to be the root way of using the literal sense, which in various forms — it is not a univocal term — has been the basic rule for biblical reading in the Christian community.
>
> The basic use of the literal sense is ascriptive rather than descriptive; it is descriptive only in a secondary way. *That this* subject — none other; not no one; not everyone; not two, one fleshly and one spiritual; not a personified quality or set of qualities — is the subject of these stories, is the basic, literal affirmation, which I find echoed theologically, that is at the level of conceptual redescription. . . . the meaning of the doctrine is the story rather than the meaning of the story being the doctrine. That is why if one thinks about Christology in a non-narrative fashion one must do so in a carefully limited, ruled sort of way.[35]

According to Frei, then, the communal consensus is a "rule-governed" consensus that focuses on the "literal-ascriptive-subject" reading of the gospel narratives about Jesus of Nazareth.

Frei's distillation of these "rules," however, is somewhat artificial.

34. Frei, *Types,* 142.
35. Frei, *Types,* 125-26.

Although Frei is in some ways at his most incisive at this point, he is also unfortunately at his most abstract. The crucial thing is the way these rules are embodied and embedded in the actual language and practices of the Christian community. For example, Rowan Greer, whose work on early Christian biblical interpretation confirms Frei's analysis, nevertheless continually highlights the liturgical locus where these rules live and are learned. As Greer writes, the early "theological controversies focus upon defining Christ, the hero of the story. Since for ancient Christianity, with the probable exception of Augustine, piety was Christocentric, it was important to define Christ as the object of Christian worship."[36] As Greer notes, the worship of the unsubstitutable person, Jesus Christ, shaped the community's reading of Scripture; the rules governing the *sensus literalis* were embodied in the worship of the church — for example, the Eucharist, where the church continually re-enacts the story about Jesus.

In short, the piety and worship of the church not only shaped the form of the canon, but also gave rise to the *regula fidei* for interpreting it. That worship is finally more important than any abstract rules for training Christians in the ascriptive logic of the gospel narratives. It is thus not surprising, as George Lindbeck has noted, that "the interpretive rules embedded in liturgy or worship have partially protected some communities against loss of canonical patterns of interpretation. . . ."[37] While Frei's abstraction of rules is enlightening, the rules should not be viewed as "floating" somewhere apart from the concrete language and practices of the Christian community, especially those embodied in worship.

I can illustrate this point with an experience I had several years ago with my five-year-old son. I was trying to teach him how to hit a baseball. After one pitch I announced, "Good! You didn't hit it, but you timed your swing just right." On the next pitch, even though my son could not possibly have known any abstract, grammatical rules for using the word "timing," he commented after he swung: "I had the timing right on that one" — which in fact he did. My son will learn how

36. Rowan Greer, "The Christian Bible and Its Interpretation," in James L. Kugel and Rowan Greer, *Early Biblical Interpretation* (Philadelphia: Westminster Press, 1986), 185; also 111-12, 189.

37. George Lindbeck, "Hans Frei and the Future of Theology in America," December 2, 1988, TMs [photocopy], 10.

"timing" is used with reference to hitting a baseball not by mastering some abstract rules for its use, but simply by learning the game — by learning to use a certain language rightly within the "form of life" of hitting a baseball.

A similar point needs to be emphasized with respect to Frei's work. The key is not our ability to abstract "the rules" for interpreting Scripture in order to set some "boundaries." Rather, the key is a community whose piety and worship is centered around the unsubstitutable person, Jesus of Nazareth, the Christ. It is in such a community that the ascriptive logic of the gospel narratives is learned through the actual use of the language in the practices of the community — including, of course, the church's preaching. To put it another way, the key is not really the abstract "boundaries," but the living center; for finally Frei's ascriptive logic calls the church to the center, the unsubstitutable person, Jesus Christ.

Thus, the interpretive community, the church, plays an increasingly important role in the interpretation of biblical narrative in Frei's later work. Scripture and community are held inextricably together. For Frei, as David Steinmetz has put it, "the church and not human experience as such is the middle term between the Christian interpreter and the biblical text."[38] Implicit in Frei's later work is a kind of "hermeneutical circle" made up of the three "marks" of the church highlighted in some strands of the Christian tradition: Word, sacrament, and discipline.[39] Frei's focus is not on general hermeneutical theories, but on the

---

38. David C. Steinmetz, "Theology and Exegesis: Ten Theses," in *A Contemporary Guide to Hermeneutics*, ed. Donald McKim (Grand Rapids, Michigan: Wm. B. Eerdmans Publishing Co., 1987), 27. At one point Frei even goes so far as to suggest the epistemological necessity of the church ("Response to 'Narrative Theology: An Evangelical Appraisal,'" *Trinity Journal* 8 [Spring 1987]: 23.

39. Frei himself was suspicious of the notion of a hermeneutical circle because it had been understood too idealistically in general hermeneutical theory (*Identity*, xvi). This ecclesial version is not open to Frei's critique, particularly if one takes seriously Frei's limitation of hermeneutics to the "rules for reading texts." Frei himself asserts that the church is constituted by Word, sacrament, and discipleship (Frei, *Identity*, 165).

Discipline has, of course, been understood in different ways in different traditions and in different historical periods. I am using the term broadly to include the practices, activities, and habits that nurture Christian discipleship — the distinctive way of life of the Christian community. Discipline need not be considered as primarily judicial in nature, but may be viewed positively as the practices that shape the virtues necessary for living as a faithful Christian community. Discipline should also not be understood primarily in individualistic terms, but as related to the life of the community.

distinctive language and practices of the Christian community as it reads its sacred text in the context of worship and discipleship. It is in the dynamic interplay of Word, sacrament, and discipline that Christians learn the communal rules for reading Scripture.[40] While these three "marks" may take different forms in particular communities and traditions, it is in their interrelation that faithful biblical interpretation takes place and Scripture exerts its authority in forming and reforming the Christian community.

Thus, as I have described it, Frei's later "communal hermeneutic" seems to be a far cry from his earlier position, in which he appears to locate "the meaning" of Scripture solidly in an autonomous text and seems to focus on a formal, analytical method through which disinterested readers may extract that meaning. The later Frei seems quite distant from the Frei whose work Lynn Poland says demonstrates the "dangers in adopting a New Critical position without qualification."[41] Nevertheless, despite the significant revisions in his work, Frei's turn to a communal hermeneutic, like his turn to a cultural-linguistic model of Christianity, represents a continuation as well as a revision of his earlier position. Although *Identity* and *Eclipse* unquestionably contain formalist elements, the seeds of Frei's later position were already present in these early works.

Several aspects of *Eclipse*, for example, point to the importance of the consensus reading of the Christian tradition in Frei's early thought.

40. I have already noted the importance of the liturgy for biblical interpretation. On the importance of discipline for biblical interpretation, see Greer, "The Christian Bible," 191; Richard B. Hays, "Scripture-Shaped Community: The Problem of Method in New Testament Ethics," *Interpretation* 44 (January 1990): 51; Stanley Hauerwas, *A Community of Character: Toward a Constructive Christian Social Ethic* (Notre Dame: Univ. of Notre Dame Press, 1981), 66-69; Stanley Hauerwas and Steve Long, "Interpreting the Bible as a Political Act," *Religion and Intellectual Life* 6 (Spring/Summer 1989): 134-42. For a more general account of the importance of virtue in all interpretation, see Jeffrey Stout, "The Relativity of Interpretation," *The Monist* 69 (January 1986): 105-6, 114. For a contemporary examination of the relationship between discipline and worship, see Michael Warren, "The Worshiping Assembly: Possible Zone of Cultural Contestation," *Worship* 163, no. 1 (1989): 2-17.

41. Lynn M. Poland, *Literary Criticism and Biblical Hermeneutics: A Critique of Formalist Approaches*, American Academy of Religion Series, no. 48, ed. Carl A. Raschke (Chico, California: Scholars Press, 1985), 108. As should be obvious by now, Frei's later work makes Poland's criticisms, which focus on the self-sufficient autonomy of the literary text, irrelevant.

Indeed, the first sentence of the book actually sets Frei's entire work within this framework:

> Western Christian reading of the Bible in the days before the rise of historical criticism in the eighteenth century was usually strongly realistic, i.e. at once literal and historical, and not only doctrinal or edifying.[42]

In this opening sentence, Frei focuses not on an abstract structural analysis of the form of the text, but on the reading tradition within the Western church. It is this reading tradition, rather than any formalist textual analysis, that Frei holds over against eighteenth- and nineteenth-century developments. "Realistic narrative" functions not simply as a formal literary category applied to a text qua text, but rather as a descriptive category for the way the church has read the gospel narratives throughout most of its history. Frei's basic point is that biblical interpretation in the eighteenth and nineteenth century, which became largely academic rather than ecclesial, departed from the consensus according to which the church had traditionally interpreted Scripture — and lost something extraordinarily significant in the process.[43] From the beginning Frei's work has been explicitly related to a reading community — the church; his later turn to the "community of interpretation" and the *sensus literalis* simply enabled him to flesh out this dimension more explicitly and fully.

It should thus not be surprising that there is significant continuity in Frei's actual understanding of the gospel narratives. His concern for the inseparability of sense and subject matter, for the ascriptive logic of the gospel narratives, and for the cumulative depiction of Jesus' identity through the interplay of character and incident are all present in his later work. However, in the later work Frei locates these concerns within the framework of the literal sense, rather than

---

42. Frei, *Eclipse*, 1.

43. Wayne Meeks suggests that *Eclipse* may be read as an account of the "fateful rupture between religious and academic readings [of Scripture] that is now so thoroughly institutionalized" (Meeks, "Unpredictable God," 119). If Meeks is on target, and I think he is, the key to *Eclipse* is not formal textual analysis, but the reading practices of different communities. In Frei's later work, the tension between the church and the academy becomes increasingly pronounced, suggesting that this tension may in fact lie at the heart of his work.

under the literary category of realistic narrative. The focus is not narrowly on the formal structure of the narratives themselves, but on the way that the Christian tradition has read those stories through its history.

In addition, Frei's emphasis on figural or typological interpretation in *Eclipse* points ahead to the development of a communal hermeneutic. A central element in the church's traditional reading of Scripture, typological interpretation is a means of discerning narrative patterns and connections among events, people, and institutions that are temporally separated in the biblical story.[44] According to Frei, typology has provided a way to unify the numerous biblical stories into a single cumulative narrative depicting a single world of one temporal sequence.[45] In addition, figural interpretation has been a way to incorporate the contemporary world into the biblical story. It has been a primary means for intratextual interpretation, a way of incorporating extrabiblical events and experiences into the world of the biblical narrative.[46]

Moreover, Frei clearly understood that typological interpretation is not a general hermeneutical technique or method that can be taught in the abstract apart from its practice within the church:

> . . . the 'method' of figural procedure was better exhibited in application than stated in the abstract. . . . Its governing rules had to remain largely implicit and are bound to look arbitrary if not nonexistent to those who are used to the statement of field-encompassing rules for the meaningful use of literary or historical congruence and comparison.[47]

---

44. Frei, *Eclipse*, 2, 28-29. Frei cites Erich Auerbach, *Mimesis: The Representation of Reality in Western Literature,* trans. Willard R. Trask (Princeton, New Jersey: Princeton Univ. Press, 1953; Princeton Paperback Edition, 1974), 73, 555. For Auerbach's discussion of figural interpretation, which influenced Frei, see Erich Auerbach, "Figura," trans. Ralph Manheim, in *Scenes from the Drama of European Literature* (New York: Meridian Press, 1959; rpt. Minneapolis: Univ. of Minnesota Press, 1984), 11-75; also Auerbach, *Mimesis,* 48-49, 73-76, 194-96, 555. For a discussion of Frei and Auerbach on this matter, see Cornel West, "On Frei's *Eclipse of Biblical Narrative,*" *Union Theological Seminary Quarterly Review* 37, no. 4 (1983): 299-302.

45. Frei, *Eclipse*, 2; also 28-37, 173-74.

46. Frei, *Eclipse*, 3; also 153.

47. Frei, *Eclipse,* 30.

With Erich Auerbach, Frei recognized that figural interpretation requires the "inspiration" of the interpreter.[48] The figural reading of Scripture depends upon the work of the Spirit in the Christian community, which has understood the biblical narrative as being fulfilled and united in the story of Jesus Christ. Figural interpretation, in short, requires the "community of interpretation"; it is part of the church's particular communal hermeneutic.[49] Although in *Eclipse* Frei does not develop the consequences of figural interpretation for a communal hermeneutic, the seeds of this later development are implicit in Frei's appreciation for typology.

Frei's later communal hermeneutic is also foreshadowed in *The Identity of Jesus Christ*, in which Frei offers an analysis of the gospel narratives. Even here, where Frei is at his most formal, he actually works "backwards" from the language and practices of the Christian commu-

48. Auerbach, *Mimesis*, 73; Frei, *Eclipse*, 28, 34. In his discussion of typology, Frei emphasizes "comprehension" as opposed simply to "creation." In particular, in *Eclipse* Frei focuses on Calvin's emphasis on figural interpretation as "inherent" in the text, rather than something "added" by the reader (Frei, *Eclipse*, 34). Poland has criticized Frei at this point, arguing that figural interpretations are necessarily "read back into" the text (Poland, 124). However, in light of Frei's later work, with its broader view of "text," Poland's criticism misses the point. Unquestionably, figural interpretation *is* dependent on the community of interpretation, the church. However, that does not mean that the community simply reads the figurative meaning back into Scripture. In fact, Poland's argument requires an understanding of Scripture apart from the Christian community; it depends on the presupposition of an objective, autonomous text into which the figural sense, as something external to that text, is read. (Here Poland seems to be the one assuming an "autonomous text"!) However, Poland's text is nothing more than a text read within a different community — the community of modern academic scholarship. In light of Frei's later work, figural interpretation is neither simplistically inherent in an autonomous text nor simplistically "read back" into the text. That very way of putting the issue misses the point: figural interpretation depends on the inseparable relationship between Scripture and the Christian community.

49. For a more extended account of figural interpretation see James Samuel Preuss, *From Shadow to Promise: Old Testament Interpretation from Augustine to Young Luther* (Cambridge, Massachusetts: Harvard Univ. Press, Belknap Press, 1969); also G. W. H. Lampe and K. J. Woollcombe, *Essays on Typology* (Naperville, Illinois: Alec R. Allenson, Inc., 1957). For a different account of typology, which emphasizes the central role of the interpretive community, see David Dawson, *Allegorical Readers and Cultural Revision in Ancient Alexandria* (Berkeley: Univ. of California Press, 1992). On the typological use of Scripture in Christian worship, see Jean Daniélou, *The Bible and the Liturgy*, University of Notre Dame Liturgical Studies, vol. 3 (Notre Dame, Indiana: Univ. of Notre Dame, 1956). I will discuss figural interpretation and its importance for preaching more fully in Chapter Nine.

nity. *The Identity of Jesus Christ,* like Anselm's *Proslogion,* operates within the framework of Christian belief and practice. Frei conducts "a series of formal hermeneutical clarifications within a larger network of Christian belief and practice"; the work is formal but by no means neutral.[50]

Drawing on insights from Frei's later work, one could say that in *Identity* Frei seeks to display the contemporary hermeneutical possibilities of the *sensus literalis* in the reading of the gospel narratives. Frei tries to demonstrate the connection between a hermeneutical procedure guided by the *sensus literalis* and the dogmatic theology of the church. In other words, *Identity* is an exercise in which Frei seeks "to describe the semiotic 'fit' between a paradigmatic text and an actual religious community's use of it. . . ."[51] In fact, in his concluding meditation, which was added to *Identity* before its publication, Frei implicitly highlights this communal use of Scripture. Focusing on the practices within which Christians rightly dispose themselves toward the gospel narratives, Frei effectively sets his reflections in *Identity* within the framework of the church's ritual reenactment and faithful discipleship — that is, within the context of a communal hermeneutic.[52]

However, Frei's appreciation for the community's role in interpretation is even more explicitly stated in his preface to *Identity.* In a revealing comment, almost an aside, Frei hints at what lies ahead in his work. Although his focus is on "reading the story itself," Frei highlights the practical, communal, dialogical character of this process within the church:

> The aim of exegesis which simply looks for the sense of a story (but does not identify sense with religious significance for the reader) is in the final analysis that of reading the story itself. *We ask if we agree on what we find there, and we discover its patterns to one another.*[53]

50. Hunsinger, "Hans Frei as Theologian," 114.
51. Schwartzentruber, 190. Schwartzentruber does not apply this description to *Identity.*
52. Frei, *Identity,* 168-73.
53. Frei, *Identity,* xv; italics mine. Poland cites this passage as an example of Frei's formalism, totally ignoring his emphasis on the actual practice of interpretation within a dialogical community (Poland, 128). Poland also does not consider carefully enough what Frei means by "reading the story itself." He does not mean here that there is an objective, autonomous text about which all disinterested readers will agree. Rather, Frei

This passage represents a seed of what will come to flower in Frei's later communal hermeneutic. The focus is on the practice of interpretation within a particular interpretive community.

Thus, Frei's mature position is in fact both a continuation and a revision of his earlier work. Within the framework of a cultural-linguistic model of Christianity, Frei turns during the final years of his life to a particularistic, communal hermeneutic, which stresses the inseparable relationship between Scripture and the community of interpretation. Nevertheless, even in his earlier work, with its more formal approach to the biblical text, the seeds of Frei's communal hermeneutic were already present, waiting to bear fruit. In addition, many of Frei's early concerns, most specifically his theological focus on the unsubstitutable identity of Jesus Christ rendered through the gospel narratives, continue to play an important role in his later position, though Frei locates these concerns within a richer, communal framework.

Critique and Development

Just as Frei's cultural-linguistic model of Christianity needs to be developed more fully, so does his understanding of the communal character of interpretation. In particular, Frei's rather narrow focus on interpretation as "meaning" needs to be supplemented by a fuller appreciation for the performative character of biblical interpretation.[54] Within a cultural-linguistic model of Christianity, one simply cannot be content with too abstract or mentalistic an understanding of biblical interpretation and the communal rules governing it. Rather, if the Christian religion is actually *constituted* and not merely expressed in its language and practices, then these practices will be much more integral to the interpretation of Scripture than Frei often suggests. Not only will these practices help to form the way the community reads Scripture, but these practices themselves will be a per-

---

simply suggests a "modest" reading of the "surface description and plot" of the story without imposing on it grand, general hermeneutical theories. In his later work, Frei's emphasis on "reading the story itself" is embedded within the community of interpretation; it amounts to reading the story according to the *sensus literalis*.

54. Frei does demonstrate some appreciation for this dimension of interpretation, but he does not develop it in any detail. See Frei, *Identity*, 154-73; Frei, *Types*, 42, 115, 117, 131, 143.

formative interpretation of Scripture. To borrow the terminology of Frei's colleague, Wayne Meeks, a development of Frei's work will need to make more explicit a "hermeneutics of social embodiment."[55] As Meeks writes,

> the goal of a theological hermeneutics on the cultural-linguistic model is not belief in objectively true propositions taught by the text nor the adoption by individuals of an authentic self-understanding evoked by the text's symbols, but the formation of a community whose forms of life correspond to the symbolic universe rendered or signaled by the text.[56]

Scripture moves the community toward social embodiment. Ultimately, "the proper context and aim of interpretation are not merely ideas or attitudes, but ethos and practice";[57] "the hermeneutical circle is not completed until the text finds a fitting social embodiment."[58] Biblical interpretation, in short, is political; it is inseparable from the formation of a particular community.[59] Within this context, mentalistic understandings of "meaning" are simply too limited.

In addition to Meeks, several other theologians and ethicists have highlighted the performative dimension of biblical interpretation. In one of the most provocative contributions to this discussion, Nicholas Lash compares the Christian community's interpretation of Scripture to the interpretation of a play through the performance of a company of actors.[60] There are, Lash notes, "some texts that only begin to deliver their meaning insofar as they are 'brought into play' through their interpretive performance."[61] The New Testament, Lash suggests, is such a text for the Christian community. Like a Beethoven quartet or a Shakespearean play, Scripture is "a text the fundamental form of the interpretation of which consists in its performance."[62]

55. Meeks, "Social Embodiment," 186.

56. Meeks, "Social Embodiment," 184-85.

57. Meeks, "Unpredictable God," 122.

58. Meeks, "Social Embodiment," 183-84.

59. Hauerwas and Long, "Interpreting the Bible as a Political Act."

60. Nicholas Lash, "Performing the Scriptures," in *Theology on the Way to Emmaus* (London: SCM Press, 1986), 40.

61. Lash, 41.

62. Lash, 41.

. . . the fundamental form of the *Christian* interpretation of scripture is the life, activity, and organization of the believing community. Secondly, . . . Christian practice, as interpretive action, consists in the *performance* of texts which are construed as "rendering," bearing witness to, one whose words and deeds, discourse and suffering, "rendered" the truth of God in human history. The performance of the New Testament enacts the conviction that these texts are most appropriately read as the story of Jesus, the story of everyone else, and the story of God.[63]

According to Lash, the primary poles in the interpretation of Scripture are not finally written texts (for example the biblical text and theological texts or sermonic texts), but rather patterns of human action: ". . . what was said and done and suffered, then, by Jesus and his disciples, and what is said and done and suffered, now, by those who seek to share his obedience and hope."[64] The interpretation of the Scriptures is a full-time affair, involving their enactment as "the social existence of an entire human community."[65] For Lash, the best illustration of the communal performance of Scripture is the celebration of the Eucharist, including the life of discipleship that it enacts.[66]

Like Meeks and Lash, Frei has highlighted the language and practices of the Christian community as the place where the church is formed and reformed through engagement with Scripture. Frei has helpfully replaced general hermeneutical theories with the church, the community in which Christians learn the rules for interpreting Scripture. However, in his work Frei did not adequately develop the performative character of biblical interpretation in the church. Nor did he explore in a concrete way the particular ecclesial practices in which the performance of Scripture is embodied in Christian communities. Any future development of Frei's position requires a more detailed treatment of these practices, such as the practice of preaching, and their role within the community of interpretation.

63. Lash, 42.
64. Lash, 42.
65. Lash, 43.
66. Lash, 46. In Chapter Eight I will examine the practice of preaching as a performance of Scripture.

Variety in Interpretation

One of the major criticisms of Frei's early work has focused on his overly simplistic harmonization of the gospel narratives.[67] This criticism is in large part on target. In *The Identity of Jesus Christ* in particular Frei does seem at times to imply that one can speak of *the* gospel narrative, which is uniformly accessible to all interpreters. In his later work, however, Frei takes more seriously not only the fourfold character of the gospel narratives, but also the polyphonous, even cacophonous, character of interpretation within the church. Along with his turn to the communal, rule-governed *sensus literalis*, Frei develops a deeper appreciation for variety in biblical interpretation. This development should come as no surprise, for, as Rowan Greer has noted, such variety was characteristic of classic ways of reading Scripture according to the rule of faith:

> That is, it [the rule of faith] excludes incorrect interpretations but does not require a correct one. Of a given passage there may be many interpretations that are valid because they do not contradict the Rule of Faith, but we cannot be sure of its true meaning. . . . Unity of belief in the early church is never confused with uniformity of belief or with assent to a definite list of theological propositions. And by the same token, the unity of valid scriptural interpretation does not require uniformity. . . . Built into the patristic understanding of exegesis is the conviction that the Christian's theological vision continues to grow and change, just as the Christian life is a pilgrimage and progress toward a destiny only dimly perceived. The framework of interpretation, then, does not so much solve the problem of what Scripture means as supply the context in which the quest for the meaning may take place.[68]

Greer's description of early Christian interpretation captures quite well the character of Frei's approach in his later work. Frei too understands the interpretation of Scripture as a communal quest within an eschatological framework.

For let us assume that the notion of a right interpretation of the Bible is itself not meaningless, but it is eschatological. The Christian com-

---

67. See, for example, James F. Kay, "Theological Table Talk: Myth or Narrative," *Theology Today* 48 (October 1991): 330.
68. Greer, "Christian Bible," 197-99.

munity is gathered in *hope*, and that extends to as ordinary a task as
that of a common way of reading its sacred text. One may take the
Church through time and space to be, among other things, not a
babble of voices talking completely past one another, but a groping
and imperfect community of interpretation. . . .[69]

Christian interpretation at best asymptotically approaches God in Jesus
Christ who is rendered in Scripture. The process, as I noted earlier, is
more like exploring a mystery than solving a problem. For Frei, the story
about Jesus, which gives the church its identity, has not yet achieved
"closure," but points ahead to a future fulfillment, with the result that
Christians today always live with a "reserve of not knowing."[70] The
eschatological character of the gospel narratives, which Frei emphasizes
even in his earlier work, provides the framework within which Frei
appreciates the polyphonic character of biblical interpretation in the
church.

Frei highlights this polyphony in several different ways. First of all,
Frei affirms variety in interpretation at the level of the "reality referent" of
the gospel narratives. Consistently distinguishing questions of textual
meaning and reference, Frei challenged the modern, historical conceptuality that understood the meaning of a text as its historical reference. By
challenging this dominant conceptuality, Frei opened the way to various
interpretations of the reality status of the gospel narratives.

In his discussion of the *literal sense* Frei makes this point clearly
and carefully.[71] According to Frei, the broad consensus regarding the
sensus literalis functions only at the hermeneutical level; it does not
extend to the extratextual referent of the gospel accounts.

> In other words, "literal" is not referentially univocal but embraces
> many possibilities. . . . *the consensus covers the literal reading or mean-
> ing of the New Testament stories about Jesus in an ascriptive mode, but
> not the reality status of the ascriptive subject Jesus* or even all the details
> of the *de*scriptive elements of the story.
>
> To summarize: The continuity of Christian tradition in the West
> [—] and now, I believe, beyond the West — lies in its textual or

69. Frei, *Types*, 56.
70. Frei, *Identity*, 164.
71. See *Types*, 84-85, 137-42.

hermeneutical reading more than in the extratextual reference of the text, where we had often hoped to find it, or in the historical continuity of an experience that is supposedly continuous because it is the experience of him. The specificity and universality of Jesus Christ and the complex simplicity of his portrait are a matter, then, of the partial reiteration, rhetorical or didactic, of the text — sometimes in an aesthetic mode, always at the disciples' distance in a form of life, and to some extent in the fragmentary conceptual redescription that is the theologian's domain.[72]

As he had done in his earlier works, Frei here challenges the equation of the literal sense with historically verifiable "fact," as if factual reporting is what language is all about. The literal sense of the gospel stories, Frei argues, is not necessarily connected with an understanding of language as "a mirror of reality or a perceptual report of our knowledge of what is extramental."[73] Rather, it is possible to read the narratives literally — according to the ascriptive logic emphasized by the Christian community — and leave the referential status of what is described in them indeterminate, open to a variety of interpretations.[74] The literal sense, as it has been understood in the Christian community, contains no univocal theory of reference; the consensus has focused not on the level of reference, but on the level of the story itself. Although Frei challenges theological positions that ignore the ascriptive logic of the gospel narratives, he affirms that in the process of contemporary conceptual redescription, a great deal of variety is possible within the framework of the *sensus literalis*.[75] As Frei concludes in *Types*, "The task of the redescription of Jesus will remain unfinished as long as history lasts. . . ."[76]

Second, even at the level of meaning Frei affirms the possibility,

---

72. Frei, *Types*, 142-43. For a brief discussion of the various ways in which the reality status of the gospel accounts might at least theoretically be understood, see Frei, *Types*, 141.

73. Frei, *Types*, 139.

74. Frei, *Types*, 138.

75. Frei, for example, criticized the work of Gordon Kaufman and David Tracy because he thought both theologians had given up the unique, unsubstitutable identity of Jesus of Nazareth.

76. Frei, *Types*, 146. Frei thus suggests the need for a "generous orthodoxy." See "Response to 'Narrative Theology,'" 21.

indeed the inevitability, of different readings of the gospel narratives. In his later work, Frei explicitly rejects the notion of a "complete or non-residual interpretation of any text," not simply because of the diversity of interpretive communities, but also because of the richness and complexity of Scripture itself.[77] In particular, Frei recognizes the fragmentary and diverse character of the depictions of Jesus' identity in the gospels. Although he affirms that we should seek to discern the unity among the four gospel narratives, he recognizes that this unity is complex, and he counsels modesty and restraint.

> The specifics of a sketch of [Jesus'] teaching as well as his being remain incomplete and fragmented and their cohesion in interpretation, as I said, a matter of restraint: Complete or non-residual interpretation of any text, but especially of a combination of juxtaposed texts, is a tempting but elusive business. Jesus is a very specific person as he emerges from the fragmentary and diverse fourfold description in which he is rendered for us, yet in that variety there is also the claim of unity which allows people of great diversity access to him, and him access to them.[78]

Although Frei continues to affirm the unique, unsubstitutable identity of Jesus Christ, and although he never rejects his earlier description of Jesus in *The Identity of Jesus Christ*, Frei here reveals a more explicit appreciation for the fragmentary character of the gospel narratives and the diverse ways in which various communities may interpret them. Most importantly, Frei explicitly emphasizes the fourfold character of the gospels — something he virtually ignored in his rather simplistic harmonizing in *Identity*. The unity in the four gospels' depictions of Jesus is at best a complex unity.

In Barth's terms, one might speak of the "onesidedness" of our knowledge of Jesus.[79] Because of the fourfold character of the gospel narratives we can never possess Jesus completely, but continually and

---

77. Frei, *Types*, 134-35.

78. Frei, *Types*, 134.

79. Karl Barth, *Church Dogmatics*, I, 1, ed. G. W. Bromiley and T. F. Torrance, trans. G. W. Bromiley (1936; Edinburgh: T. & T. Clark, 1975), 174-81. Barth speaks here of the onesidedness of the Word in its "divine content and secular form." I do not mean to imply here that there are only two sides, but rather a variety of "sides" in Jesus' complex unity, which cannot be captured theoretically or systematically.

inevitably wrestle with one side or another of his multifaceted, complex unity. As Frei suggests even in *Identity,* Jesus' presence is always "indirect."[80] In more contemporary terms, we might say that while the narratives do not present us with four different Jesuses, they nevertheless do present us with a "decentered" Jesus, who as the resurrected and living one will not be possessed by any theory or community, but continually surprises even the church. This "decentered" Jesus of Nazareth "is able to resist all human formulations and eludes the grasp of all our discourses." He is "thus able to be the fathomless source of disruptive significations which 'interrupt' our unredeemed condition, and which are in consequence the source of our true hope."[81]

In fact, the fourfold gospel has this disruptive character *only* as the church seeks to read the gospel narratives according to the ascriptive logic of the *sensus literalis.* If one reads the gospels according to some other logic (for example as mythical or symbolic expressions of general human experience), they more easily lose their disruptive force. As expressions of general truths or experiences the gospels are more easily harmonized — and tamed. However, as stories about the unique, unsubstitutable person, Jesus of Nazareth, the four gospel narratives are less easily harmonized; they remain in tension with each other and consequently possess the kind of disruptive power I have noted.[82]

---

80. Frei, *Identity,* 155-57.

81. Kenneth Surin, "The Weight of Weakness: Intratextuality and Discipleship," in *The Turnings of Darkness and Light: Essays in Philosophical and Systematic Theology* (Cambridge: Cambridge Univ. Press, 1989), 220. Surin here distinguishes the Second Person of the Trinity, who is "subtextual," from Jesus of Nazareth, who is fully textualized in Christian Scripture. According to Surin, it is the Second Person of the Trinity who cannot be fully textualized and thus is the source of disruption. Contrary to Surin, I am suggesting that the fourfold character of the gospel narratives themselves actually "textualizes" Jesus of Nazareth in such a way as to enable such disruptions. I do not think it is necessary to make the rather sharp distinction that Surin makes between Jesus and the Second Person of the Trinity in order to affirm the disruptive power of the gospel narratives.

82. Paul Schwartzentruber has argued that it is the impossibility of capturing Jesus' identity through general theories that provides the theological warrant for Frei's rejection of general hermeneutical theory. Schwartzentruber focuses on the fact that the unique, unsubstitutable identity of Jesus Christ can be rendered only through a particular narrative, not through any general theory (Schwartzentruber, 191-93). In addition, I would argue, the disruptive, "complex unity" of Jesus in the fourfold gospel narrative provides a further theological warrant for rejecting general hermeneutical theory in favor of the church's communal hermeneutic.

In short, the ascriptive logic of the gospels sets some limits, but does not provide any single correct interpretation. Jesus simply cannot and will not become the possession of any interpretation, but continually interrupts and disrupts them all. The journey of the Christian community involves an ever-growing faithfulness to Jesus Christ, a continual wrestling with the narratives rendering his identity, but never a possessing or controlling of him. The fourfold gospel assures this kind of disequilibrium.

Finally, in his later work Frei asserts the value and legitimacy of interpretations that move beyond the literal sense (in its grammatical/syntactical aspect). Reflecting a move in a different direction from the Reformers, who were the "heroes" of *Eclipse*, Frei even affirms the validity of allegorical readings. Although the stories about Jesus are not allegorized, other parts of Scripture may be interpreted allegorically. Frei does not provide a detailed explanation at this point, largely because he is concerned with the exegetical practice of the Christian community, rather than with abstract methods of interpretation. What is important, however, is the fact that Frei's understanding of the literal sense does not exclude other valid ways of interpreting texts, as long as they remain subordinate to the literal sense of the central story of Jesus of Nazareth.[83]

At several points in his later work, then, Frei is quite explicit about the polyphonic character of biblical interpretation in the church. It is through the ongoing conversation among many voices that Scripture forms and reforms the community of faith. However, Frei's explicit recognition of variety in interpretation should not be viewed simply as a revision of his earlier position. There is continuity here as well.

For example, in "Theological Reflections" and *Identity* Frei explicitly affirms variety in interpretation. In both of these works Frei notes the necessity of reading with some conceptual tools, apart from which we could understand nothing at all.[84] Completely neutral description is impossible; some redescription is inevitable. In addition, Frei asserts that his particular formal reading of the gospel narrative is but "one

---

83. For Frei's discussion of these matters, see *Types*, 137-43. With Augustine, Frei does defend a general moral constraint on allegorical interpretation: it must contribute to the love of God and neighbor (Frei, *Types*, 137-38).

84. Hans W. Frei, "Theological Reflections on the Gospel Accounts of Jesus' Death and Resurrection," *The Christian Scholar* 49 (Winter 1966): 274-75; Frei, *Identity*, 45.

possible arrangement" of it.[85] Before presenting his own arrangement in *Identity*, he states that "it may be possible to find a variety of such formal ordering schemes, some of which may be in conflict with others."[86] In fact, not only are other descriptions possible, but Frei even admits that Barth's description of the narrative is "quite different" from his own.[87]

In "Theological Reflections" Frei even speaks of the "mystery" that always surrounds the identity of Jesus Christ. Writing of the "apparently contradictory" tendencies of power and powerlessness that "converge in the gospel narrative," Frei rejects any simple, theoretical harmony between them: ". . . heresy is often the sign that orthodoxy has sacrificed the elements of mystery, and along with it tentativeness or open-endedness, to an oversimplified consistency."[88] Indeed, it is at this very point that the gospel narratives are so important. Only in the narratives do power and powerlessness fit together "naturally and easily" in the ascriptive subject, Jesus of Nazareth, without succumbing to an oversimplified consistency.[89] The gospel narratives actually protect the mystery of Jesus Christ from all of our general theories and abstract, conceptual redescriptions.

Thus, even in his earlier work Frei not only respects, but affirms, the inevitably polyphonic character of biblical interpretation within the church. Indeed, as several people have recently noted, Frei pioneered a general approach to Scripture and theology that is compatible with great diversity.[90] In his appreciation for variety in interpretation, as in his turn to a cultural-linguistic model of religion and a communal hermeneutic, Frei's later work represents both a continuation and a revision of his earlier position.

---

85. Frei, "Theological Reflections," 293, 277.
86. Frei, *Identity*, 127-28.
87. Frei, *Identity*, 128. See Barth's account in *Church Dogmatics*, IV, 1, 224-28.
88. Frei, "Theological Reflections," 266.
89. Frei, "Theological Reflections," 266.
90. Lindbeck, "Frei and the Future of Theology," 2. As early as his dissertation Frei notes that the "realistic" reading of the Bible represents a "general approach," not a specific set of conclusions (Hans W. Frei, *The Doctrine of Revelation in the Thought of Karl Barth, 1909-1922: The Nature of Barth's Break With Liberalism* [Ann Arbor, Michigan: University Microfilms, 1956], 489).

Conclusions

Throughout his life Frei sought to confine "hermeneutics" to its rather low-keyed definition as "the rules and principles for determining the sense of written texts, or the rules and principles governing exegesis."[91] This is precisely the path that Frei follows in his later work. Within the framework of a cultural-linguistic understanding of Christianity, Frei seeks to discern and describe not some universal set of rules for reading all texts, but rather the consensual rules that the church has used in reading Scripture. Being a member of the Christian community involves learning to use these rules of interpretation in reading and performing Scripture. One must thus conclude that Frei has no general "narrative hermeneutic." Rather, Frei develops a specialized communal hermeneutic, which describes the rules for reading a particular narrative within a particular historical community.

For Frei, the church's theology and hermeneutic belong inseparably together. In his later work Frei simply supplements his theological particularity, focused on the identity of Jesus Christ, with a hermeneutical particularity, which approaches the interpretation of Scripture from within the community of faith.[92] This move is essential because no general hermeneutical theory, but only a particular narrative read according to an ascriptive logic, can render the unique, unsubstitutable identity of Jesus, who is the center of the church's worship and life.[93] Just as Frei's theological position challenges liberal approaches to theology, which begin with general human experience, rather than with Jesus of Nazareth, so Frei's "communal hermeneutic" challenges general hermeneutical theories, which seek to provide a "foundation" for biblical interpretation apart from the concrete language and practices of the Christian community.

For both theological and hermeneutical reasons, Frei rejects any "global foundational scheme for reading texts so that the reading of biblical material would simply be a regional instance of the universal procedure."[94] Indeed, Frei even rejects his earlier literary approach as

91. Frei, *Identity*, xvi.
92. Frei, "Literal Reading," 67.
93. Schwartzentruber, 191-93.
94. Frei, "Literal Reading," 59.

too much a general theory, which tends to subsume the biblical stories under the more general category of realistic narrative.[95] As Frei writes, "the less high powered general theory that upholds the literal or realistic reading of the Gospels may be just as perilously perched as its more majestic and pretentious hermeneutical cousin."[96] It is time, Frei argues, to lower our theoretical sights.[97] The actual practice of interpretation within the Christian community is primary, not general theories of "meaning" or "understanding" or "narrative."[98]

Frei thus does not provide a general hermeneutical theory to explain how ancient biblical texts can become "meaningful" for contemporary persons. Indeed, Frei has been criticized for this theoretical omission.[99] However, it is not that Frei has ignored this issue. Rather, he simply has not answered it with a general hermeneutical theory, but has dealt with the issue in terms of a concrete people, the community of faith. Frei refuses to substitute hermeneutical theory for the church, the community in which Christians learn the rules for reading and performing Scripture. In moving beyond the general categories of "text" and "interpreter," Frei points explicitly to the language and practices of the Christian community as the place where persons are formed and reformed through their ongoing engagement with Scripture.

In his analysis of *The Eclipse of Biblical Narrative*, George Schner briefly suggests that Frei's real concern in that book is a rediscovery or restatement of the particularity of the gospel.[100] Here Schner captures a central thread that runs through Frei's work early and late, through both his theology and his hermeneutics. Although Frei's work itself, with the exception of *Identity* and "Theological Reflections," remains far too general and abstract, he is clearly concerned with particularity — the particularity of Jesus of Nazareth, whose identity is rendered in a specific narrative, and the particularity of a nonfoundational communal hermeneutic, which guides the church's reading of that narrative. In a time

95. Frei, "Literal Reading," 67.
96. Frei, "Literal Reading," 64. That high-powered cousin is phenomenological hermeneutics, represented particularly by the work of Paul Ricoeur.
97. Frei, "Literal Reading," 67.
98. Frei, "Theology and Interpretation of Narrative," 101-2; Frei, *Types*, 56-57.
99. Poland, 120-37.
100. Schner, 159.

when the danger facing the church, as Frei perceived it, is accommoda-
tion to the surrounding culture, Frei calls the church back to its own
distinctive identity, which is shaped by the identity of Jesus of Nazareth.
Finally, it is this unapologetic theological and hermeneutical particularity that stands as Frei's challenge to all who turn to narrative, including
preachers.

PART TWO

Narrative Homiletics:
A Postliberal Critique

"A few summers ago, we all heard a sermon in which the preacher waxed eloquent about a 'whale watch' in which he had participated off the New England coast and had declared after viewing the whales, 'It was the greatest experience in my life!' The rest of us were led to doubt the authenticity of that statement. Later and without being at all unctious [sic] Hans said that he was glad to hear anyone attempt to preach about Jesus Christ these days. He did not mention whales!"

Letter from John Woolverton,
September 19, 1991

Chapter Five

Narrative Preaching
and Experiential Events

. . . we preachers forget that the gospel itself is for the most part a simple narrative of persons, places, happenings, and conversation. It is not a verbal exposition of general ideas. Nine-tenths of our preaching is verbal exposition and argument, but not one tenth of the gospel is exposition. Its ideas are mainly in the form of a story told.[1]

With these words H. Grady Davis, in 1958, signaled the turn to narrative in contemporary, mainline Protestant preaching.[2] Shifting the focus of homiletics from sermon content, which had been the emphasis of neo-orthodox homiletics, to sermon form, Davis's book significantly shaped homiletical developments in the second half of the

1. H. Grady Davis, *Design for Preaching* (Philadelphia: Fortress Press, 1958), 157.
2. I am focusing on mainline Protestant homiletics. I am not dealing with the African-American preaching tradition, which in some ways comes closer to Frei's position. Nor am I dealing with Roman Catholic homiletics, which takes more seriously than Protestant homiletics the liturgical context of preaching and the character of the preacher. For more detailed discussions of the development of contemporary narrative homiletics, see George M. Bass, "The Evolution of the Story Sermon," *Word and World* 2 (Spring 1982): 183-88; and Billy Joe Bennett, *The Development of a Story-Form Homiletic, 1958 to 1985: Retelling the Story of God in Community* (Ann Arbor, Michigan: University Microfilms International, 1988). For a discussion of a similar turn to narrative in the nineteenth century, see David S. Reynolds, "From Doctrine to Narrative: The Rise of Pulpit Storytelling in America," *American Quarterly* 32 (Winter 1980): 479-98.

twentieth century. Indeed, in his brief treatment of the story form, Davis highlighted many of the themes developed more fully by contemporary narrative homileticians.[3]

During the sixties and early seventies, which was a period of struggle and experimentation in homiletics, the relationship between narrative and preaching began to be explored in earnest, the most notable contributions being Charles Rice's *Interpretation and Imagination* and, less directly, Fred Craddock's *As One Without Authority*.[4] Influences such as the New Hermeneutic, communications theory, literary criticism, linguistic theory, and narrative theology furthered the interest in the relationship between narrative and preaching. By the late seventies and early eighties, narrative preaching had become the most popular and influential movement in contemporary homiletics, and numerous significant contributions had been published in the field.

Among these contributions, several books have emerged as seminal works and will serve as the focus of the discussion that follows. The first is the book mentioned earlier, Charles Rice's *Interpretation and Imagination,* which "more than most other works in homiletics or related fields, turned the attention of preachers in the direction of narrative sermon forms."[5] In addition, the early works of Fred Craddock, *As One Without Authority* and *Overhearing the Gospel,* have been formative.[6] Although not considered by some to be a "narrative homiletician," Craddock has exerted enormous influence on recent developments in homiletics in general and on narrative preaching in particular.[7] *As One Without Authority,* which popularized the "inductive method" and the New Hermeneutic for preaching, is undoubtedly the most important

---

3. Davis cites as potential *weaknesses* of this form the very things that contemporary writers highlight as its strengths: the "indirect" conveyance of meaning, the necessity of active listening by the hearers, and the need for hearers to draw their own conclusions and make their own applications (Davis, 161).

4. Bass, 184.

5. Bass, 185.

6. Fred B. Craddock, *As One Without Authority,* 3rd ed. (Nashville: Abingdon, 1979); *Overhearing the Gospel* (Nashville: Abingdon, 1978).

7. Within her broad definition of narrative preaching as preaching that enables "participation in an experience that's open-ended," Lucy Rose has included Craddock as a key representative of that genre. Lucy Rose, "The Parameters of Narrative Preaching," in *Journeys Toward Narrative Preaching,* ed. Wayne Bradley Robinson (New York: Pilgrim Press, 1990), 34-35.

homiletics text in the past twenty-five years.[8] *Overhearing the Gospel,* though generally less influential, has made an important contribution to narrative preaching. Much of the work in this field, though taking new directions and new forms, is thoroughly indebted to Craddock's groundbreaking books, as the number of references to Craddock in the literature suggests. Indeed, contemporary homiletics often seems to involve little more than variations on themes that Craddock made popular. In addition to Craddock's and Rice's works, three other influential books require close examination: Steimle, Niedenthal, and Rice's *Preaching the Story* and two important books by Eugene Lowry, *The Homiletical Plot* and *Doing Time in the Pulpit.*[9]

Although none of these books necessarily represents the author's final position, the works are historically the most influential ones in the area of narrative preaching.[10] Moreover, the books represent various positions that remain prevalent today in the field of narrative homiletics.[11] Indeed, as even a cursory glance at the books reveals, there is no simple way to define "narrative preaching." In general, the field may be broken down into two major positions, represented by those who argue for the actual telling of stories or a single story in the sermon and those

8. Craddock's appropriation of the New Hermeneutic was preceded by David Randolph in *The Renewal of Preaching* (Philadelphia: Fortress Press, 1969). However, Craddock's work popularized this approach.

9. Edmund Steimle, Morris Niedenthal, and Charles Rice, *Preaching the Story* (Philadelphia: Fortress Press, 1980); Eugene Lowry, *The Homiletical Plot: The Sermon as Narrative Art Form* (Atlanta: John Knox Press, 1980); Eugene Lowry, *Doing Time in the Pulpit: The Relationship Between Narrative and Preaching* (Nashville: Abingdon, 1985). Lowry's more recent book, *How to Preach a Parable: Designs for Narrative Sermons* (Nashville: Abingdon, 1989), focuses on details of technique and adds little to his earlier theoretical works. I am not examining one influential book, Richard Jensen's *Telling the Story: Variety and Imagination in Preaching* (Minneapolis: Augsburg Press, 1980). Jensen's work is somewhat different from the others in that he argues that story sermons should take the form of a single "parabolic story." However, Jensen's position is thoroughly dependent on Craddock's work. All of the issues discussed below are present in *Telling the Story.* There is thus no need to discuss Jensen's book in detail.

10. Charles Rice's most recent book, in particular, represents some important new developments in his thought, particularly with respect to the matter of "translation" and to the liturgical context of preaching. However, the book has to date exerted little influence on narrative preaching. See Charles Rice, *The Embodied Word: Preaching as Art and Liturgy* (Minneapolis: Fortress Press, 1991).

11. In the course of my discussion of these books, I will note connections between them and more recent books.

who emphasize narrative form in more general terms — the narrative shape of sermons in one respect or another. However, even within these two broad positions, there is much variety. Narrative homiletics is not one thing, but actually represents a large umbrella under which several different, but related, approaches are generally lumped.[12]

None of the authors whom I will discuss understands the significance of narrative for preaching in exactly the same way. Charles Rice, for example, emphasizes the importance of nonbiblical narratives for preaching and focuses on the character of narrative as extended metaphor. Fred Craddock, on the other hand, argues that inductive sermons should "move like a good story" and that stories provide the best vehicle for "indirect" speech and "overhearing the gospel." In yet another way, Edmund Steimle argues that preachers should weave together the biblical story and "our stories" and suggests that sermons should formally embody various characteristics of a good story. Finally, Eugene Lowry argues that every sermon should have a "plot," understood as the movement from disequilibrium through reversal to equilibrium. In short, there is no one thing called "narrative preaching."

However, despite their differences, these authors share some significant common ground. All of them, in reaction against cognitive-propositional preaching, give a central place to human experience in preaching; at the heart of narrative preaching in its various forms is the "experiential event" evoked by the sermon. In addition, all of the authors struggle to relate two different stories or worlds — the "biblical world" and the "contemporary world" — through the sermon. Finally, all of the writers offer a formal understanding of the role of narrative in preaching, with a specific emphasis on parable and plot. These three matters are central to the various forms of narrative preaching. However, in each of these three areas Frei's cultural-linguistic theology offers both a critique of and an alternative to current positions. This critique and alternative will be the focus of the remainder of this book.

In what follows, however, I do not want to imply that narrative

---

12. See John McClure, "Narrative and Preaching: Sorting It All Out," *Journal for Preachers* 15 (Advent 1991): 24-29. Although McClure does highlight several different appropriations of narrative in contemporary homiletics, his distinctions are too rigid; there is more common ground than he suggests.

homiletics has not made significant, positive contributions to preaching in the United States. In fact, just the opposite has been the case. First of all, the turn to narrative has unquestionably included a turn to Scripture. Narrative preachers generally reject topical sermons and emphasize the importance of the biblical text. Indeed, the turn to narrative was in part a result of insights regarding the narrative form of much of the Bible. When one finds modern, liberal presuppositions underlying narrative preaching, one discovers just how deeply these presuppositions are rooted in contemporary homiletics. Second, narrative homileticians have enriched the form of the sermon. The deductive, three-point sermon has been supplemented (if not completely displaced) by a variety of new forms, many of them related to the forms of the biblical literature itself. Third, narrative homiletics has brought with it a new appreciation for the indicative character of the gospel. Frei himself would surely have approved of the more descriptive, less explanatory and moralistic, orientation that characterizes narrative preaching. Fourth, the holistic character of preaching, which addresses not just the intellect but also the emotions, has been recaptured; logical argument no longer dominates homiletics texts as it once did. Finally, the poetic and metaphorical dimensions of the language of preaching have been highlighted and the role of the imagination in preaching has been recovered. Although none of these contributions is as new as many of the authors make them sound, and although the older, more "deductive" homiletics is frequently treated as a kind of straw figure, one should not overlook these positive developments in recent homiletical thought, to which narrative homiletics has contributed greatly.

However, despite these contributions, one can hardly argue that these developments have resulted in a more vital and faithful church. Indeed, the mainline church has itself been in decline during the period in which narrative preaching has thrived. In addition, it is questionable whether many forms of narrative preaching are adequate for the current American context, in which a biblically illiterate church finds itself in an increasingly minority situation in an increasingly secular culture. Finally, serious theological reflection has been sorely lacking; there has been no careful examination of the theological and hermeneutical presuppositions behind narrative preaching. Such reflection is long overdue, and Hans Frei's postliberal theology provides a helpful perspective from which to undertake this task. With these issues in mind I now turn to a critique of contemporary narrative homiletics, beginning, in this chapter, with the emphasis on "experiential events."[13]

The Individual, Experiential Event

Although narrative homiletics takes a variety of forms, at the center of the major works in the area is an emphasis on human experience. To borrow Lindbeck's categories, narrative homiletics represents a turn away from cognitive-propositional preaching to experiential preaching. The authors in the field uniformly reject older models of preaching such as shared information or logical argument or propositional knowledge. Unlike these older cognitive models, narrative preaching seeks to touch the hearer at the "level of experience" rather than intellect.[14] Narrative is valued for its distinctive ability to produce or evoke experience.[15]

Along with this emphasis on experience, narrative homileticians have also generally accepted the New Hermeneutic's emphasis on the existential "Word-event"; preaching is understood as a creative, transforming "happening."[16] This "Word-event," however, is understood primarily in experiential terms; the sermon becomes an "experiential event" in which transformation is supposed to happen experientially in individuals.

This understanding of preaching as an "experiential event" represents a very different orientation from Frei's cultural-linguistic model. As I will demonstrate in what follows, the experiential orientation in narrative preaching leads not only to an overly individualistic understanding of preaching, but also to a tendency toward the very experiential-expressivist understanding of Christianity that Frei critiques.

---

13. In Chapter Six I will examine the ways narrative homileticians seek to relate the biblical and contemporary "worlds"; and in Chapter Seven I will discuss their formal understanding of the role of narrative in preaching, particularly their preoccupation with parable and plot.

14. Don M. Wardlaw, "Introduction: The Need for New Shapes," in *Preaching Biblically: Creating Sermons in the Shape of Scripture*, ed. Don M. Wardlaw (Philadelphia: Westminster Press, 1983), 19, 21.

15. Rose, 39.

16. Charles Rice is an exception. In his treatment of preaching as "event," he draws (problematically) on the early work of Karl Barth.

Homiletics has not yet made the "postliberal" move to a cultural-linguistic approach to preaching, but continues to operate within a modern, liberal framework.[17]

Charles Rice

The emphasis on the "experiential event" can be seen in all of the major works of narrative homiletics, despite their different appropriations of narrative for preaching. Most extreme in this regard, and closest to a purely experiential-expressivist position, is Charles Rice's influential early work, *Interpretation and Imagination*. According to Rice, religion is fundamentally a general human experience, which is expressed both in particular religious traditions and in the general culture. Religion, Rice writes, is "the depth of all experience," and theological language is fundamentally the expression of this deep human experience.[18] Rice's work signals the clear shift from a cognitive-propositional understanding of religion to what Lindbeck would call an experiential-expressivist model.

Rice explicitly notes the influence of Schleiermacher, through Tillich, on his position: ". . . Tillich appreciated Schleiermacher's great contribution: the redirection of theology away from propositional dogmatism toward the realm of human experience."[19] "Tillich asks the church to show a proper humility, consonant with the nature of religious experience, to keep in mind that doctrine, institutional forms, and Holy Scripture are at best efforts to articulate the sense of God in the depths of man's life."[20]

---

17. As McClendon and Murphy note, an emphasis on the authority of individual experience is a characteristic of modern theology, as is the link between individualism and expressivism (Nancey Murphy and James William McClendon, "Distinguishing Modern and Postmodern Theologies," *Modern Theology* 5 [April 1989]: 196-98). I do not intend to argue that experience is the sole emphasis of narrative homiletics. Many of the writers do speak of "seeing the world" differently through new images and metaphors. But the vehicle for this is the experiential event. And, as I will note below, metaphor and image are often understood in experiential-expressivist ways.

18. Charles Rice, *Interpretation and Imagination: The Preacher and Contemporary Literature* (Philadelphia: Fortress Press, 1970), 51, 57.

19. Rice, *Interpretation*, 64.

20. Rice, *Interpretation*, 5. Rice's emphasis on experience continues in his contribution to *Preaching the Story*, which he wrote with Edmund Steimle and Morris

Appropriately, a critique of Barth is part and parcel of this position:

> Barth denied Schleiermacher's major premise, that Christian faith is grounded in man's general experience of God. Had Barth been more open to Schleiermacher, as was Tillich, he would not have equated homiletics with textual exegesis and narrow exposition. If Barth had entertained more seriously Schleiermacher's idea that all men have a sense of God, then he would have expected the Word of God not exclusively in connection with texts but wherever men live with feeling.[21]

Barth, Rice argues, could not accept that that to which the Bible spoke and speaks "resides in the depths" of human life.[22] Thus, the key for Rice is not the biblical text, but the human experience "behind" it, which is expressed in the text. Rice can even suggest that Jesus himself is "an expression of the religious," completely sacrificing the ascriptive logic of the gospel narratives.[23]

The one thing that Rice retains from Barth is the latter's emphasis on the "eventfulness" of preaching.[24] In Rice's work, however, this emphasis on the eventful character of the sermon is placed within an experiential framework; the sermon becomes an *experiential* event. The preacher must find ways to evoke an experiential "happening" for the hearers.[25]

Despite his discussion of "general religious experience," however,

---

Niedenthal (Philadelphia: Fortress Press, 1980). There too, preaching is an "experiential event"; Rice even speaks of the "celebration of experience" (*Preaching the Story*, 9, 67, 30-32). Although Rice has a greater respect for the biblical text in his later work, his position with regard to experience remains virtually unchanged in *Preaching the Story*.

21. Rice, *Interpretation*, 14.

22. Rice, *Interpretation*, 17.

23. Rice, *Interpretation*, 17.

24. Rice, *Interpretation*, 13.

25. Rice thinks Barth abandoned this emphasis in his later work and his own preaching. According to Rice, Barth's textual preaching simply cannot create the "experiential event." Indeed, Rice views textual sermons as a form of "propositional didacticism" (*Interpretation*, 61-63). Rice understands "event" differently from Barth. Barth's understanding of "event" is more focused on the activity of God and less on human experience; it is more linguistic and "objective," less dependent on existential experience. Indeed, for Barth the "effect" of preaching is not even constitutive of its definition. See Karl Barth, *Homiletics*, trans. Geoffrey W. Bromiley and Donald E. Daniels (Louisville, Kentucky: Westminster/John Knox Press, 1991), 49.

the experience Rice seeks to create in the sermon is presented in individualistic terms. Narrative allows each individual to relate to the story through his or her own experience.[26] The movement is two-way, from the written word to *one's own* experience and from *one's* experience back to the literature.[27] The sermon is directed to the individual.[28] Rice's experiential emphasis leads to an extremely individualistic understanding of the preaching event.[29]

Rice thus moves preaching away from propositional logic to the realm of individual human experience. "Preaching betrays its theology by the form it takes. In the homiletical movement from religious experience to confessional expression, what one has experienced will determine how one expresses it."[30] In Rice's work one finds the seeds of the dominant emphasis on "existential experience" in narrative preaching.[31] One of the primary reasons for the use of story is its ability to evoke this religious experience in the hearers.

Fred Craddock

Fred Craddock's two important books, *As One Without Authority* and *Overhearing the Gospel,* reflect a similar emphasis on individual experience in the preaching event, though within a different theological framework from that of Rice. In discussing these books, however, one must be careful. First of all, the books do not represent a final statement of Craddock's understanding of preaching.[32] They are, as Crad-

---

26. Even more recent authors who have stressed the retelling of *biblical* stories in the sermon remain captive to this individual experiential-event model. See, for example, John C. Holbert, *Preaching Old Testament: Proclamation and Narrative in the Hebrew Bible* (Nashville: Abingdon Press, 1991), 49.

27. Rice, *Interpretation,* 16; italics mine.

28. Rice, *Interpretation,* 79.

29. I am not saying that there is never a social dimension to Rice's message. Rice will preach in relation to social problems, but the experience of the individual hearer remains the goal of the sermon.

30. Rice, *Interpretation,* 60.

31. Rice, *Interpretation,* 64-65.

32. Craddock's other major homiletical work, *Preaching* (Nashville, Abingdon, 1985), a general homiletics text, differs in some important respects from the earlier books. However, *As One Without Authority* and *Overhearing the Gospel* are the books that have influenced the development of narrative homiletics.

dock himself notes, intended as correctives, rather than full-blown homiletics.[33] Second, no criticism should ignore the positive contributions and salutary effects of many of Craddock's insights, particularly his concern to effect a new hearing of the gospel.[34] Craddock's exploration of the method — the "how" — of the sermon has been a creative and positive contribution to Christian preaching. His work unquestionably breathed new life back into the practice of preaching and the discipline of homiletics at a time when the pulpit was in woeful shape.[35] Third, Craddock repeatedly affirms the dynamic relation between Scripture and the church as central to the preaching event.[36] He is unquestionably committed to Scripture as the church's book, though, as I will discuss below, his method seems at odds with this affirmation, and his understanding of the church is limited. Finally, Craddock seeks to hold in tension the Bible and the contemporary situation; he seeks to avoid both a narrow biblicism and trendy relevance. Craddock's goal is faithful biblical preaching, not shallow entertainment.

In addition, *As One Without Authority* and *Overhearing the Gospel* should not simply be lumped together; there are important differences between the two books. For example, in *Overhearing the Gospel* Craddock draws more heavily on narrative, affirms more strongly the authority of Scripture, and demonstrates a more positive attitude toward the biblical idiom in preaching. In addition, in the later book Craddock reveals a stronger turn to literary criticism, including even Frei's work, which moves him beyond a "meant"-"means" hermeneutical framework and toward a greater appreciation for the present literary form of the canon.[37] Indeed, Craddock even critiques historical criticism in ways consistent with Frei's work.[38] All of these developments represent positive changes in Craddock's position. However, despite these qualifica-

33. Craddock, *Overhearing*, 58-60.

34. Craddock, *Overhearing*, 16, 19.

35. For example, his emphasis on the hearers' participation in the sermon, including the important role of movement, anticipation, and concreteness in preaching, is important. Likewise, Craddock's affirmation of the role of imagination and his stress on the oral character of preaching have proved valuable in homiletical developments, as has his challenge to moralistic preaching. Craddock, *Authority*, 58, 62-63.

36. Craddock, *Authority*, 126-28.

37. Craddock, *Overhearing*, 75-77.

38. Craddock, *Overhearing*, 75-76; 143 n. 16.

tions, which create some tensions within his work, an individualistic, existentialist, experiential framework remains basic to Craddock's homiletical thought.

Most fascinating, however, are the different presuppositions behind *As One Without Authority* and *Overhearing the Gospel.* In *As One Without Authority* the basic presupposition is that Christendom is dead and that ministers can no longer rely on the authority of their position or the authority of the church or the authority of Scripture.[39] Therefore the inductive method, which moves from the particulars of human experience to the gospel, is necessary.

However, in *Overhearing the Gospel* the presupposition is that Christendom remains alive.[40] That is, the Christian language and tradition are so familiar that they have lost their power. There "is an illusion of participation in the Christian faith where actually little or none exists."[41] People are immersed in the tradition and language of the faith, but it has lost its life.[42] What is needed is the "intimate realization of the significance of what [is] already known."[43] Therefore, the "indirect method," best embodied in stories, is necessary to evoke or bring to life this knowledge that is within the hearers;[44] the method enables the hearers to appropriate the inward truth already at hand.[45] Indeed, were such information lacking, were people not already thoroughly grounded in the Christian tradition, a direct method, which both provides information and enables a direct "I-Thou" encounter, would be essential.[46] Paul, for example, used the direct method because he was involved in evangelism. However, in our current situation, which parallels Kierkegaard's "Christendom," more information is not what is necessary; what is needed is something else: an experience of the information we already possess.[47]

Obviously, there are serious issues regarding Craddock's presuppositions, particularly those in *Overhearing the Gospel.* In recent years

39. Craddock, *Authority,* 14-15.
40. Craddock, *Overhearing,* 22, 25, 30-31, 37-38.
41. Craddock, *Overhearing,* 24.
42. Craddock, *Overhearing,* 22, 26.
43. Craddock, *Overhearing,* 91.
44. Craddock, *Overhearing,* 84.
45. Craddock, *Overhearing,* 91.
46. Craddock, *Overhearing,* 84.
47. Craddock, *Overhearing,* 104, 22.

numerous theologians have argued that Christendom is dead. The church, they contend, is not only no longer deeply grounded in its primary language and tradition, but also finds itself in an increasingly minority position in an increasingly secular culture.[48] Lesslie Newbigin has even suggested that modern Western culture must now be understood as a mission field.[49] These readings of the situation of the contemporary church in the West suggest that Craddock's indirect method may not be at all what the church needs right now. Indeed, if Newbigin is correct, we are actually once again in a situation similar to Paul's, which, Craddock himself argues, requires a direct method of communication. If people are not as immersed in the Christian tradition as Craddock suggests in *Overhearing the Gospel*, then the whole idea of evoking something that is already within them becomes extremely problematic. One has to wonder what our stories are evoking — the Christian faith or the general cultural presuppositions that have become dominant.

Craddock himself recognizes that Christendom is dead in his most recent thought. In his 1991 Sprunt Lectures at Union Theological Seminary in Virginia, Craddock discussed the importance of the hearers being grounded in the church's Scripture and tradition.[50] However, he then acknowledged that congregations today are not biblically literate, and he argued that we must therefore ground our preaching in human experience. That is, he returned to a position similar to that in *As One Without Authority*. In the Sprunt Lectures Craddock not only undermined the presuppositions behind his indirect method, but also confirmed the fundamentally experiential orientation of his position. This orientation is further confirmed by a close examination of *As One Without Authority* and *Overhearing the Gospel*.

Like Rice, Craddock's fundamental challenge is to cognitive, propositional preaching, which begins with a general propositional conclusion and then applies it to the situation of the hearer. Such preaching,

48. See, for example, Stanley Hauerwas and William Willimon, *Resident Aliens* (Nashville: Abingdon Press, 1989).

49. Lesslie Newbigin, *Foolishness to the Greeks: The Gospel and Western Culture* (Grand Rapids, Michigan: Wm. B. Eerdmans Publishing Co., 1986).

50. Fred Craddock, "The Sermon as a Twice-Told Tale," Sprunt Lectures (Union Theological Seminary, Richmond, Virginia, February 4-6, 1991, Reigner Recording Library, Union Theological Seminary, Richmond, Virginia).

Craddock contends, is deductive and authoritarian; it encourages passiveness in the hearers rather than participation.[51] Craddock rejects this "downward" authoritarian movement of deduction in favor of the "upward" experiential movement of induction.[52] Like Rice, he seeks to redirect preaching away from propositional dogmatism or shared information to the realm of human experience. As an alternative to a cognitive-propositional understanding of Christian preaching, Craddock develops his inductive method, which emphasizes contemporary human experience. The preacher seeks not primarily to convey propositional information or develop a logical argument, but rather to effect an experience of the gospel in the hearers.[53] Like other contemporary homileticians, Craddock again and again emphasizes the experiential purpose of preaching. The sermon begins and ends with human experience:

51. Craddock, *Authority,* 54-55. The assertion about the passiveness of the listeners in deductive preaching is interesting, but hardly documented. Surely an argument could be made that hearers of earlier deductive, logical, "point" sermons were quite actively engaged with them. Following a careful argument requires a significant amount of participation by the hearers. Indeed, these earlier, deductive sermons were often the focus of discussion around Sunday dinner following the service of worship — precisely the kind of ongoing engagement and involvement in the sermon that Craddock seeks. What Craddock appears to want to avoid are certain *kinds* of participation: e.g. anger, defensiveness, direct opposition, conflict, intellectual struggle (Craddock, *Overhearing,* 84). These kinds of participation inhibit the effectiveness of preaching; they prevent the gospel from being heard. While there may be some truth in this assertion, one must wonder why Jesus was crucified if he avoided these kinds of "participation" by his hearers.

52. Craddock, *Authority,* 57.

53. Craddock uses the term "experience" rather loosely. Unlike Rice, Craddock does not have in mind some general "religious experience" in human beings. Rather, he speaks much more mundanely of experience in everyday life — common experiences that all human beings share (*Overhearing,* 123). In other places in his work Craddock uses "experience" to mean simply "holistic" — that is, an "experience" involves affective, intellectual, and aesthetic faculties (*Authority,* 85, 90; *Overhearing,* 133). Here, however, there is some confusion in Craddock's work, as others have pointed out. At times Craddock will speak of the central *idea* of the sermon or the pursuit of an *idea* (*Authority,* 151-55). Craddock also argues that preaching involves the creation of new images in the hearts of the hearers, which transform their lives (*Authority,* 78-80); in general these new images are drawn not from Scripture, but from the contemporary world of experience that is familiar to the hearers (*Authority,* 78-79; 92). I am arguing that experience is more fundamental for Craddock than either ideas or images, though I do not want to discount these other aspects of Craddock's position. At the very least, Craddock has not adequately spelled out how all of these are related.

Because the particulars of life provide the place of beginning, there is the necessity of a ground of shared experience. . . . these common experiences, provided they are meaningful in nature and are reflected upon with insight and judgment, are for the inductive method essential to the preaching experience.[54]

As Lucy Rose has accurately summarized Craddock's inductive method, it seeks to enable "participation in an experience that is open-ended."[55]

The centrality of experience becomes evident in Craddock's rejection of any primary Christian language or distinctive biblical idiom for preaching.[56] Craddock bemoans the "hesitation to lay aside old terms and phrases," including the biblical idiom itself; he argues that the Church needs a "retirement program for old words," which simply do not work anymore.[57] Craddock, however, does not discuss with any care how we go about finding a new language, other than suggesting implicitly that it must somehow express and evoke the same experience once

54. Craddock, *Authority,* 58; also 29, 45, 54, 128, 129, 147-51. Despite their apparently different understandings of "experience," Rice cites Craddock's inductive method as the appropriate method for preaching because it begins both in preparing and in delivering the sermon "where people are" — i.e., with "experience" (Steimle, Niedenthal, and Rice, *Preaching the Story,* 33). Morris Niedenthal also affirms the experiential starting point of inductive preaching (Steimle, Niedenthal, and Rice, *Preaching the Story,* 76).

55. Rose, "Parameters," 35. Having argued that the preacher can no longer presuppose the general recognition of his or her authority as a clergyperson, or the authority of the church, or the authority of Scripture, Craddock, despite his disclaimers, locates authority in individual human experience (*Authority,* 12, 14-15, 58, 61, 72). Craddock's emphasis on experience continues in *Overhearing.* There too the key is to evoke fresh experiences, to move from information about faith to the experience of faith, to get people to experience what they already know (*Overhearing,* 97, 99-100). The listener's experience, he asserts, is the "alpha and omega of the whole effort," the fundamental presupposition being the general similarity of human experiences (*Overhearing,* 104, 123).

56. Craddock's position in *As One Without Authority* is moderated somewhat in *Overhearing the Gospel.* In the latter volume Craddock even critiques Bultmann's project of demythologizing. He recognizes that people may need to return to the biblical idiom for some "imaginative depth" (*Overhearing,* 134). Even in *Overhearing the Gospel,* however, Craddock gives no sustained attention to the use of the biblical idiom in preaching. In fact, part of the problem is that the old language of Scripture and tradition, in which people are already supposedly immersed, no longer carries any power (*Overhearing,* 69).

57. Craddock, *Authority,* 7; see also 95-96.

expressed in the old one.[58] The key, finally, is the experience expressed in or evoked by language, and a new language, a contemporary idiom, is required to create that experience today.

However, because of his strong emphasis on language, Craddock cannot simplistically be lumped into the "experiential-expressivist" camp. He does not defend the kind of universal religious experience that lies at the heart of Rice's work. Rather, Craddock asserts that we understand through language and that words "create and give meaning to human experience."[59] Nevertheless, although his position appears at points to resemble Frei's, this resemblance is superficial; Craddock's position actually remains quite different from the cultural-linguistic approach.

This difference has been pinpointed by George Lindbeck in a review of Gerhard Ebeling's book *Dogmatik des Christlichen Glaubens*. Although not writing about Craddock, Lindbeck's critique of Ebeling applies equally to Craddock, whose work depends on that of Ebeling and the New Hermeneutic:[60]

> Something more must be said, however, regarding [Ebeling's] view of language. This view — the most novel and baffling aspect of his thought — has superficial resemblances to, but yet is fundamentally different from, that associated with Wittgenstein. The primacy of, for example, prayer for Ebeling is reminiscent of the emphasis on ordinary language in Anglo-American linguistic analysis, and the fusion of language and experience in *Sprachgeschehen* is not totally dissimilar to the close relation between language games and forms of life. On the other hand, Ebeling does not look at languages as instances of ruled behavior, but rather, at least in their religious uses, as collections of evocative and expressive symbols. Therefore the God of Christianity or of any other religion is not identified by the role he plays in the stories told of him (or, more generally, by his function within the language games in which he operates), but only by reference to the experiences with which talk to or from him is associated.

58. Craddock, *Authority*, 7.

59. Craddock, *Authority*, 34; also 42.

60. The influence of the New Hermeneutic upon Craddock is obvious throughout *As One Without Authority*. Craddock wrote the book while at Ebeling's Institute for Hermeneutic at Tübingen (Craddock, *Authority*, vi).

Correspondingly, experience for Ebeling is less behavioral and more private and affective than in a form of life.[61]

Lindbeck here captures Craddock's position beautifully. Although Craddock affirms the "fusion of language and experience," he nevertheless maintains the centrality of experience in his discussions of the language of preaching, even in *Overhearing the Gospel,* where he is more positive toward the biblical idiom. For Craddock too, Christian language is a collection of evocative and expressive symbols, rather than an instance of ruled behavior. God is identified relationally through experience, which Craddock understands more privately and affectively than in a form of life. As Craddock writes about the existentialism that informs his position:

> . . . the only path from thought to reality is through existence, my existence, with all the variables of my experiences coloring the picture. In view of this, many have thought it most honest if they spoke only of that which was verified in experience and remained neutral and silent about metaphysics. If God is mentioned, it is either in the passive voice or only in terms not of his being but of our experience of his "toward manness."[62]

As Craddock makes clear here, the identity of God is known primarily in experience, not by the role God plays in the stories that are told of God.[63] Craddock's understanding of the function of Christian language, though not simplistically experiential-expressivist, remains fundamentally different from that of Frei.

Within this experiential framework, the sermon becomes for Craddock, as for Rice, an "experiential event." Like Rice, Craddock emphasizes the eventfulness of preaching. The language of Christian preaching is performative; it is creative; it "makes something happen."[64] However, this understanding of the power of the Word is intimately linked with Craddock's experiential emphasis; the "event" involves ex-

---

61. George Lindbeck, "Ebeling: Climax of a Great Tradition," *Journal of Religion* 61 (1981): 313.

62. Craddock, *Authority,* 12.

63. My distinction here, like Frei's, is between the biblical narrative and experience, not metaphysics and experience.

64. Craddock, *Authority,* 5, 35-36, 112-14.

pressing or evoking an experience.[65] For Craddock as for Rice, the goal of preaching is to evoke an "experiential word event" in the hearers.

In addition, Craddock's emphasis on experience, like Rice's, results in an individualistic orientation to his homiletical thought, despite his assertions of the importance of the church. This orientation can be seen in various ways. To begin with, the purpose of open-ended, inductive preaching is to allow individuals the freedom to experience the sermon for themselves, to feel their own feelings and think their own thoughts.[66] The focus of preaching is finally the individual hearer. Each person is to draw his or her own conclusions.[67] Craddock's use of the "rights" language of modern liberalism to describe the hearer's role in the sermon further highlights this individualistic orientation.[68]

In addition, and somewhat ironically, Craddock's emphasis on the "priesthood of all believers" confirms the individualism inherent in his method. Craddock argues that his method affirms the priesthood of all believers because it gives each individual hearer the "right" to draw his or her own conclusions.[69] However, this understanding of the priesthood of all believers represents a gross distortion of that doctrine. As Robert McAfee Brown has noted, the doctrine of the priesthood of all believers is actually meant to serve as a "corrective to understandings of grace focused on individual 'religious experience.'"[70] The point of the doctrine is not that each person can serve as his or her own priest, but that every person is a priest to every other person.[71] Craddock's position actually represents what Brown calls a "widespread *misunderstanding* of the doctrine."[72] Although seeking to affirm the community of faith through his emphasis on the priesthood of all believers, Craddock inadvertently reveals the fundamental, underlying individualism in his thought.[73]

65. Craddock, *Authority*, viii.
66. Craddock, *Authority*, 157.
67. Craddock, *Authority*, 146.
68. Craddock, *Authority*, 17, 62, 93, 149.
69. Craddock, *Authority*, 67.
70. Robert McAfee Brown, *The Spirit of Protestantism* (New York: Oxford Univ. Press, 1965), 94-95.
71. Brown, 97.
72. Brown, 97; italics mine.
73. In *As One Without Authority* Craddock also seeks to affirm the communal character of preaching in two other ways, each of which turns out to be very limited.

In *Overhearing the Gospel* Craddock speaks even more elo-
quently of the community. Indeed, the evocative power of the indirect
method requires that the hearers be repeatedly exposed to the Christian tradition and, apparently, be involved in a Christian "form of
life."[74] However, the individualistic purpose is, if anything, even more
pronounced in this book, in part because of Craddock's reliance on
Kierkegaard. The most important concern is to respect the "privacy"
of the individual hearer.[75] The key for preaching is the "inwardness
of each person's life," the experience of the individual self.[76] In the
end, the goal of preaching is to enable every hearer to "stand alone"

First, Craddock argues that the church is a linguistic community, which sounds pro-
mising at first. However, Craddock's linguistic community exists primarily in the
moment of preaching; it is an "event," which is not surprising in light of Craddock's
reliance on the New Hermeneutic. Gerhard Ebeling, for example, understands the
church itself as a "word-event" (Gerhard Ebeling, *Theology and Proclamation: Dialogues With Bultmann*, trans. John Riches [Philadelphia: Fortress Press, 1966], 94-106).
In addition, Craddock's linguistic community shares not a distinctive Christian discourse, but rather a common vernacular language, a view consistent with Craddock's
uneasiness with a distinctive Christian speech (*Authority*, 95-97). This understanding
of community is at best a bit "thin." Second, Craddock affirms the communal character
of oral communication (*Authority*, 43). Although this oral-communal understanding
of preaching does highlight one significant dimension of the practice of Christian
preaching, this model is also too "thin"; it says nothing about the distinctiveness of
the Christian community or the larger linguistic and practical skills within which
preaching occurs. For example, the speeches at the Republican National Convention
create a "community" in terms of the oral communication model. Yet, surely, the
church is not "community" in the same way as the Republican National Convention.
Craddock's "community" is finally little more than a collection of individuals who
share no distinctive discourse or practices and who draw their own conclusions about
the meaning of the gospel apart from any recognition of communal authority or any
process of communal decision making.

  74. Craddock, *Overhearing*, 104, 50. Craddock does not, however, spell out the
connection between the practices of the Christian community and the ways in which
sermons are "experienced." In *Overhearing the Gospel* Craddock does provide an
insightful discussion of the importance of Christian discipline for the *preacher;* he
affirms a close connection between form of life and use of language (*Overhearing*, 50).
However, Craddock does not carry this over to the hearers in the church. Finally,
Craddock expects each individual to bring to the sermon little more than his or her
own personal experiences, on which the preacher must build in order to bring the
gospel back to life.

  75. Craddock, *Overhearing*, 109.

  76. Craddock, *Overhearing*, 84, 57.

before God.[77] In short, experience for Craddock, as Lindbeck notes of Ebeling, is less behavioral and more private and affective than in a form of life.

Thus, Craddock, like Rice, emphasizes the "experiential event" of preaching within an individualistic framework. The experience of the individual is the focus of inductive preaching and the indirect method. Although Craddock's work does contain some tensions and does suggest some possible correctives to this orientation, the personal experience of the individual hearer remains as Craddock's most basic concern in his most influential works.

Preaching the Story (Steimle, Niedenthal, and Rice)

As I noted earlier, the contributions of Rice and Niedenthal to *Preaching the Story* give this book, like the others I have discussed, an orientation to the "experiential event." However, this general assertion cannot be the final word on *Preaching the Story*. Although the book is often mentioned as if it presented a uniform position, no fewer than eight authors contributed to the volume, which prevents any singular summary of the book's approach to narrative preaching.

In fact, this proliferation of authors results in some interesting contradictions in the work. Consider a couple of examples. First, in his chapter on "Preaching from a Liturgical Perspective," Gilbert Doan argues that the liturgy takes the form of a narrative patterned after the life of Jesus.[78] The service of the Word is parallel to Jesus' ministry in Galilee and provides a "period or module of information, instruction, and edification by Scripture and sermon."[79] This "module" is followed by the Lord's Supper, which "remembers, rehearses, and recapitulates" the paschal mystery.[80] Thus, by viewing the liturgy as a narrative shaped by the story of Jesus, Doan makes sermonic "instruction and edification" one part of a larger narrative. Information and instruction, however,

77. Craddock, *Overhearing*, 91, 93.

78. Gilbert Doan, "Preaching from a Liturgical Perspective," in Steimle, Niedenthal, and Rice, *Preaching the Story*, 97. The important thing about Doan's essay is his emphasis on the way the liturgy forms the congregation after the storied identity of Jesus.

79. Doan, 96.

80. Doan, 96.

are the very characteristics of traditional preaching that narrative homileticians have rejected. Indeed, Rice's approach directly contradicts Doan's understanding of preaching.[81]

Second, in his chapter on the preacher, Charles Rice is highly critical of a young man who adopts the "role" of preacher in his sermon and does not let his individual person appear. In contrast, Rice praises a young woman who preaches a sermon in which "it was Mary and her world that came through."[82] In another chapter on the preacher, however, Steimle affirms the importance of the vocational role of the ordained minister, who does not preach simply out of his or her own experience, but rather preaches from, for, and to the church.[83] While these two emphases are not necessarily incompatible — Steimle certainly does not want the preacher to "hide" behind a role — the differences are significant and not in any way integrated with each other.

Because of the multiple authors, then, it is difficult to discern a single, coherent position in *Preaching the Story*. This fact also accounts for two other significant problems in the book. First of all, "story" is used primarily as an image or metaphor for preaching, which provides a lens through which preaching can be viewed holistically — in terms of the preacher, the hearers, the context, and the message.[84] The key point is that various "stories" come together in preaching — that of the preacher, the hearers, and Scripture. Admittedly, it is a nice image. However, while the term "story" is ubiquitous in the book, it remains very formal and does little distinctive work. Rather, the book mainly affirms traditional insights under a new image: the preacher's honest, personal engagement with the message; exegesis of the cultural and congregational contexts; the relation between the biblical story and

---

81. Doan, however, makes an important point. Most of the works in narrative homiletics have been concerned with the homiletical method of the individual sermon, with little or no consideration for the liturgical context. Doan's suggestion that the entire liturgy is a narrative into which the worshipers enter gives room for a piece of that narrative to be instructional or informational. (Consider, for example, the significant "instructional" sections contained within the overarching biblical narrative.) Doan thus raises the question of whether the individual sermon or the overarching liturgy is the primary locus of narrative in Christian worship.

82. Steimle, Niedenthal, and Rice, *Preaching the Story,* 31.

83. Steimle, Niedenthal, and Rice, *Preaching the Story,* 37-42.

84. Steimle, Niedenthal, and Rice, *Preaching the Story,* 1.

these contexts. "Story" does not add much that is unique to all of this.[85] Instead, because of the multiplicity of authors, "story" becomes a general, umbrella term that does little distinctive work.

The second issue revolves around the notion of preaching as an "experiential event." As I have noted, both Rice and Niedenthal affirm this experiential orientation of preaching. Steimle, however, does not emphasize this particular approach in his essays. Nor does he emphasize this aspect of preaching in a somewhat earlier essay in which he states his general position.[86] In fact, Steimle actually rejects the "Word-event" model that has been so dominant in narrative homiletics.[87] He states his purpose more generally as that of interweaving the biblical story with our stories in so sensitive a way that light is shed on both.[88] Quoting Amos Wilder, Steimle rejects an experiential understanding of the gospel: "The new movement of the Gospel was not to be identified with a new teaching or a new experience but with an action and therefore a history. The revelation was an historical drama."[89] Steimle's sermons tend to be more cognitively oriented than those of many other narrative homileticians. Indeed, Steimle, who uses theological language unapologetically, has been referred to as the last of the "didactic preachers."[90] While it is certainly overstated to call Steimle a "didactic" preacher, his contribution remains somewhat at odds with the dominant trend that I am examining, as well as in some tension with the other voices in *Preaching the Story* itself.[91]

---

85. The one place where "story" does make a significant difference is in Steimle's essay on sermon form (Steimle, Niedenthal, and Rice, *Preaching the Story,* 163-75).

86. Edmund Steimle, "Preaching and the Biblical Story of Good and Evil," *Union Seminary Quarterly Review* 31 (Spring 1976): 198-211.

87. Steimle, "Good and Evil," 199.

88. Steimle, "Good and Evil," 199, 201.

89. Amos N. Wilder, *Early Christian Rhetoric: The Language of the Gospel* (New York: Harper and Row, 1964; reissue, Cambridge, Massachusetts: Harvard Univ. Press, 1971), 76-77; cited in Steimle, "Good and Evil," 200.

90. Robert G. Hughes, "Narrative as Plot," in *Journeys Toward Narrative Preaching,* ed. Wayne Bradley Robinson (New York: Pilgrim Press, 1990), 55.

91. Bass, 188. As I will make clear in the next two chapters, Steimle's approach nevertheless differs significantly from Frei's.

Eugene Lowry

No one has done more to highlight the role of narrative in preaching than Eugene Lowry. His three books, *The Homiletical Plot, Doing Time in the Pulpit*, and *How to Preach a Parable*, represent some of the most interesting reflection to date on narrative preaching. There is no question that many of his insights about the temporal character of preaching and the structure of the sermon can be of immense importance to contemporary preachers. Nevertheless, the issues that arise in the other works are equally present in Lowry's books as well. In fact, in Lowry's work the issues are present in an extreme form, for Lowry argues that his method of preaching is the *only* appropriate method. Every sermon, he asserts, should take the form of his homiletical plot.[92]

Lowry explicitly emphasizes the experiential character of preaching throughout his work. Indeed, no one has highlighted the move from cognitive-propositional preaching to experiential preaching more strongly than Lowry. Although in his first book, *The Homiletical Plot*, he often discusses the "generative idea" of the sermon, Lowry nevertheless stresses the experiential purpose of preaching.[93] Even in this first book the heart of his "homiletical plot" is the "experience of the gospel"; the hearer should experience the gospel existentially, rather than know it propositionally.[94] The sermon should be an experiential event, rather than a cognitive conceptualization.[95] The goal is to preach so that "the experiencing of the word can occur as *event*."[96]

In his second book, *Doing Time in the Pulpit*, Lowry carries out this experiential emphasis even more strongly and consistently. The key to his homiletical method, he writes, is a shift from ideas to experience.[97] He seeks to develop a form of preaching that orders

92. Lowy, *Plot*, 16, 76, 78; *Parable*, 25.

93. Lowry, *Plot*, 8. The notion of the generative idea is taken from Davis, *Design for Preaching*. Richard Eslinger has criticized Lowry for this early focus on the idea of the sermon. See Richard Eslinger, *A New Hearing: Living Options in Homiletic Method* (Nashville: Abingdon Press, 1987), 86.

94. Lowry, *Plot*, 33. See the chapter entitled "Experiencing the Gospel," 62-66.

95. Lowry, *Plot*, 33, 64.

96. Lowry, *Plot*, 66.

97. Lowry, *Doing Time*, 13. Lowry does not deny the ideational content of experience.

experience rather than ordering ideas.[98] Lowry argues that the Christian revelation as originally experienced simply cannot be contained in propositions:

> At *best,* propositional statements viewed formally can be no more than dead skeletons of what once was lived experience. The *life* of the Good News runs so deep and spreads so broad that the linguistic form of conceptual thought only points in the direction of truth. The *more* of which we are all witnesses becomes *so much more* that at long last it is truer to speak of the difference in qualitative rather than quantitative terms.
>
> At *worst,* propositional thought by its very nature distorts and even reforms the experiential meaning so that it is scarcely recognizable.[99]

Lowry thus rejects discursive knowing as inadequate to the gospel experience. He prefers to speak of what he calls "aesthetic knowing," which he describes as the difference between reading a book and experiencing a painting. In the former activity, according to Lowry, one is actively seeking meaning, the propositional thought. In the latter one is "grasped" by an "experience" of the work of art; a kind of conversion or abrupt change takes place, as the work of art is experienced as an "event" at an intuitive level.[100] The gospel, he concludes, is finally not understood, but experienced; the goal of the sermon is to create a transforming, revelatory, experiential event for the hearers.[101] Here again, one finds an emphasis on the Word-event combined with an experiential orientation, resulting in an understanding of preaching as a transforming, experiential event.

More specifically, this experiential event takes place through Lowry's "homiletical plot," which helps to clarify the "experience" that Lowry has in mind. The experience takes the form of a narrative plot, which begins with an initial discrepancy (or disequilibrium); moves to a deepening conflict; then comes to a surprising twist or reversal, which resolves the discrepancy and creates an experience of the gospel; and concludes with a denouement, which highlights the implications of the

98. Lowry, *Doing Time,* 8, 11, 25.
99. Lowry, *Doing Time,* 79-80.
100. Lowry, *Doing Time,* 82.
101. Lowry, *Doing Time,* 36.

resolution for the future.[102] This experience of narrative movement is what Lowry means by the "ordering of experience in time." Central to this movement is the "experience of the gospel," which for Lowry involves a resolution of ambiguity, a release of tension; it has the character of a "Whee" experience.[103] In this experience the gospel "happens"; it is not just understood as an idea.[104] A transforming, "watershed experience" occurs.[105] As Lowry concludes, "When the sermon by its very form is narrative this power turns words into events, preachers into poets, and God language into religious experience."[106]

Moreover, this experience has a decidedly individualistic orientation, despite Lowry's comments on the importance of story for forming communal identity.[107] In fact, Lowry consistently employs the images of doctor-patient or therapist-client to describe the preacher-congregation relationship in the preaching event.[108] He seeks fundamentally to analyze problems of "interior motivation" and to offer the gospel as a "cure": "The purpose of sermonic analysis is to uncover the areas of interior motivation where the problem [disequilibrium, ambiguity] is generated, and hence expose the motivational setting toward which any cure will need to be directed."[109] What Lowry finally means by plot is "the logic of the heart searching for wholeness."[110] Consistent with this approach, when Lowry writes about the characters in the biblical stories, he, unlike Frei, emphasizes their "inner subjectivities."[111] And in suggesting the way hearers identify with these characters, he concludes, "the most important character in the narrative becomes oneself. I am the one finally discovered . . . within the text I find *me* as I never knew me before."[112] For Lowry, as for the other authors I have examined, an

---

102. The development of this understanding of plot, which is essentially the movement from problem to resolution, with a "reversal" in the middle, is the focus of *The Homiletical Plot*; it is discussed in less detail in *Doing Time in the Pulpit*.

103. Lowry, *Plot*, 24-25, 29, 67.

104. Lowry, *Doing Time*, 25.

105. Lowry, *Doing Time*, 23, 26, 32.

106. Lowry, *Doing Time*, 85.

107. Lowry, *Doing Time*, 39-41.

108. Lowry, *Plot*, 37-38, 40, 62, 64.

109. Lowry, *Plot*, 40.

110. Rose, 30.

111. Lowry, *Doing Time*, 47.

112. Lowry, *Doing Time*, 49.

emphasis on the experiential event and an individualistic orientation go together.

Limitations of the Individual, Experiential Event

The turn away from narrow, cognitive-propositional approaches to preaching has unquestionably been a positive one. In the shift to experience, the holistic character of preaching has been affirmed; sermons are no longer understood primarily as cognitive enterprises, but are also addressed to the emotional and volitional life of the hearers — to the heart as well as the head. None of my criticisms should be taken as arguments for a return to cognitive-propositional preaching. However, despite this positive contribution, the turn to individual experience raises several issues that contemporary narrative homileticians have not adequately examined.

Thomas Long has raised the most basic issue, highlighting the limitations and dangers of a simplistic reliance on human experience:

> There is a deep theological danger in measuring preaching by its capacity to generate religious experience. Theologian Hendrikus Berkhof has reminded us that, in the Old Testament, one of the reasons why Israel was continually abandoning Yahweh for Baal was that Baal was always more available, more visible, providing blessings that were more predictable. One could always count on Baal for a religious experience, but not so Yahweh. Yahweh tended, on many occasions, to have a hidden face, to be absent in those times when the people yearned for a more readily available God. In sum, God does not always move us when we desire to be moved, and everything that moves us deeply is not God.[113]

As Frei would put it, the emphasis on experience brings with it the danger of theological "relationalism" — a relationalism that dares to make no claims for God apart from the experience of human beings. Human experience becomes the focus of the sermon, rather than God in Jesus Christ, whose identity is rendered in the biblical narrative. In Lindbeck's terms, the God of Christianity is not identified by the role

---

113. Thomas G. Long, *The Witness of Preaching* (Louisville: Westminster/John Knox Press, 1989), 40-41.

God plays in the biblical stories, but only by reference to the experiences with which God is associated.[114]

Within this framework the preacher speaks about God primarily by speaking of human beings, or by speaking of how God is reflected in human existence or experience. Preachers, as Craddock argues, speak only about "our existence as it is in the liberating light of God's graciousness toward us"; they present "the way life is experienced now held under the light of the gospel."[115] Focusing on a "way of being in the world," this hermeneutical position tends to lose the ascriptive subject, Jesus of Nazareth. The primacy of the relational "presence" of Christ in human experience results in the loss of the unique, unsubstitutable identity of Jesus as the ascriptive subject of his own predicates. Jesus becomes too easily a cipher for human experience and in the process can virtually evaporate as a unique identity who "turns to us."

This kind of experiential relationalism can be clearly seen in the emphasis on evocative preaching, which seeks to draw out something that is already within the hearers. If it cannot be evoked from experience, it cannot be preached. There is no place for the kind of "irrelevant" preaching that Stanley Hauerwas affirms:

> . . . [Will Willimon] recently preached on the preexistence of Christ. I must admit I think we need more of that kind of preaching, as its virtue is that it lacks almost all existential relevance to people's immediate lives. But in the process we are reminded as faithful followers of Christ that our salvation is cosmic in scope, and that is just the wonder of it.[116]

In short, the experiential focus of contemporary narrative homiletics can result in a theological relationalism that makes God too dependent on immediate human experience.

In addition to this basic theological limitation of experiential preaching, several more issues need to be noted. First of all, in contrast to Frei's emphasis on the public, social character of Christianity, the emphasis on individual experience tends to locate the Christian faith

114. Lindbeck, 313.

115. Craddock, *Authority,* 80, 92.

116. William H. Willimon and Stanley Hauerwas, *Preaching to Strangers* (Louisville, Kentucky: Westminster/John Knox Press, 1992), 13.

in the private sphere, where American liberal society has wanted to keep it. Craddock, as I noted, emphasizes the importance of respecting the hearer's "privacy" in preaching. And Lowry argues that preaching should focus on the "interior motivations" of the hearers. The sermon, all assert, is to be open-ended so each individual hearer can experience his or her own feelings and think his or her own thoughts. When preaching focuses on individual experience in this way, the Christian faith all too easily gets relegated to the private realm. The gospel becomes divorced from serious, radical, public claims and from a concrete, public community of faith. By succumbing to this private-public split and focusing preaching on "private" experience, contemporary homiletics runs the danger of selling out to the presuppositions of modern, liberal, American culture.[117]

Second, by linking the notion of the "Word-event" to human experience, contemporary narrative homileticians understand the language of preaching too narrowly. From this perspective sermonic language tends to be viewed primarily as a symbolic expression of experience. This understanding of language appropriately supplements merely cognitive or scientific views of language that emphasize intellectual propositions or verifiable "facts." However, this position completely ignores Frei's cultural-linguistic understanding of language as the ruled behavior or learned skill of a community. Again, in contemporary homiletics, the move has been made from a cognitive-propositional approach to an experiential-expressivist one. The cultural-linguistic model, which has rich implications for preaching, remains unexplored.

Third, the emphasis on the individual, experiential event has limited the attention that contemporary narrative homileticians have given to the role of preaching in building up the community of faith.[118] The problem here is not the rather unexceptional recognition of the variety of ways that people hear, interpret, and respond to sermons. No one who has ever preached would deny this variety, which occurs with

117. For a discussion of the private-public split that is relevant for contemporary preaching see Newbigin, 13-14, 40-41, 61.

118. Two quite different authors have recently argued that the "event" model of preaching is inherently individualistic and cannot take seriously the communal dimensions of preaching. See Richard Lischer, *A Theology of Preaching: The Dynamics of the Gospel*, rev. ed. (Durham, North Carolina: Labyrinth Press, 1992), 85; and Rebecca Chopp, *Power To Speak* (New York: Crossroads Publishing Co., 1991), 6.

any kind of sermon. Rather, the problem is that up until now narrative homiletics has provided no resources for thinking carefully about the ways preaching contributes to the upbuilding of the church — the formation of the people of God — *beyond* the individual hearer. One reads the literature with the impression that, where the sermon is concerned, the church is simply a rather loose collection of individuals who share some similar experiences and participate in the event of oral communication. Although everyone affirms at least in passing the importance of stories in forming communal identity, the focus remains on individual experience. No consideration is given to the Christian faith as a set of communal practices and skills, including linguistic ones, and to the ways in which preaching functions at this level. Unlike Frei's cultural-linguistic theology, the privatistic, individualistic, experiential approach of narrative homiletics simply cannot address adequately the communal dimensions of preaching.

Finally, in all of the works I have discussed there is a rather naive confidence in homiletical technique to bring about transforming, experiential events. In contrast to Frei's work, there is little appreciation for the larger cultural-linguistic context that shapes "experience" and indeed makes it possible. Further, this confidence in technique is frequently accompanied by an equally naive confidence in individual experience and choice, just at a time when the very notion of the free, autonomous "self" is being questioned in the postmodern world. What is thoroughly absent in these homiletical works is any profound sense of the "tyranny" of American culture over the individual, which inhibits the hearing of the gospel.[119] Indeed, as I will argue in more detail below, in its focus on the individual, "private" experiential event, contemporary homiletics has itself succumbed to the "tyranny" of modern culture and more specifically to the "tyranny" of liberal individualism in America.

By focusing narrowly on homiletical technique, contemporary narrative homileticians have not given adequate attention to the larger context of preaching, particularly the context of the community of faith within which preaching takes place. They have ignored the communal practices that are essential for a truthful hearing of the gospel. In their

---

119. Craddock rightly wants to avoid the "tyranny" of the preacher, but says nothing about the various other "tyrannies" within which the hearers (and homileticians) may live. Craddock, *Authority,* 64.

focus on discrete experiential Word-events, contemporary homileticians have neglected the intimate relationship between preaching, polity, and discipleship. They have overlooked not only the political nature of Christian preaching, but also the importance of a disciplined community for a "new hearing" of the Word.

Obviously, these are enormous issues. However, they are precisely the issues that arise when the Christian faith is understood not primarily as an individual experience, but as a larger set of skills and practices within a distinctive, cultural-linguistic community. And they are precisely the kinds of issues that Frei's cultural-linguistic understanding of Christianity may enable homileticians to address.

Chapter Six

Between Two Worlds?

In narrative preaching one of the key concerns is to bring together the "world of the Bible" and the "contemporary world" — the biblical story and the hearers' stories. The fundamental presupposition is that the preacher stands in "two worlds" that need to be related hermeneutically. The issue, as Richard Thulin has noted, is how to maintain the "dual centrality" of both the biblical and nonbiblical stories.[1] Despite the importance of this matter, however, there has been too little careful discussion about how these "two stories" are brought together — or about whether this framework is the best way to pose the issue. For the most part these two stories are related in rather unclear ways. However, all too often the stories end up being related in good, liberal fashion; the biblical story is too often "translated" into the independent, purportedly "broader" world of human or cultural experience. Although important tensions and contradictions exist in the authors I will discuss, in subtle and not-so-subtle ways narrative homiletics has continued the hermeneutical "great reversal" that Frei critiqued.

Charles Rice

In *Interpretation and Imagination* Rice states quite clearly that the preacher stands in two worlds, the "world of the Bible" and the world

1. Richard L. Thulin, "Retelling Biblical Narratives as the Foundation for Preaching," in *Journeys Toward Narrative Preaching,* ed. Wayne Bradley Robinson (New York: Pilgrim Press, 1990), 13.

of contemporary human experience, each of which has a kind of autonomy in relation to the other. The preacher's task is a "bifocal" one; he or she seeks to relate the Christian, biblical-historical tradition to contemporary experience — "the way it is with people" — which is discernable apart from the biblical witness.[2]

In his attempts to relate these two worlds Rice's work becomes somewhat muddled. At times Rice does seem to give the "world of the Bible" the primary position. There is no question that the preacher must take Scripture and tradition seriously. Christian theology will inevitably shape the way one sees contemporary culture. At times, Rice even seems to suggest that "the way things are" is known only from within the "world of the Bible."[3] In *Preaching the Story* he writes, "Preaching is the event in which our particular stories are caught up into The Story to be judged, redeemed, and enlarged in purpose."[4] However, at other times the relationship between these two worlds is simply left rather vague and unclear. Rice suggests that the two worlds "collide"; they come together in "living tradition." One is left completely in the dark as to how this takes place in preaching, other than through the individual experience of the preacher, who is grounded in the Christian tradition and "interpret[s] holy history by personal history and expose[s] personal history to holy history."[5]

Finally, however, Rice comes down on the side of the great "reversal" that Frei argues has taken place in modern theology. The goal of preaching, Rice argues, is to "translate" the more particular Christian tradition into the terms of "broader" human experience. The preacher seeks to express the Christian tradition in the idiom of the culture so that it can become meaningful to contemporary hearers. Echoing Tillich, Rice asserts that the distinctive language of the Christian faith is incapable of carrying the gospel to contemporary people; the peculiar

---

2. Charles Rice, *Interpretation and Imagination: The Preacher and Contemporary Literature* (Philadelphia: Fortress Press, 1970), 26, 16-17. Rice follows precisely this "correlational" method in *Preaching the Story*, where he first analyzes various characteristics of our culture independently of the gospel and then correlates the gospel message to the issues that arise from his analysis (Charles Rice, Edmund Steimle, and Morris Niedenthal, *Preaching the Story* [Philadelphia: Fortress Press, 1980], 55-73).

3. Rice, *Interpretation*, 73-74.

4. Steimle, Niedenthal, and Rice, *Preaching the Story*, 35.

5. Rice, *Interpretation*, 11.

vocabulary of Christians is the problem.[6] The preacher, Rice asserts, stands in two worlds, the world of contemporary cultural experience and the world of the Bible; and it is up to the *former* to renew the latter.[7] Rice thus rejects any primary language of the Christian faith and understands the "preacher as translator": ". . . the preacher's vocation is translation, the apt and artful presentation of the gospel in contemporary idiom."[8] Contemporary "unimpeachable human experience," Rice concludes, is "theology's interpreter and the Bible's exegete."[9] What the preacher must *not* do is, like Barth, "withdraw into the world of the Bible."[10]

These assertions are striking because Rice simultaneously takes the opposite position when dealing with contemporary literature. When using contemporary literature in the sermon, he argues, preachers must stick close to the language and idiom of the poem or novel. To "translate" literature is to distort it, for form and content are intimately linked. Reflection on a poem, Rice writes, "is almost necessarily in the idiom of the poem itself"; one must use the words and images of the artist.[11] The very assertions he makes about the interpretation of contemporary literature are unequivocally rejected in relation to Scripture. The Bible must be translated into another, "secular idiom"; literature must not be "translated" in this way. However, Rice gives no rationale for this position, other than the "obvious" inability of contemporary people to experience existentially the biblical idiom.

Within this framework Rice turns to narrative, and particularly to contemporary literature, as the crucial vehicle for presenting the gospel in contemporary idiom. Drawing on Tillich's theology of culture, particularly Tillich's assertion that "religion is the substance of culture and culture the form of religion," Rice affirms that a culture's art and literature create a recognition of the fundamental religious dimension of experience and help evoke that experience again.[12] This deep experience,

6. Rice, *Interpretation*, ix. Rice cites *The Shaking of the Foundations* as a model for preaching (*Interpretation*, 3).
7. Rice, *Interpretation*, 92-93; viii, ix.
8. Rice, *Interpretation*, xi.
9. Rice, *Interpretation*, 3, 29.
10. Rice, *Interpretation*, 3.
11. Rice, *Interpretation*, 91.
12. Rice cites Tillich in *Interpretation*, 6.

which is expressed in the artistic works of the culture, is itself broader, less "parochial," than the Christian faith, and thus crucial for preaching. Unlike the church, the true artist has a "clear-eyed detachment from culture," which enables the artist both to depict "universal human experience" and to provide a prophetic critique of a particular culture.[13] Therefore, literature becomes the crucial avenue both for translating the gospel into the contemporary idiom and for critiquing contemporary culture.[14] Unlike later advocates of narrative preaching, Rice even takes the extreme step of advocating a "nonbiblical sermon" preached from texts of contemporary literature.[15]

Finally, then, Rice opts for a translation model. Human experience and contemporary culture, which are "less parochial" than the church's Scripture and tradition, provide the terms within which the preacher makes the gospel meaningful. In Frei's terms, the world absorbs the biblical story, rather than the biblical story absorbing the world.

Nevertheless, there are significant contradictions in Rice's work at

13. Rice, *Interpretation*, 32, 53.

14. Although at this point my concern is not Rice's use of the term "culture" or his understanding of the artist, I do need briefly to note the problems here. First, Rice seems confused in his use of the term "culture." On the one hand, "culture" (here used, it seems, as a "whole way of life") is understood very positively as the bearer of deep religious experience and meaning. The gospel needs to be translated into the idiom of the culture, which is broader than the parochial tradition of the church. On the other hand, however, Rice primarily values the artist as one who is detached from the "culture" — even "against" it — and able to provide a prophetic critique of it; here "culture" in terms of artistic works, is over against "culture" as a whole way of life. Second, Rice's understanding of the artist is far too idealized and simplistic — and indeed culturally shaped. The notion of the artist as the isolated, individual, "prophetic" genius, detached from culture and offering critique, is shaped by American culture. The idea of the individual artist transcending the culture to tap universal human experience is idealistic and naive. Further, it is disturbing to have the preacher linked with the artist in this sense; the individual preacher can too easily become the "artistic genius" detached from the church. For a discussion of the cultural embeddedness of literature, see Jane Tompkins, *Sensational Designs: The Cultural Work of American Fiction, 1790-1860* (New York: Oxford Univ. Press, 1985).

15. Rice, *Interpretation*, 97. Rice's position is not representative at this point. Indeed, he himself moves closer to Scripture in his later writings. Nevertheless, the approach he presents in an extreme way in *Interpretation and Imagination* appears in more subtle forms in much of contemporary homiletics, as well as in Rice's later essay, "Shaping Sermons by the Interplay of Text and Metaphor," in *Preaching Biblically: Creating Sermons in the Shape of Scripture,* ed. Don M. Wardlaw (Philadelphia: Westminster Press, 1983), 101-20.

this point, especially when he discusses his experience with specific communities. For example, at one point he shares an experience he had among the Maori tribe, a tightly knit Polynesian community in New Zealand:

> The Maori religious meeting which I attended lasted for three days, during which the people ate and slept together as conscientiously as they shared worship and speechmaking. Their deliberations were quite unlike what we know in America. Rather than taking sides and attempting to convince each other of one position or another, the people lived together through three days of storytelling, both as verbal story and as living experience. The speeches were given mostly by the elders and were *largely rehearsals of Maori history*. At the end of the encampment, the community arrived at consensus, bound together not by subscription to propositional creed but by a shared story, one inherited and one ongoing.[16]

What is important here is that the members of the tribe told the *traditional* stories; there is no indication of the kind of "translation" that Rice advocates throughout his work. It was apparently a particular, traditional story, not its translation into contemporary idiom, that bound the people together. Rice's central example of the importance of storytelling actually counts against the approach he takes throughout the rest of *Interpretation and Imagination*.

In an important later essay, "Shaping Sermons by the Interplay of Text and Metaphor," Rice shares yet another telling experience he had in an African-American church.

> The preaching of the black church almost invariably derives its primary metaphor from the Bible itself. I recall preaching for a black congregation at the dedication of their new building in one of the suburbs of Newark, New Jersey. I had gone there with a rather long text from II Corinthians 4–5, and an image from the movie *Question 7*, intending to elaborate the movie's picture of an East German preacher, drenched by rain pouring through the leaky roof, reading the text at hand. But when I read verse 7 of chapter 4, "For we have this treasure in earthen vessels," the congregation let me know imme-

---

16. Rice, *Interpretation*, 86-87; italics mine.

diately that that was the image for the day and metaphor enough. The people connected those words immediately with their new building and their experience as God's people in that place. The biblical image itself took over, as it were, the imagination of both the congregation and the preacher, within the first few minutes of give-and-take.

What would it take, by way of teaching and preaching the Bible, for the Bible's own images, its distinctive language, to function as altogether competent metaphor? That Sunday morning there was no doubt at all about the depth of meaning carried by the simple image of a clay pot; translating from "earthen vessels" to modern terms would not have heightened the meaning at all. Whatever it takes, we can only hope that the Bible will be recovered as itself a metaphor, a book of imagination whose narratives and poetic language could be experienced with all the power and feeling that came flooding out in that black church.[17]

Rice here almost wistfully hopes for a renewal of the distinctive idiom of the Bible in the church. However, in the sample sermon that concludes his essay, Rice follows his earlier theory rather than his experience in the African-American church. He tells the story of the movie *Ordinary People,* incorporating within it a few, brief theological asides. By the end of the sermon not only has the distinctive language of the Christian tradition been lost, but the message of the text (Matthew 6:19-34) has been coopted by modern American culture. Contrary to the opening statement in the sermon ("What ordinary people need, of course, is God"), what "ordinary people" finally seem to need is not God, but a good therapist.[18] Indeed, God plays no essential role whatsoever in the sermon.[19] Once again, Rice's own experience in a particular

---

17. Rice, "Text and Metaphor," 108. In this essay Rice treats narrative as "extended metaphor."

18. Rice, "Text and Metaphor," 111-20. There is also no church in this sermon; no community of faith is even remotely important. The "Ordinary People" are upper class, individualistic Americans (an interesting assumption about who is "ordinary"). Further, the "good news" offers little more than a way to help these people cope. Despite the emphasis of the text on "seeking the kingdom first," Rice simply encourages upper-class Americans to take time to "smell the roses." The "narrative" of upper-class American life takes over the narrative of the gospel in the process of translation. Jesus is no place to be found.

19. The grammar of Rice's opening assertion, "What ordinary people need, of

community counts against both his homiletical theory and the sermon he offers.

In contrast, however, Frei's postliberal, cultural-linguistic theology suggests that preachers need to take much more seriously the particular communities that Rice mentions. Preachers need to do more than simply hope that the Bible will be recovered in the church; they need to do more than simply wonder wistfully what it would take, "by way of teaching and preaching the Bible, for the Bible's own images, its distinctive language, to function as altogether competent metaphor." Instead, Frei suggests, preachers need to think seriously about the relationship between preaching and the larger life and discipline of the church in order to enable this to happen. They need to concentrate on the formation of a people able to hear the story truthfully and use the language rightly, rather than simply seeking a new idiom "relevant" to "where people are." To borrow from Stanley Hauerwas, preachers need to be about the task of forming a people worthy of the story, rather than telling a different story "more relevant" to the people.[20] What Rice rather wistfully longs for, Frei suggests a specific direction for pursuing.

One thing this renewal will require, Frei implies, is the virtue of patience — the patience of once again learning and practicing the Christian language. However, this kind of patience is precisely what seems to have no place in Rice's homiletical model, which is governed, like the other models, by the understanding of preaching as an existential, experiential event. The goal of preaching, as I noted above, is to enable a "happening," which is understood in experiential terms. However, because the biblical idiom seems incapable of creating this existential experience today, except in some African-American congregations, translation becomes the necessary hermeneutical model. Rather than exploring ways in which the church may reclaim and renew the distinctive biblical idiom, rather than

---

course, is God," is revealing. The "needs" of "ordinary people" (as if those terms were clear) are the subject of the sentence — and the subject of the sermon. The "of course," discloses the "natural theology" of the sentence. Here is no "miraculous nevertheless," in Barth's terms, but only a "natural therefore." Finally, at the end of the sentence one comes to "God" in a passive position as a predicate noun, a mere complement to the needs of "ordinary people." The grammatical movement of the sermon is from the human situation to, "of course," a God who does not do anything.

20. Stanley Hauerwas, "The Church as God's New Language," in *Christian Existence Today* (Durham, North Carolina: Labyrinth Press, 1988), 60.

working to form a people worthy of that language, and rather than questioning the experiential-event model of preaching itself, Rice and others opt for an apparently simpler and more immediate solution: a translation hermeneutic. Immediacy and "the moment" come to govern the notion of preaching as an event, with the result that there is no place for thinking about the way a language is learned in a cultural-linguistic community or about the role preaching may play in that process. However, it is precisely this alternative that Frei's work requires.

Fred Craddock

One discovers similar issues in Craddock's inductive method, which moves from the particulars of human experience to the gospel.[21] The structure of Craddock's most important book, *As One Without Authority,* is itself an excellent example of the nature and problems of the inductive method. In Part I of the book, entitled "The Present Situation," Craddock examines the cultural situation within which preaching takes place today, highlighting the problems with contemporary models for preaching and noting developments that signal the possible renewal of preaching.[22] Craddock begins not with the gospel or theological reflection, but in good liberal, correlational fashion with the contemporary situation, which is somehow self-evident and which defines what is possible for preaching. Then, in the later chapters Craddock develops his inductive method as a "solution" to the problem, largely on the culture's own terms. The book itself thus takes the old problem-solution form of liberal preaching.[23] Craddock seeks a method of preaching that is more in tune with the speaker-hearer relationship in American culture.

Just as American culture finally captures the gospel in Rice's ser-

---

21. Rice cites Craddock's inductive method as crucial for the kind of narrative preaching he espouses. See Steimle, Niedenthal, and Rice, *Preaching the Story,* 33.

22. Fred Craddock, *As One Without Authority: Essays on Inductive Preaching,* 3rd ed. (Nashville: Abingdon Press, 1979), 1-50.

23. Thomas Long has argued that Craddock's inductive method itself follows the problem-solution format. The key issue is how to "bridge the gulf" between Scripture and people — how to solve the "problem" of getting modern people to hear an ancient text (Thomas G. Long, *The Witness of Preaching* [Louisville: Westminster/John Knox Press, 1989], 98).

mon "Ordinary People," so the "American way of life" plays a crucial role Craddock's inductive method. The starting point for Craddock is not the gospel preached to the baptized in the worship of the church, but rather the "present speaker-hearer relationship" in American culture.[24] This relationship, Craddock notes, is characterized by openness and conversation. He cites as supporting examples our open-ended style of life featuring dialogue and discussion, spontaneity and conversation; the insights gained through the therapeutic model; the pedagogical method in schools, which stresses dialogue and sharing; and our contemporary openness in matters of faith themselves.[25]

Because of these cultural factors a new homiletical method is required — one that is relevant to this new and different cultural situation.[26] Cultural, not theological or biblical, considerations provide the starting point for Craddock's method, which is directly correlated to these characteristics of American culture.[27] As Craddock summarizes his position, "Relevant sermons we all want and need, but what is painfully lacking is a mode of proclamation that is relevant to the present speaker-hearer relationship."[28] And Craddock concludes, "the inductive method is fundamental to the American way of life."[29] American culture is the starting point, and the preaching of the gospel must

24. Craddock, *Authority,* 19, 56.

25. Craddock, *Authority,* 29-30. In *Overhearing the Gospel,* Craddock argues for an indirect method of communication, which is a species of the inductive method, not because this form of communication is integral to American cultural life, but because the culture is dominated by a *different* form of communication — that of direct confrontation and encounter (Fred B. Craddock, *Overhearing the Gospel* [Nashville: Abingdon, 1978], 116-17). Craddock's widely different readings of "culture" in his two books, written just a few years apart, make one wonder about the self-evident character of "situations," which Craddock seems to assume in his work.

26. Craddock, *Authority,* 18, 56.

27. I do not wish to deny that such cultural considerations play some role in the method of preaching. However, Craddock gives them too central a place in his homiletical method. The speaker-hearer relationship in the church's worship and preaching may in fact be different from that prevalent in the culture at large. Indeed, I would suggest that the preacher must presume that both speaker and hearer stand together under the authority of Scripture, a stance that Craddock himself asserts, but one that is in tension with his understanding of the inductive method, which begins not with Scripture and baptism, but with some purported "common human experience" (*Authority,* 58).

28. Craddock, *Authority,* 19.

29. Craddock, *Authority,* 58.

be made relevant to it. The danger, of course, is that American culture will finally take over the speech of the church.

The same danger lurks in the application of the method in individual sermons. The movement in the sermon, like the development of Craddock's inductive method itself, is "from the particulars of experience that have a familiar ring in the listener's ear to a general truth or conclusion."[30] "Homiletical induction," Craddock writes, "begins with an interpretation of human existence today and then moves to the text."[31] One moves from human experience, which can be understood apart from the gospel, to the gospel, which is correlated with or sheds light on that experience.

In light of Frei's work, several issues arise in relation to Craddock's inductive method of preaching. First, Craddock argues that the inductive method contains an explicit theology; the movement of the sermon from experience to gospel, Craddock asserts, embodies a theological position. As he writes, "The method is the message. So is it with all preaching: *how* one preaches is to a large extent *what* one preaches."[32] Within this understanding of the sermon, what Craddock's inductive method finally preaches is not the identity of Jesus Christ rendered in the gospel narratives, but rather a liberal theology of human experience. The inductive form of the sermon, which moves from "familiar human experience" to general conclusions, embodies the kind of liberal theology critiqued by Frei. Even if Craddock, in *preparing* his sermons, actually begins with Scripture, that is irrelevant. For Craddock himself argues that the *form of the sermon,* not the method of preparation, embodies his theology; form and content are one in the sermon.[33] The theological significance of sermon form cannot be overemphasized in Craddock's position; if he gives that up he gives up everything. And Craddock's inductive method is fundamentally an embodiment of the liberal theological tradition that Frei has challenged.

Second, even though Craddock clearly wants to hold the Bible and the contemporary situation in tension, he remains, like Rice, at best very vague about how they are related. At times he can sound quite "intratex-

---

30. Craddock, *Authority,* 57.
31. Craddock, *Authority,* 55.
32. Craddock, *Authority,* 52.
33. Craddock, *Authority,* 3.

tual." In interpreting Scripture, he writes, drawing on the New Herme
neutic,

> One does not begin with the idea that we have in the New Testament
> verbal statements that are obscure into which we must introduce the
> light of understanding; rather one listens to the Word hopeful that it
> will shed light on our own situation which is obscure. The Word of
> God is not interpreted; it interprets. Here a radical reversal in the
> direction of traditional hermeneutics occurs. The goal of biblical
> study is to allow God to address man through the medium of the
> text.[34]

At other times, however, Craddock is less clear, as when he writes, "the
situation addressed precedes the Word of God; the Word of God
precedes the situation";[35] and when he affirms in one place that human
experience is the "primary data" and in another place that Scripture is
the "raw material" of the sermon.[36] Here again there is a confusing "dual
centrality" of the biblical story and other "stories." Finally, at other times
Craddock suggests that, if he has to come down somewhere, the "situation" — human experience — is primary; "the congregation speaks
first."[37] Although Craddock is not clear about his priorities at this point,
his inductive movement points to the priority of the "situation."

Third, the inductive method assumes that preachers must begin
"where people are"; and the assumption is that the familiar ground
shared by the congregation is "the situation" or "human experience."
However, this assumption is oversimplified. To begin with, Craddock's
confidence in the rather self-evident situation creates problems for him.
The "situation" is not so simplistically self-evident as he supposes; it is
not the "primary data" that Craddock touts. "Situations" are not simply

---

34. Craddock, *Authority,* 42.

35. Craddock, *Authority,* 110.

36. Craddock, *Authority,* 73, 117. Here Craddock is discussing the biblical study
of the preacher in sermon preparation. He is not discussing the form of the sermon, in
which the situation addressed comes first.

37. Craddock, *Authority,* 132. While Craddock wants to avoid the "tyranny of
ideas" that he thinks is implicit in deductive preaching, one must ask whether or not
he has succumbed to a "tyranny of the situation" or a "tyranny of the congregation" or
a "tyranny of the individual," not to mention the "tyranny" of American culture. William H. Willimon has raised this issue in *Peculiar Speech: Preaching to the Baptized*
(Grand Rapids, Michigan: Wm. B. Eerdmans Publishing Co., 1992), 49.

"out there." Rather, they are understood within the narratives and practices that give them meaning. As John Howard Yoder has argued, "There is no such thing as a simple situation dictating a particular line of action. No situation is self-interpreting. Only within the context of prior assumptions about how to take the measure of a given situation can the situation itself have any meaning."[38]

In addition, questions need to be raised about Craddock's understanding of "where the people are." Craddock assumes that the preacher must bring the hearers to Scripture inductively from somewhere else — from "experience." In Craddock's approach, unlike Frei's, human experience and not the church becomes the middle term between the preacher and the biblical text. However, contrary to Craddock's assumptions, what the hearers share in the context of Christian worship is not some general human experience or situation, but rather baptism and Scripture.[39]

Within the church the appropriate movement begins with baptism and "the world of the Bible," which is precisely what Christian worshipers share in common. From the perspective of Frei's work, in which the biblical world is the one real world, this movement can be understood as *inductive* when it takes place within the particular cultural-linguistic community of the church. Within the church the "starting point" for moving *inductively* is not "human experience," but rather baptism and Scripture, which describe both the hearers and human experience. Further, the "goal" of the sermon is not a "general conclusion," but rather the ongoing story of the church — the future life of the people of God in and for the world.

The presupposition that this kind of preaching is deductive and authoritarian is absurd, based on the assumption that what is most basic is "human experience," rather than baptism and Scripture. There is no

---

38. John Howard Yoder, " 'What Would You Do If . . . ?' An Exercise in Situation Ethics," *Journal of Religious Ethics* 2 (Fall 1974): 82. In contemporary scientific terms, "inductive movement" takes place within the paradigms and practices of a communal discipline. No induction takes place apart from a paradigm within which data are understood. See Garrett Green, *Imagining God: Theology and the Religious Imagination* (San Francisco: Harper and Row, 1989), 51-52, 114.

39. Both baptism and Scripture together are important. Through baptism believers enter into particular communities of interpretation, in which, through training and discipline, they learn to read the Bible in particular ways. I am not arguing for a disinterested reading of Scripture, but rather for a reading informed by the disciplined life of particular Christian communities.

authoritarianism here, just the ecclesial presupposition that when people join the church they accept baptism and the biblical world as their life and their world. The preacher moves inductively from there. What the church takes from the sermon is not simply a "moving experience" and the memory of contemporary stories or anecdotes, but rather the story of God in Jesus of Nazareth, who shapes the church's life in and for the world. Through this approach some of the strengths of Craddock's work can be retained without the problematic theological framework within which he develops them.

Edmund Steimle

Edmund Steimle also seeks to relate the biblical story — The Story — and the hearers' stories. Like the two previous authors, however, he too either states this relationship in rather vague terms or, when he gets specific, actually moves in the direction of the reversal that Frei has described, though in a somewhat different way from Rice and Craddock. The primary image he uses for the way in which the two stories are related is "interweaving." The preacher seeks to interweave the biblical story and our stories in so sensitive a way that light is shed on both.[40]

The image of interweaving is interesting, though not very clear or precise. At times Steimle can emphasize the side of the biblical story. The biblical stories, he writes "locate us in the very midst of the great story and plot of all time and space and therefore relate us to the great dramatist and storyteller, God. . . ."[41] The goal is for the biblical story to become our story.[42] At other times, however, Steimle appears to take a more correlational approach: The calling of the preacher is to "interpret the biblical story *in terms* of their [the hearers'] world and their stories."[43] One is not exactly sure what Steimle has in mind.

However, what Steimle has in mind becomes clear when he offers a summary of the biblical story — "the story of good and evil." In fact, Steimle is the only person among the writers I am discussing who shares

40. Edmund Steimle, "Preaching and the Biblical Story of Good and Evil," *Union Seminary Quarterly Review* 31 (Spring 1976): 199, 201.
41. Steimle, "Good and Evil," 201-202.
42. Steimle, Niedenthal, and Rice, *Preaching the Story,* 129.
43. Steimle, Niedenthal, and Rice, *Preaching the Story,* 38; italics mine.

his understanding of what the biblical story actually is; he is the only one who attempts to provide any content at all. In doing so, he reveals what he means by "interweaving," and the result is precisely the hermeneutical reversal of which Frei speaks. The biblical story is explained and made meaningful in terms of a general, existentialist anthropology drawn from Reinhold Niebuhr.

Steimle begins telling the biblical story with a discussion of the creation and fall in Genesis. However, at this point Steimle gets uneasy. Although the Bible takes evil seriously, he writes, Scripture is not concerned about providing any *explanation* of the evil in the world.[44] Steimle feels the need to correct this omission, so he turns to Reinhold Niebuhr's *Nature and Destiny of Man,* which offers the best explanation Steimle has found. Drawing on Niebuhr's analysis of the existential structure of human beings, Steimle argues that the explanation of evil in the world lies in the anxiety of human existence in freedom and finitude, which leads inevitably but not necessarily to sin.[45]

With this meaningful explanation in hand, Steimle proceeds to tell the remainder of the biblical story in these terms — the biblical story according to Reinhold Niebuhr's existentialist anthropology, one might call it. Everything is explained in terms of the overcoming of anxiety. Even Jesus is presented in these terms: "the Christ figure is content to live with his anxiety as a mortal creature who knows that he is a mortal creature and to trust God and thus to be obedient, even if it meant death and darkness."[46] Finally, the good news becomes the fact that God "has freed you, at least in part, from your anxiety about who you are and what the future holds for you and thus opened for you the possibility of obedience and even of having something of the mind of Christ in you."[47] Not surprisingly, when Steimle turns to an analysis of the contemporary situation in order to discover how the gospel might be correlated to that situation, he discovers that the fundamental problem facing human beings today is anxiety.[48]

If this is what Steimle means by "interweaving" the biblical story

---

44. Steimle, "Good and Evil," 205. This focus on anthropological explanation rather than redescription is precisely the move that Frei challenges.

45. Steimle, "Good and Evil," 205.

46. Steimle, "Good and Evil," 205. Steimle is commenting on Philippians 2:6-8.

47. Steimle, "Good and Evil," 206.

48. Steimle, "Good and Evil," 208.

and our stories, it is precisely the kind of move that Frei rejects. Steimle first of all *explains* the biblical story in terms of Niebuhr's general, existentialist anthropology (a kind of "natural theology" of sin). Explanation takes the place of description or redescription in order to make the gospel "meaningful" to modern human beings. In the process Christology becomes a function of soteriology, understood as freedom from existential anxiety. A general anthropology sets up the soteriological problem for which Christology becomes the solution. Jesus becomes a good existentialist.

From Frei's perspective, there are numerous issues in Steimle's reading of the story. Most importantly, the ascriptive logic of the gospels is lost, as Jesus becomes a mere cipher for a general anthropology. Equally significant, however, is the extraordinarily individualistic turn of Steimle's reading, which is not surprising in light of Niebuhr's existentialist orientation. There is no essential place for Israel or the church in the biblical story, which is also the case in Niebuhr's ethics. The key is relief from individual, existential anxiety, not the formation of a people. Frei's two essential concerns, Jesus and the community of faith, are distorted or lost in Steimle's "meaningful explanation" of the biblical story in terms of our stories. Steimle's "interweaving" of the Biblical story and our stories is something very different from Frei's intratextual approach.

Eugene Lowry

The work of Eugene Lowry is somewhat more interesting and complicated. In his *Homiletical Plot* Lowry affirms a dual movement in preaching. The sermon, he writes, should begin with the liberal, inductive approach of raising a problem from the human situation, but then, following a "surprising reversal," should conclude with a Barthian, "deductive" approach to preaching the Word. In his emphasis on the "reversal," which turns the human situation "upside down" and enables the hearers to experience and see life differently, Lowry seeks to highlight the gospel's overagainstness to the culture and to our "common sense" understandings of life.[49] Repeatedly, Lowry wants to emphasize Barth's

---

49. Eugene Lowry, *The Homiletical Plot: The Sermon as Narrative Art Form* (Atlanta: John Knox Press, 1980), 48, 53.

"Nein!" to the questions we bring to Scripture, which are all too often the wrong questions.[50]

Lowry seeks a compromise between liberal induction and Barthian deduction. Lowry's "plot"

> begins with establishment of contact with the congregation at the point of their human predicament and moves through stage two (analysis) inductively in good liberal tradition form. But rather than mobilize the resources of the gospel to fulfill human aspirations, it reveals such aspirations for the dead ends they are. By disclosing the clue to resolution, which typically involves some kind of reversal, it opens a new door, and prepares the context in which the word of God can be proclaimed — deductively ordered in good Barthian fashion.[51]

Lowry wants to avoid the approach of Harry Emerson Fosdick, "who spoke of 'the garnered wisdom of the ages' which can help meet the problems of human existence.'"[52] At the same time, he also sets his method in sharp contrast to that of the neo-orthodox preacher Paul Scherer, who opposes the inductive method and admonishes the preacher not to meet the listeners where they are because too often they are "in the wrong place."[53] In contrast to both of these approaches, Lowry views the gospel as continuous with human experience *after* that experience has been turned upside down by the gospel.[54]

Lowry thus seeks a middle ground. Further, in many of his sermons, usually those from narrative texts or parables, Lowry does not begin with general human questions or problems. Rather, he begins with the text of Scripture. The biblical text *both* upsets the hearers' equilibrium at the beginning of the sermon *and* provides the new equilibrium at the end; that is, the biblical text *both* raises the "problem" and provides the "solution." This approach actually comes close to Frei's position. The biblical text does not simply answer a general human question, but also poses the question itself. Furthermore, in Lowry's

---

50. Lowry, *Plot,* 60-61.

51. Lowry, *Plot,* 61.

52. Lowry, *Plot,* 65-66; citing Harry Emerson Fosdick, *The Living of these Days* (New York: Harper and Brothers, Publishers, 1956), 95.

53. Lowry, *Plot,* 66; citing Paul Scherer, *The Word God Sent* (New York: Harper and Row, 1965), 19.

54. Lowry, *Plot.*

sermons of this type there are, in good Barthian fashion, no "introductions."[55] He simply begins with the biblical story.

Nevertheless, despite Lowry's suggestive approach, his attempt to
"have his cake and eat it too" leads to some confusion. To begin with,
as I noted above, even when he starts with a text, Lowry's analysis tends
toward the psychological, focusing on the subjectivities and interior
motivations of the characters. The questions posed by the text thus tend
to take an individualistic, psychological form, which is quite different
from Frei's approach to the narrative as rendering Jesus' identity through
the interplay of character and incident.

In addition, as Thomas Long has noted, when Lowry does *not*
begin with a biblical text his approach becomes the old "problem-solution" method in a new guise.[56] Unfortunately, this approach is the one
Lowry develops most thoroughly in his books; he emphasizes the movement of the sermon "from the human predicament to the solution born
of the gospel."[57] The problems with this approach become evident in
Lowry's discussion of the sermon's movement from stage 2, the "analysis
of the discrepancy," to stage 4, the "experience of the gospel"; here the
differences between Lowry and Frei become apparent. According to
Lowry, the key to the experience of the gospel is the proper analysis of
the human situation. The shape of the analysis — the diagnosis — of
the human condition will shape the form of the gospel that is proclaimed.[58] Lowry cites Craddock's inductive method as a positive example of what he has in mind.[59] The preacher does not begin with Jesus

55. Barth rejects the use of "introductions" that prepare the hearers for the
reception of the gospel (Karl Barth, *Homiletics,* trans. Geoffrey W. Bromiley and
Donald E. Daniels [Louisville, Kentucky: Westminster/John Knox Press, 1991], 121-25).

56. Long, *Witness,* 99-101.

57. Lowry, *Plot,* 21.

58. Lowry, *Plot,* 36. Lowry is wrong to claim Barth as an ally for this approach,
for Barth rejects any human preparation, even a negative one, for the hearing of the
Word. Lowry is actually much closer to Brunner's "negative contact point" than to
Barth's position. In addition, Lowry misrepresents Barth when he asserts that "neo-orthodox" preaching is wrongheaded because the "application" is preceded by lengthy
exposition (*Plot,* 60-61). Barth is quite clear both in his theory and in his practice that
exposition and application belong together *throughout* the sermon. Lowry simply does
not know what to do with Barth; he cannot figure out why Barth did not properly attend
to "upsetting the equilibrium" in order to prepare the context for the effective hearing
of the Word (Lowry, *Plot,* 78).

59. Lowry, *Plot,* 50.

and move to the human condition, but rather vice versa. As Lowry concludes, "The question of the human condition is, I believe, the most fundamental and consequential question of all."[60] As a result, the method of correlation becomes central. "Precision of analysis will determine the correlation of the gospel and the human condition."[61]

Further, in analyzing the human condition, the preacher, at least as Lowry explains it, can progress quite "naturally" apart from the gospel.[62] In "analyzing the discrepancy" the preacher continually asks the question "why?" in order to move beneath surface behavior to internal motivations.[63] In asking this question and moving deeper into the "human condition," however, what Lowry relies on is not the biblical text, but rather his own personal experience. Time and again as he seeks to move deeper and deeper into a problem, he cites his own personal experience and introspection to take the next step.[64] This process comes to an end when the preacher finally feels a peculiarity or a strange angle in the problem. This peculiarity, which is arrived at independently of the gospel, provides the clue to resolution and signals the surprising turn of the gospel.[65]

The danger in this process, as Frei has pointed out, is that the independent analysis of the human condition too easily shapes the gospel that can be preached and heard. Even if the gospel does apparently reverse "common sense," the analysis has determined the character and shape of the reversal. Lowry unquestionably seeks a "critical correlation," but his personal analysis determines the kind of critique the gospel is able to make. Christology becomes a function of soteriology, which is shaped by an independent analysis of human existence. The ascriptive logic of the gospels is lost, as Jesus becomes a cipher for the preacher's insightful solution to a problem.

These issues become most pronounced in *Doing Time in the Pulpit.*

60. Lowry, *Plot,* 37.
61. Lowry, *Plot,* 42.
62. I do not want to deny a certain circularity here, which is focused in the person of the preacher who is doing the analysis. Obviously, this analysis will be colored by the theology of the preacher and is not completely divorced from a prior understanding of the gospel.
63. Lowry, *Plot,* 40.
64. Lowry, *Plot,* 40-43.
65. Lowry, *Plot,* 48. For an example of this process see pp. 54-56.

In the penultimate, though climactic, chapter of the book, entitled "The Bible and Time," Lowry makes extraordinary claims for human experience. He argues that preaching creates the experiential event by evoking "preconscious images" that are already within us. These preconscious images, "some from the relatively common experiences of one's own group and others drawn from the universals of human experience," are the basic raw material that make aesthetic experiences, including preaching, so powerful.[66] The key for the preacher, it seems, is to evoke these universals of human experience: ". . . once sermon preparation has begun, the story can unfold according to the dictates of those universals we know at the preconscious level."[67] In this way the biblical story is located within a "broader" context of human experience, rather than itself absorbing the world. Such a conclusion comes as a surprise. Lowry appears to contradict other parts of his work, suggesting at least some confusion in his theological-hermeneutical position.

Despite its rich possibilities, Lowry's theory not only highlights the experiential emphasis at the heart of contemporary homiletics, but also reveals the modern theological liberalism that continues to underlie narrative preaching. In narrative homiletics, as represented by Lowry, Rice, Craddock, and Steimle, the "great reversal" of liberal theology continues in subtle and not-so-subtle ways. The world absorbs the Bible, rather than Scripture absorbing the world; Christology becomes the function of an independently generated soteriology. This result is not surprising when one discovers the extraordinarily small role that Jesus of Nazareth plays in narrative preaching, an issue that will occupy me in the next chapter.

66. Eugene Lowry, *Doing Time in the Pulpit: The Relationship Between Narrative and Preaching* (Nashville: Abingdon, 1985), 87-91.
67. Lowry, *Doing Time*, 90.

Chapter Seven

Whose Story? Which Narrative?

From Plot to Character

The different understandings of narrative in the work of Frei and that of narrative homileticians can be examined in a number of ways. First, one might, as Mark Ellingsen has done, note the structuralist approach to narrative that has characterized contemporary homiletics, as opposed to Frei's focus on the particular biblical narratives.[1] There is truth in this critique. Narrative homiletics, as Ellingsen points out, has tended to begin not with the particular biblical narratives that are the church's Scripture, but rather with general theories about narrative and the ways it works. Narrative has been valued because it is rhetorically effective in engaging the congregation and enabling participation in the sermon; because everyone likes a good story; because stories are "open-ended" and allow everyone to make his or her own meaning; because much of the Bible takes narrative form; because individuals and communities have their identity in stories. The specifics of the biblical narrative tend to be subordinated to these general considerations, which is precisely the reverse of Frei's approach. Nowhere is the inadequate appreciation for Frei's work more evident than in the homiletical inattentiveness to the specific narrative character of the gospels and the implications of that for preaching.

---

1. Mark Ellingsen, *The Integrity of Biblical Narrative: Story in Theology and Proclamation* (Minneapolis: Fortress Press, 1990), 55-57.

167

Of the authors I have examined, for example, only one, Edmund Steimle, even considers the specifics of the biblical story. Rather, in the literature one finds a more general approach to narrative as a genre. Craddock argues that the sermon should move like a good story and that stories are the primary vehicle for indirect speech, which enables people to overhear the gospel. Steimle, in addition to using "story" as a metaphor for the preaching event, suggests that story is the general form of Scripture and highlights certain characteristics of sermon form that follow from that fact.[2] Lowry has focused exclusively on formal matters, distinguishing between telling a particular story and using a narrative plot in the sermon. Although there is no question that the narrative form of Scripture contributed to the turn to narrative in homiletics, the homiletical reflection has remained general and formal. Contemporary homiletics has not taken seriously Frei's approach, which has been summed up very well by John Howard Yoder: ". . . the particular narrative is prior to the general idea of narrativeness."[3]

Ellingsen understands this difference as a distinction between a New Critical approach to the biblical narrative, which takes the particularity of the text seriously, and a structuralist approach, which focuses on the deep structures that all narratives share in common.[4] Although, as will be evident below, I do not agree with Ellingsen's emphasis on New Criticism, he does make a good point about the problems inherent in a structuralist approach to narrative, particularly with regard to some rather simplistic assumptions about the use of nonbiblical stories in preaching:

> If one uses a secular story to make the same points [or create the same experience] as a biblical text, the working suppositions . . . are those of structuralism. If two different stories (the biblical and the secular one) can mean the same thing, one must assume that they have something in common. But if they are different stories about different (albeit similar) people, their literal content cannot be identical. What holds them together, it seems, can only be a common flow

---

2. Charles Rice, Edmund Steimle, and Morris Niedenthal, *Preaching the Story* (Philadelphia: Fortress Press, 1980), 163-75.

3. John Howard Yoder, "The Hermeneutics of Peoplehood," in *The Priestly Kingdom* (Notre Dame, Indiana: Univ. of Notre Dame Press, 1984), 36.

4. Ellingsen, 55-57; 78.

in the action they narrate, common structures. Insofar as the stories' structures are deemed to be the main conveyers of meaning, the compatibility with or dependence of this mode of preaching on structuralist analytic technique is readily apparent.[5]

In short, it is simplistic to assume that different stories, much less a general narrative form, create the same — or even similar — meanings or experiences.

As the quotation from Ellingsen suggests, a second way of putting this issue is that homiletics has focused far more on narrative form than on the content and function of the biblical narrative. Despite the constant affirmations that form and content are inseparable, discussions of narrative in preaching have simply not taken that affirmation seriously. It is amazing how loosely various authors can play with this entire issue. For example, Charles Rice, while affirming that form and content are inextricably linked, nevertheless suggests that in preaching we must now tell *different* stories because the old stories no longer work — they no longer evoke the religious experience. However, Rice offers no reflection on the following question: If form and content are so intimately linked, when you tell a different story, do you not in fact have a different content — and create a different experience? Similarly, Lowry asserts that every sermon, even those from non-narrative texts, should take the form of his homiletical plot. However, if form and content are so intimately linked, is this appropriate? Even Craddock, despite his affirmation of a variety of forms, does not address clearly the relationship between form and content when developing his inductive method.

In short, rather grand assertions about the unity of form and content are made to support the turn to narrative, but the implications of these assertions have been ignored in rather cavalier moves to non-biblical stories and narrative sermon structures. Although the writers surely presume that the content of the sermon will be given with each individual text,[6] there is little or no consideration of the specific content

---

5. Ellingsen, 56. Paul Ricoeur has argued that structuralist analysis is incapable of adequately interpreting the gospel narratives. See Paul Ricoeur, "Interpretative Narrative," trans. David Pellauer, in *The Book and the Text*, ed. Regina Schwartz (Cambridge, Massachusetts: Basil Blackwell, 1990), 237-57.

6. Eugene Lowry states as much in *How To Preach a Parable: Designs for Narrative Sermons* (Nashville: Abingdon, 1989), 25, 27.

and function of the biblical narrative in general or the gospel narratives in particular. It is an astonishing omission in the literature.

This omission can have disastrous consequences. In a paper submitted in a preaching class a student briefly summarized the children's story *Are You My Mother?* [7]

> Once upon a time, there was a baby bird who was lost. The bird went from animal to animal, and machine to machine asking, "Are you my mother?" "Are you my mother?" He finally wound up in front of a bulldozer, asking, "Are you my mother," as the giant teeth of the machine lifted the bird skyward to ultimate annihilation. At the last second, the bird's mother rescued him from the bulldozer and brought him back safely to the nest.

Then the student concluded, "The young bird is lost and alone. He thinks a bulldozer is his mother. His real mother saves him from being hurt and brings him home. The gospel is told." [8] The conclusion that the gospel is told is based on the formal characteristics of this story, which, like the gospel stories, contains elements of tragedy, comedy, and fairy tale. [9] The story also serves all the functions of narrative highlighted by Craddock and Lowry. In particular, it includes the five steps of Lowry's narrative plot. However, the assertion that *Are You My Mother?* proclaims the gospel is ridiculous. [10]

Now, of course, none of the writers I have been discussing would disagree with my assessment of this student's paper; they too would probably be horrified. However, this extreme example reveals the danger when general reflection on the value of narrative replaces more focused and careful attention to the content and function of the particular narratives at the heart of the Christian faith. As Nicholas Lash has written,

> To put it very simply: as the history of the meaning of the text continues, we can and must tell the story differently. But we do so

---

7. P. D. Eastman, *Are You My Mother?* (New York: Random House, 1960).

8. Shannon Smith, TMs, 4.

9. Fredrick Buechner, *Telling the Truth: The Gospel as Tragedy, Comedy, and Fairy Tale* (New York: Harper and Row, 1977).

10. To her credit, the student sensed the problems with this approach before I pointed them out to her.

under constraint: what we may *not do*, if it is *this* text which we are to continue to perform, is to tell a different story.[11]

Although the issues are much more subtle and complex in homiletical narratives by contemporary narrative preachers, the question of when we begin to tell another story has simply not been addressed with any care.

While Ellingsen has raised this issue in a general way, Frei's work enables one to address this matter more precisely. In fact, the fundamental issue can be stated within the framework of narrative itself: while contemporary narrative homiletics has been concerned with formal matters of *plot*, Frei's work shifts the focus to the particular matter of *character*. This simple shift of focus has significant implications. Whereas for homileticians the narrative shape of the gospels has led to a focus on plot and sermon form, for Frei the narrative shape leads to an emphasis on character and Christology. According to Frei, Christians are interested in narrative only because Jesus is what he does and undergoes, not because of anything magical about narrative form per se. Frei, however, has been ignored by most homileticians at this point. In none of the above works, for example, is the rendering of God's or Jesus' identity considered to be crucial for the particular narratives of the Christian community.[12] At just this point Frei's work can provide a needed corrective and additional depth to recent homiletical developments.

Moreover, Frei's focus on character is an appropriate way to highlight the particularity of the gospel narratives. As Scholes and Kellogg have noted in their classic work on narrative, it is with regard to

11. Nicholas Lash, "Performing the Scriptures," in *Theology on the Way to Emmaus* (London: SCM Press, 1986), 44.

12. Craddock does mention once that the central character of the biblical narrative is God (Fred B. Craddock, *Overhearing the Gospel* [Nashville: Abingdon, 1978], 140). The only major homiletician who has stressed the link between the biblical narrative and the identity of Jesus Christ is David Buttrick. See David Buttrick, *Homiletic: Moves and Structures* (Philadelphia: Fortress Press, 1987), 13-17. It is not surprising that Buttrick's last two books have been on Christology: *Preaching Jesus Christ: An Exercise in Homiletical Theology* (Philadelphia: Fortress Press, 1988) and *The Mystery and the Passion: A Homiletic Reading of the Gospel Traditions* (Minneapolis: Fortress Press, 1992). Buttrick's work, however, is quite different from Frei's. Buttrick loses the ascriptive logic of the gospels, as Jesus becomes merely a "living symbol" that discloses "Gratuitous Love" (*Homiletic*, 15).

character that plots must become particular. One can discuss plot in general (as homileticians usually do), but once one turns to character one must get specific: "Plot is only the indispensable skeleton which, fleshed out with character and incident, provides the necessary clay into which life may be breathed."[13] Character thus provides a helpful lens through which to view Frei's particularistic approach to the biblical narrative.

Indeed, it is not surprising that Ellingsen, who seeks to base his work on the "Yale School," quite naturally focuses more on character than on plot. At one point he even captures the centrality of the identity of Jesus Christ as the crucial issue that must be considered in telling stories in preaching.

> To tell another story about other actions is to describe characters other than Jesus and the patriarchs of Scripture. There is no place for "Christ-figures," for mere secular storytelling in an approach to preaching which respects the unique literary character of Scripture's narrative accounts.[14]

Here and in other places Ellingsen argues that the unique, unsubstitutable identity of characters is central to an understanding of biblical narrative.[15] Again, Ellingsen is onto an important point. However, as I will argue below, his approach to character is itself problematic in light of Frei's work and is not developed as fully as it could be.

Much more serious attention to the specifics of the gospel narratives is needed in contemporary homiletics. As Frei reminds us, it is not narrative form that is the key to Scripture. Rather, as Frei would put it, it is the One whose identity is rendered by the narratives in the Bible who is the key. "Story" cannot save us or empower us. Rather, it is God in Jesus Christ, whom the biblical narratives identify, who saves and empowers. Character, not plot, is primary. General structural parallels between sermon form and certain biblical materials do not provide an adequate way to reflect on the relationship between narrative and preaching.

---

13. Robert Scholes and Robert Kellogg, *The Nature of Narrative* (New York: Oxford Univ. Press, 1966), 239. See also Richard Lischer, "The Limits of Story," *Interpretation* 38 (January 1984): 29.

14. Ellingsen, 79.

15. For other references see Ellingsen, 20, 32, 33, 37, 38, 43.

In Frei's approach to biblical narrative, form and content are both more closely related and more loosely related than a simplistic structural parallelism suggests. Form and content are more closely related because "narrative form" cannot be easily abstracted from the particular gospel stories and the specific agent they identify through the interplay of character and incident. However, form and content are more loosely related because once the identity of Jesus Christ is rendered through the gospels, other forms may in fact proclaim that identity, though always inadequately and always with the need to return to be judged by the biblical narratives. In short, Jesus of Nazareth is the inescapable link between form and content and between the gospel narratives and the sermon.

The gospel narratives — and the biblical narrative as a whole, which renders the identity of God in Jesus Christ — point us beyond formal considerations of sermon structure to the crucial matter of Christology. It is the central character rendered by the gospel narratives, not narrative plot in general, that is at the heart of preaching shaped by the biblical story. An older, discursive sermon that focuses on the identity of Jesus Christ within the framework of the gospel narratives can be more faithful to those narratives than a "narrative sermon" that fails to render the identity of God in Jesus Christ in any concrete way. The current obsession with sermon form (or plot), despite its numerous contributions to the field of homiletics, now needs to yield to a focus on the central character rendered by the biblical narratives. In Scholes and Kellogg's terms, flesh needs to be put on the skeleton.

If You've Got a Good Parable, You Don't Need Jesus[16]

It is not simply because of their focus on plot that the narrative homileticians pay little attention to the matter of character. There is also another reason. When they do turn to the biblical material they do not hold up the "literal sense" of the gospels as the key for narrative preach-

---

16. The title of this subsection is based on a comment by the character Hazel Motes in Flannery O'Connor's short story "Wise Blood": "Nobody with a good car needs to be justified. . . ." Flannery O'Connor, "Wise Blood," in *Three* (New York: New American Library, 1962), 64.

ing. Rather, they turn almost exclusively to the parables. In narrative preaching it has generally been the case that narrative equals parable. And in the parables, of course, Jesus himself is not a character, except as the narrator.

The title of one of Eugene Lowry's books is a good example of the homiletical appropriation of narrative in recent years: *How To Preach a Parable: Designs for Narrative Sermons.* Implicit in this title is the equation of narrative and parable for the purposes of preaching. What is equally revealing about this book is the fact that only one of the sermons examined by Lowry is actually based on a New Testament parable. Every sermon, for Lowry, should be "parabolic"; it should have a plot leading from disequilibrium through reversal to a new equilibrium.[17]

Like Lowry, Craddock also focuses almost exclusively on the parables. Virtually every example of narrative cited in *As One Without Authority* and *Overhearing the Gospel* is a parable.[18] In fact, Craddock's inductive method appears to be nothing more than an application to preaching of his understanding of the way parables work. He cites Dodd's classic definition of a parable, which, with a stronger experiential emphasis, could serve as a good definition of Craddock's inductive method. As Dodd writes, a parable is "a metaphor or simile drawn from nature or common life, arresting the hearer by its vividness or strangeness, and leaving the mind in sufficient doubt about its precise application to tease it into active thought."[19] Here is Craddock's method in a nutshell. He begins with "common human experience" and moves to

17. Lowry, *Parable*, 21-23. For other references to the parables in Lowry's work, see Eugene Lowry, *The Homiletical Plot: The Sermon as Narrative Art Form* (Atlanta: John Knox Press, 1980), 14, 15, 32, 45, 56-58, 89; Eugene Lowry, *Doing Time in the Pulpit: The Relationship Between Narrative and Preaching* (Nashville: Abingdon, 1985), 8, 13, 16, 68-69, 85-90.

18. See Fred Craddock, *As One Without Authority: Essays on Inductive Preaching*, 3rd ed. (Nashville: Abingdon Press, 1979), 52, 59, 65, 67, 104, 132, 146, 150; Craddock, *Overhearing*, 16, 63, 77, 90, 112, 123.

19. C. H. Dodd, *The Parables of the Kingdom* (New York: Charles Scribner's Sons, 1961), 5; cited in Craddock, *Authority*, 65. At another place Craddock reveals that he holds a view of the parables as having one point, which may account for his emphasis on the sermon having a single point (*Authority*, 104). For a discussion of Dodd's definition within the framework of the New Hermeneutic, see Robert W. Funk, *Language, Hermeneutic, and Word of God* (New York: Harper and Row, 1966), 133-62.

an open-ended, experiential "point," which forces the individual hearer to decide in his or her existential situation.[20] As Craddock writes in *Overhearing the Gospel:*

> The parable is the example par excellence of a piece of literature that is not designed to convey information but by its very form arrests the attention, draws the listener into personal involvement, and leaves the final resolution of the issue to the hearer's own judgment.[21]

For Rice the parables are similarly central. Narrative and parable are virtually equated as "extended metaphors."

> Increasingly preachers are having success with one sermon form that is rooted in this kind of listening, seeing, and moving — the extended metaphor. The sermon relies upon a story or an extended narrative to carry the meaning, as Jesus did in his parables.[22]

For Rice, narrative sermons function as parabolic extended metaphors in order to evoke the experiential event.[23]

This emphasis on the parable should come as no surprise. After all, the parables have received intense scrutiny in recent years. Furthermore, the New Hermeneutic, which has so profoundly influenced developments in homiletics, has focused its work on the parables.[24] The New Hermeneutic's understanding of the parables as "existential, experiential events" has been the dominant understanding of the parables in contemporary narrative preaching — and has contributed to the similar understanding of the "preaching event" itself.

---

20. This metaphorical understanding of the parables as existential, experiential Word-events is only one recent way of understanding the parables. For a brief history of parable interpretation see John Dominic Crossan, *In Parables* (San Francisco: Harper and Row, 1973), 7-22. See also Thomas G. Long, *Preaching and the Literary Forms of the Bible* (Philadelphia: Fortress Press, 1989), 87-106.

21. Craddock, *Overhearing,* 77.

22. Charles Rice, "Shaping Sermons by the Interplay of Text and Metaphor," in *Preaching Biblically: Creating Sermons in the Shape of Scripture,* ed. Don M. Wardlaw (Philadelphia: Westminster Press, 1983), 106. See also Charles Rice, *Interpretation and Imagination: The Preacher and Contemporary Literature* (Philadelphia: Fortress Press, 1970), 2, 16, 19, 46, 53, 108.

23. Steimle is the only one who does not emphasize the parables.

24. Craddock, *Authority,* 52; see Funk, 123-222.

The work of John Dominic Crossan reveals the experiential-expressivist orientation of these recent approaches to the parables.[25] What becomes important is not Jesus as an agent rendered through the interplay of character and incident in the gospel narratives, but rather Jesus' "religious experience" linguistically expressed in the parables. As Crossan writes, reflecting the parabolic orientation of contemporary narrative homiletics,

> Poetic experience terminates only with its metaphorical expression so that the two are inseparably linked. So also religious experience involves both "the moment of disclosure or perception itself" and the "embodiment of the experience in symbolic form," to quote from Thomas Fawcett. This means that the experience and the expression have a profound intrinsic unity in the depths of the event itself. The fact that Jesus' experience is articulated in metaphorical parables, and not in some other linguistic types, means that these expressions are part of the experience itself. . . . There is an intrinsic and inalienable bond between Jesus' experience and Jesus' parables. A sensitivity to the metaphorical language of religious and poetic experience and an empathy with the profound and mysterious linkage of such experience and such expression may help us to understand what is most important about Jesus: his experience of God.[26]

The hearers are thus invited to enter into a symbolically expressed experience. Disclosive metaphor replaces Jesus as agent; Jesus as the ascriptive subject of the gospel narratives is lost.

This emphasis on the parables, as well as the particular understanding of the parables implicit in narrative homiletics, deserves detailed study. The issues here are numerous, and I obviously cannot examine them in any detail. Rather, I simply want to highlight two crucial issues that arise in light of Frei's work. First, there is a tendency in homiletics to isolate the parables from their context in the gospel narratives. This approach, influenced by form and redaction criticism, has characterized much recent interpretation of the parables. As Crossan writes, "Modern biblical scholarship has taught us to distinguish between the stories of Jesus in their original intentionality and in their present interpretations within the

---

25. Crossan, *In Parables*, 17-22.
26. Crossan, *In Parables*, 22.

gospel texts."[27] Even the immediately surrounding "interpretive" material is often dismissed as a secondary addition — secondary both temporally and qualitatively. Following this procedure, homileticians have tended to make the parables into discrete aesthetic objects divorced from the larger narratives in which they are located. In this discrete form, the parables have functioned as models for preaching.

Even Mark Ellingsen falls into this trap with regard to the parables. Unlike most other homileticians he makes a sharp distinction between the "realistic narrative" portions of Scripture and the parabolic and poetic ones. However, while he rejects "experiential-expressivist" readings of the realistic narratives, he affirms this approach with regard to the parables. He too isolates the parables from their literary context and seeks the experience expressed in them.[28] Further, Ellingsen gives no serious reasons for distinguishing between his New Critical analytic approach to the "realistic narrative" portions of Scripture and his different approach to the parables.[29]

Unlike these other approaches, Frei's literary approach to Scripture, which focuses on the gospel narratives as primary, suggests that the parables need to be interpreted in relation to their larger literary context.[30] Frei intentionally offers a different approach to the parables, which takes more seriously the larger narratives in which they are located. For Frei, the parables must be seen

> in the light of the story identifying Jesus of Nazareth rather than (reversely) providing the clue for the theme of that story. In the context of the *full* narrative — pericopes together with passion and

---

27. John Dominic Crossan, *The Dark Interval: Towards a Theology of Story* (Niles, Illinois: Argus Communications, 1975), 98. In addition to Crossan's works, see Joachim Jeremias, *The Parables of Jesus*, 2nd ed., trans. S. H. Hooke (New York: Charles Scribner's Sons, 1972). For a different approach see John R. Donahue, *The Gospel in Parable: Metaphor, Narrative, and Theology in the Synoptic Gospels* (Philadelphia: Fortress Press, 1988).

28. Ellingsen, 80-81.

29. Obviously, different kinds of material may require different interpretive procedures. However, Ellingsen's rejection of the New Critical approach to the parables and other "poetic" material is strange because New Criticism focused not on narrative, but on poetry. Ellingsen asserts that the analytic methods of New Criticism, which he so strongly affirms in relation to "realistic narrative," are inappropriate with respect to the very types of literature on which the New Critics focused.

30. Richard Lischer has made a similar point about the larger context of the parables (Lischer, "Limits," 27-29).

resurrection — Jesus identifies the Kingdom of God and is only sec-
ondarily identified by his relation to it: He is himself the parable of
the Kingdom.[31]

That is, the parables cannot be isolated from the identity of their
teller, rendered in the story of his life, death, and resurrection; Jesus of
Nazareth defines the parables, not vice versa. For Frei, the parables are
more inseparably connected with rest of the gospel narratives than in
the homiletical literature. In this way Frei actually takes narrative interpretation more seriously than the homileticians. He refuses to dissect
the gospels through form and redaction criticism in order to isolate
parabolic gems that may serve as aesthetic models for Christian preaching. Frei's work suggests that a focus on the parables as models for
narrative preaching is simply too narrow, not only because they represent too small a portion of the biblical literature, but because they need
to be understood within the larger narrative framework of the gospels.

The second major problem with the homiletical appropriation of
the parables can be seen in the title of a recent preaching text: *Learning
to Preach Like Jesus.*[32] In this title one finds the crucial turn that takes
place in contemporary homiletics: Jesus becomes a *model preacher,*
rather than the *one preached.* Jesus preached in parables, the argument
goes, so the parables serve as a model for our preaching today.[33]

---

31. Hans W. Frei, "Theology and the Interpretation of Narrative: Some Hermeneutical Considerations," in Hans W. Frei, *Theology and Narrative: Selected Essays,* ed.
George Hunsinger and William C. Placher (New York: Oxford Univ. Press, 1993), 104.
Others have also understood Jesus as the parable of the Kingdom: Crossan, *Dark Interval,*
123-28; Sallie McFague, *Speaking in Parables: A Study in Metaphor and Theology*
(Philadelphia: Fortress Press, 1975). However, Frei's approach differs from these because
he does not equate parable and metaphor, though he does admit that parable is closer
to metaphor than to allegory. In addition, Frei does not view the parables primarily as
"innovative" or "expressive," but rather understands them as having a strong descriptive
component; they are, in short, connected closely with the "literal sense" of the gospel
narratives, which render the identity of Jesus of Nazareth (Frei, "Theology and Interpretation," 104). Frei's work is too cryptic at this point to be of great help, but he does
make the point clearly that the parables must be read within the larger context of the
gospel narratives.

32. Ralph L. Lewis and Gregg Lewis, *Learning to Preach Like Jesus* (Westchester,
Illinois: Crossway Books, 1989).

33. On Jesus as a model preacher see Lowry, *Doing Time,* 28, 68-69; Craddock,
Authority, 59; *Overhearing,* 26; Rice, *Interpretation and Imagination,* 46, 89, 93.

Biblically and theologically, this turn to Jesus as a model preacher is problematic, even if one assumes that the "historical Jesus" did preach in parables.[34] Frei's emphasis on the way the gospels preach Jesus by rendering his unique, unsubstitutable identity is more on target. After the resurrection, as even Crossan notes, Jesus becomes the one preached, not the preacher.

> The evangelists have accustomed us to reading Jesus' stories as apologues, that is, as allegorizing how God acts toward us or as exemplifying how we should act before God and towards one another. Such a change in interpretation is not inexplicable. Jesus spoke of God in parables, but the primitive communities spoke of Jesus, the Crucified One, as the Parable of God.[35]

> The parabler becomes the parable. Jesus announced the Kingdom of God in parables, but the primitive church announced Jesus Christ, the Parable of God. . . . Jesus died as parabler and rose as parable.[36]

Frei's approach to the gospels is consistent with Crossan's point; the gospels render the identity of the risen Jesus and locate the parables within this larger narrative. It is not accidental, as Frei notes, that the church did not just save the parables; its Scripture did not become a collection of metaphorical sayings, but rather an extended narrative. The Gospel of Thomas, a collection of Jesus' sayings, was not made part of the canon.[37] Further, it is also not accidental that in the rest of the New Testament, including Acts and the Pauline letters, we do not find little parabolic stories, but rather the presentation of Jesus Christ and the implications for the church that lives into his ongoing story. The story of Jesus' encounter with the disciples on the Emmaus road, which is clearly liturgically shaped, represents a better understanding of the church's post-resurrection preaching than the parables. In that story Jesus does not tell a parable, but rather "interpret[s] to them the things

---

34. It is not my purpose here to argue with the claim that the "historical Jesus" preached in parables. However, one can certainly argue that *as he is rendered in the gospel narratives,* Jesus unquestionably uses other forms of preaching and teaching besides the parable.

35. Crossan, *Dark Interval,* 10.

36. Crossan, *Dark Interval,* 124-26.

37. Crossan, *Dark Interval,* 110-11.

about himself in all the scriptures."[38] In Frei's terms, preaching serves to identify Jesus, who is not primarily a "model preacher," but the one preached.

When Jesus becomes primarily a model preacher, as he does in the contemporary emphasis on the parables, the stance of preaching changes. The preacher becomes not one who points to Jesus Christ, but one who stands in the place of Jesus and "preaches like Jesus preached." This understanding of the place of Jesus in preaching is not only inconsistent with the content and function of the gospel narratives, but also with the preaching that we find in the rest of the New Testament.[39]

Thus, in their approach to the biblical narrative, as well as in their emphasis on the experiential event and their methods of relating the biblical story to the contemporary world, the most influential writers in narrative homiletics represent a position quite different from that of Hans Frei. Despite their turn to narrative, these homileticians remain within the modern, liberal theological framework that Frei critiqued. Frei's cultural-linguistic understanding of Christianity, his "intratextual," communal hermeneutic, and his emphasis on the ascriptive logic of the gospel stories have yet to be taken seriously by the major figures in narrative homiletics.

The Limits of Ellingsen's "Postliberal" Homiletic

As I noted earlier in this chapter, Mark Ellingsen, more than other writers in the field, has emphasized the particularity of the biblical story — the "integrity of biblical narrative." As the first person to develop a

38. Luke 24:27. New Revised Standard Version (Division of Christian Education of the National Council of the Churches of Christ in the United States of America, 1989).

39. The New Hermeneutic, which is largely responsible for the homiletical turn to the parables, sought to keep together the identity of Jesus Christ and the parables. As I discussed earlier in connection with the New Quest of the Historical Jesus, the New Hermeneutic, through a complicated theory of language, saw in the parables a vehicle for discerning the "historical Jesus," who was what he proclaimed. Frei himself criticized the inadequacies of this approach. However, what is significant is that this aspect of the New Hermeneutic has been lost completely in contemporary narrative homiletics. What is central in the parables is the disclosive metaphor or "experiential event," and not in any way, shape, or form the identity of Jesus Christ.

homiletical position based on the work of the "Yale School," Ellingsen appropriately highlights this crucial dimension of Frei's work. Unfortunately, however, Ellingsen has not taken equally seriously other dimensions of Frei's thought, with the result that *The Integrity of Biblical Narrative* remains both limited and flawed. The book cannot be taken as an adequate development of a "postliberal" homiletic.[40]

The most problematic characteristic of Ellingsen's work is his failure to appreciate the cultural-linguistic turn of Frei's later thought.[41] Ellingsen fails to recognize that the integrity of biblical narrative is inseparably related to a particular community of interpretation. Although Ellingsen mentions this aspect of Frei's position in passing, his approach to biblical narrative not only represents a narrow reading of Frei's early work, but also remains torn between two fundamentally modern hermeneutical options.

Ellingsen's failure to appreciate Frei's cultural-linguistic turn can be seen clearly in his insistence upon a single, objective, normative reading of the realistic narratives in the Bible. He repeatedly defends the possibility of a "single, descriptive meaning, which is not materially conditioned by the interpreter's perspectives."[42] Such a normative reading, Ellingsen asserts, is not dependent on any faith commitment or

40. While completing the revisions to this manuscript I received a copy of Richard Eslinger's recent book, *Narrative and Imagination: Preaching the Worlds that Shape Us* (Minneapolis: Fortress Press, 1995), which is the second book seeking to develop a "postliberal homiletic." Although Eslinger does not deal adequately with Frei's theology, his work is the best appropriation to date of a "postliberal narrative hermeneutic" (though Frei eschewed that phrase) for preaching. The book is superior to Ellingsen's and deserves serious attention. The fundamental issue for Eslinger is whether the "two beginnings" of the book — a "postliberal narrative hermeneutic" (chapter 1) and a phenomenological analysis of consciousness and imagination (chapter 2) — are as compatible as he asserts. At points, "imaginative consciousness" seems to replace "narrative consciousness" as a foundational element in Eslinger's work, despite his attempt to locate imagination within his postliberal hermeneutic. In addition, Eslinger's treatment of Frei's "narrative hermeneutic" apart from his theology creates problems. Not surprisingly, in the practical section of the book, Eslinger focuses on "preaching narrative and imagery" (p. 141), rather than on "preaching Jesus." With regard to narrative, he remains more concerned with plot than with character. Theologically speaking, the question is whether Eslinger can be a postliberal disciple of David Buttrick, whose recent work has been written in explicit opposition to postliberalism.

41. Eslinger avoids this pitfall and takes seriously the cultural-linguistic character of postliberal hermeneutics.

42. Ellingsen, 35; see also 59, 77, 80.

form of life, but can be arrived at by any disinterested reader, whatever his or her context.[43] This single, normative reading carries enormous weight for Ellingsen. Such a reading is necessary to assure the transcendence of God, to affirm the public character of Christian theology, and to guarantee that the preacher stands on certainties, rather than mere opinions, when he or she preaches.[44]

However, Ellingsen's work at this point not only misrepresents Frei's position, but also contains internal problems.[45] To begin with, time and again Ellingsen has to admit that various presuppositions must be in place for such a "normative" reading to take place. He simultaneously affirms both the possibility of a single, normative reading available to all disinterested readers *and* the necessity of certain formal presuppositions about how to construe the text (i.e., as a unified, realistic narrative with Jesus as the central character).[46] Such presuppositions are hardly disinterested; as Frei himself argues, they are deeply grounded in the Christian tradition and community.

Ellingsen's confusion surfaces further in the contradictory ways in which he understands the "literal sense" of Scripture. At times the literal sense is precisely the public, normative meaning that any disinterested reader can, at least in principle, discern. At other times, however, the "literal sense" is the "obvious meaning of the text which the whole church endorses over time; it is a matter of the consensus of the Christian community."[47] Here Ellingsen has simply not worked through the complex way in which Frei himself understood the "literal sense" of Scripture. Nor has he taken seriously the cultural-linguistic framework within which Frei developed his understanding of the *sensus literalis*. Ellingsen's work is confused and confusing at this point.

In addition, throughout the book it is clear that Ellingsen's own understanding of Scripture shapes his approach to the biblical text. His defense of an objective, neutral reading is primarily an attempt to defend the Reformed principle of *sola scriptura;* the cultural-linguistic interpretive community, the church, though affirmed at various points, must

43. Ellingsen, 31.
44. Ellingsen, 32, 40-41, 63-64, 77.
45. In earlier chapters I have critiqued this understanding of Frei's work. Here I will examine the internal problems in Ellingsen's position.
46. Ellingsen, 29-35.
47. Ellingsen, 10-11, 61, 65, 75.

not get in the way of this principle.[48] Ellingsen's "neutral" reading is thus not only dependent on a particular construal of Scripture grounded in the Christian tradition, but also on his particular understanding of *sola scriptura*.

Yet another source of Ellingsen's confusion can be seen in his limited understanding of faith as spiritualistic and psychologizing and subjective.[49] Ellingsen must reject the role of faith in interpretation because, unlike Frei, he does not understand faith as intimately related to the language and practices of the church, but rather views faith as the existential subjectivity of an individual believer. In this way as well, Ellingsen has not fully appreciated Frei's cultural-linguistic turn.

Finally, however, it is in his understanding of the available hermeneutical options that Ellingsen reveals most clearly his distance from Frei's postmodern, cultural-linguistic position. For Ellingsen there are two hermeneutical options, both of them grounded in modernity. On the one hand there is "Kantian subjectivity," in which the individual's perspective and experience shape and even control the meaning of the text.[50] This view of interpretation, Ellingsen argues, leads to total relativism.[51] Ellingsen is correct in affirming Frei's rejection of this approach and in criticizing the frequent homiletical reliance on individual experience.

However, over against this subjective approach and as a protection against it, Ellingsen can only offer a rather feeble and confused defense of a single, normative, objective meaning for each text. It is to this end that he affirms the analytic procedures of New Criticism. What Ellingsen fails to recognize, however, is that he has simply succumbed to the other pole of the modern axis — "scientific objectivity."[52] Over against individual subjectivism Ellingsen seeks the security and certainty of a scientifically objective analytic procedure. The irony of New Criticism at this point has been noted by Terry Eagleton. Whereas the New Critics

48. Ellingsen, 19, 85.
49. Ellingsen, 59, 64.
50. Ellingsen, 57.
51. Ellingsen, 58.
52. Ellingsen's options represent what Murphy and McClendon call the "expressivist" and "representationalist" poles of modernity. See Nancey Murphy and James William McClendon, "Distinguishing Modern and Postmodern Theologies," *Modern Theology* 5 (April 1989): 193-96.

sought to break with a scientific understanding of the world, they in fact bought into its presuppositions.[53] Ellingsen is pulled between two modern options: individual subjectivity or scientific objectivity; and he opts for a defense of the latter.

What Ellingsen completely overlooks, however, is Frei's cultural-linguistic turn and his emphasis on the community of interpretation, which, as Stanley Fish has contended, avoids both subjective relativism and neutral objectivity.[54] Ellingsen continues to speak primarily about the individual interpreter and the text, and he struggles to free interpretation from relativistic subjectivism. Frei, however, focuses instead on Scripture and community, emphasizing the linguistic and practical skills in which believers receive training to read Scripture in the community of faith. Whereas Frei moved to a postmodern approach, Ellingsen seeks to interpret Frei within a modern framework.

The second limitation of Ellingsen's work lies in his understanding of typology. Although Ellingsen rightly highlights this aspect of Frei's work as central for preaching, particularly for absorbing the hearers into the world of the Bible, his understanding of typology is not only flawed, but quite unlike that of Frei. Contrary to Frei's approach, Ellingsen's view of typology leads to an emphasis on individuals and individual experience that is not that much different from other writers in contemporary homiletics. Rather than understanding typology Christologically and ecclesiologically, Ellingsen argues that the various characters in the biblical narratives are "analogues" to contemporary persons.[55] That is, the characters depicted in the biblical narrative are analogous to individuals today, linked by the "common human experience" they share.[56] Preachers are supposed to discern the "correlation" between these analogous situations, so "present-day readers [can] discover themselves in the biblical characters."[57] Typological interpretation functions

53. Terry Eagleton, *Literary Theory: An Introduction* (Minneapolis: Univ. of Minnesota Press, 1983), 46-49. In fact, this understanding of science is itself no longer widely held.

54. Stanley Fish, *Doing What Comes Naturally: Change, Rhetoric, and the Practice of Theory in Literary and Legal Studies* (Durham, North Carolina: Duke Univ. Press, 1989), 138.

55. Ellingsen, 72, 89.

56. Ellingsen, 47.

57. Ellingsen, 47; also 44.

individualistically; contemporary individuals are understood as figures of various biblical characters.

The best example of this approach can be seen in the sermon with which Ellingsen concludes his book.[58] The sermon is based on the "dry bones" passage in Ezekiel 37:1-10, and Ellingsen's "typological" move is revealing. He begins by telling the story from the prophet, faithful to his argument that the biblical narrative must have priority over other stories that are used in the sermon.[59] However, rather than moving typologically through Jesus Christ to the church, which would be consistent with Frei's approach, Ellingsen proceeds immediately and directly to identify individual hearers with individual skeletons in the valley of dry bones. The text is addressed directly to the "spiritual dryness" of individuals, rather than announcing the reconstitution of a political community. Despite his repeated criticism of the psychologization of American culture, Ellingsen moves directly to the spiritual and psychological lives of individuals.

Ellingsen's approach here is better characterized as a kind of "analogy" rather than typology. In preparing the sermon the preacher seeks to discern an analogy between the characters in the biblical narrative and the contemporary hearers.[60] However, this individualistic use of analogy and character is not at all what Frei means by typology. Rather, a better approach involves a Christological-ecclesiological typology, in which Jesus and the church shape the key hermeneutical moves, rather than other characters in the narrative and contemporary individuals.

The third problem in Ellingsen's position, as the preceding discussion suggests, is his failure to develop sufficiently his understanding of Frei's focus on character. Frei nowhere suggests, as Ellingsen does, that each character in the narratives has a "unique, unsubstitutable identity." Indeed, Frei would certainly have argued that few, if any, of these characters are fully enough developed to make this kind of assertion on their behalf. Rather, the key is the unique, unsubstitutable identity of Jesus of Nazareth, which Ellingsen recognizes, but fails to develop homiletically. Further, the crucial homiletical move, so evident in *The*

---

58. Ellingsen, 97-101.
59. Ellingsen, 90.
60. Ellingsen, 89-90.

Identity of Jesus Christ, is from this central character, Jesus of Nazareth, to the church that is formed by his identity. It is the church, the body of Christ, that carries forward the narrative by becoming a character in the ongoing story of Jesus. While Ellingsen rightly highlights the importance of character in Frei's reading of the gospel narratives, when it comes to preaching he moves too simplistically to various individual characters rather than to the central character and his formation of the church.

Thus, although his work is provocative, Ellingsen's constructive proposal leaves much to be desired; it does not represent the best appropriation of Frei's work for contemporary homiletics. In my critique of narrative preaching in the previous chapters, I have already hinted at the directions such a constructive proposal will take. In Part Three I will attempt to sketch more fully some new directions for preaching growing out of Frei's postliberal theology.

PART THREE

New Directions for Preaching

"*. . . Jesus of Nazareth has in all ages been at the center of Christian living, Christian devotion, and Christian thought.*"

Hans W. Frei, *Types of Christian Theology,* 140

"*. . . what can one preach if individual appropriation is the crucial element in religion? Is there anything to be proclaimed beyond one's own experience?*"

Hans W. Frei, *Doctrine of Revelation,* I, 14.

Chapter Eight

Preaching Jesus

In his most telling statement about the role of narrative for theology, Frei wrote that Karl Barth was a "narrative theologian" only to the extent that Jesus was what he did and underwent.[1] For Frei, as for Barth, the gospel narratives function to render the unique, unsubstitutable identity of Jesus through the cumulative interplay of character and incident.[2] Neither narrative structure in general nor other stories in particular are of real interest to Frei. Rather, his focus is on the specific gospel narratives that render the identity of Jesus of Nazareth. This function of the gospels is reinforced by Frei's consistent use of the appellation "Jesus of Nazareth" in *The Identity of Jesus Christ*. This descriptive identification, which includes both a specific name and a particular place, emphasizes the unique, unsubstitutable character of Jesus in the gospel narratives. Frei's emphasis on "Jesus of Nazareth" serves as a check to all attempts to turn Jesus into merely a symbol or a myth.[3]

In this chapter I will delineate some of the homiletical implications of a paraphrase of Frei's comment about Barth: We are narrative preach-

1. Hans W. Frei, "Barth and Schleiermacher: Divergence and Convergence," in *Barth and Schleiermacher: Beyond the Impasse,* ed. James O. Duke and Robert F. Streetman (Philadelphia: Fortress Press, 1988), 72.

2. One could go on to make the case that the function of the biblical narrative is to render the identity of God in Jesus Christ. However, I will simply focus on the New Testament in this chapter.

3. Hans W. Frei, *The Identity of Jesus Christ: The Hermeneutical Bases of Dogmatic Theology* (Philadelphia: Fortress Press, 1975), 131, 136-38.

ers only to the extent that Jesus is what he does and undergoes. In a postliberal homiletic, narrative is important neither because it provides a "homiletical plot" for sermons nor because preaching should consist of telling stories. Rather, narrative is important because it is the vehicle through which the gospels render the identity of Jesus of Nazareth, who has been raised from the dead and seeks today to form a people who follow his way. Accordingly, preaching from the gospels begins with the identity of Jesus. In this chapter I will explore the homiletical implications of these assertions in relation to the content, form, and "performance" of sermons.

The Story of Jesus and Sermon Content

As I argued in the previous chapter, Frei shifts the focus of contemporary narrative homiletics in two significant ways. First of all, Frei directs preaching away from an almost singular focus on the parables to a focus on the gospel narratives. Frei even goes so far as to suggest that the parables cannot and should not be understood outside the larger narratives that render Jesus' identity. It is the person of Jesus who gives meaning to the parables and not vice versa. Second, Frei shifts the focus from plot to character, in particular to the central character in the gospels, Jesus of Nazareth. Obviously, plot and character are inseparably related in the gospels as Frei understands them; character and incident render each other. However, whereas contemporary homiletics has tended to define narrative preaching in terms of plot, whether that is embodied in particular stories or shapes the overall structure of the sermon, Frei directs preaching to a primary emphasis on character. The most important consideration for preaching is that the plots of the gospel stories render the identity of Jesus.

This dual redirection of focus from parable to gospel and from plot to character is consistent; each move reinforces the other. As long as the parables remain the central focus for preaching, then plot can remain the primary concern; after all, Jesus is not a character in the parables (at least, directly), but rather tells them. One can study the ways the narrative structure of parables functions and apply those findings in general to preaching, which is precisely what many narrative homileticians have done. However, once one turns to the gospel narratives as primary, the matter of character moves to the center because the function of the gospels is to render the identity of Jesus of Nazareth. One cannot simply emphasize narrative structure, but must come to terms with the particular character who is rendered through these specific narratives. These two changes alone, from parable to gospels and from plot to character, mark a significant shift from previous reflection on narrative preaching.

The implications of this shift are significant, particularly when considered with reference to Frei's understanding of the ascriptive logic of the gospel narratives. According to Frei, as I have noted, the church has generally read the gospels according to an "ascriptive logic." In the broadest sense this simply means that the stories are about Jesus. However, in a more specific and carefully delineated way, this logic asserts, in grammatical terms, that Jesus is the subject of his own predicates. The predicates applied to Jesus cannot be abstracted from his unique, unsubstitutable enactment of them in the gospel narratives. Jesus cannot be "identified" primarily in terms of abstract qualities applied to him (e.g., love), but rather Jesus himself as rendered in the gospel narratives owns and defines those qualities as a unique, unsubstitutable person.[4]

A good example of this logic is highlighted by Frei with reference to the place of both power and powerlessness in Jesus' identity. As Frei argues, there is both a coincidence of power and powerlessness and a transition from power to powerlessness in the narrative rendering of Jesus' identity.[5] What Frei notes, however, is that one cannot therefore move from Jesus as an enactment of this relationship to a general discussion of the paradoxical relationship between the abstract concepts of power and powerlessness in human life. Rather, the relationship is narratively rendered in Jesus of Nazareth. While that relationship may be described with reference to the narrative of Jesus, and even more importantly embodied in the lives of disciples, it cannot be *explained* in general, anthropological terms. Jesus embodies the relation between power and powerlessness at the heart of the gospel; he is not himself a symbol or cipher of the paradoxical relationship of two abstract qualities. To repeat, Jesus is the subject of his predicates.

4. Hans W. Frei, *Types of Christian Theology,* ed. George Hunsinger and William C. Placher (New Haven: Yale Univ. Press, 1992), 141-43.
5. Frei, *Identity,* 104.

In addition, Frei's understanding of the ascriptive logic of the gospels focuses not on Jesus' inner life — his consciousness or self-understanding — but on his public enactment of his mission. It is through Jesus' intentional actions in the midst of particular circumstances that his unique, unsubstitutable identity emerges. The focus, that is, is not "behind" or "beneath" the biblical text, but on the surface depiction of Jesus' identity through the interplay of character and circumstance. Through this interplay Jesus is rendered as an independent character — one "extra *nos*" — who will not be reduced to rational propositions or absorbed into general human experience.

The significance of this ascriptive logic for preaching begins to become apparent when Frei distinguishes this understanding of Jesus from "myth."

> Myths are stories in which character and action are not irreducibly themselves. Instead they are representations of broader and not directly representable psychic or cosmic states — states transcending the scene of finite and particular events subject to causal explanation. The deepest levels of human existence, the origin and destiny of the universe, including humanity, are the themes that myths evoke through storytelling. Myths are convincing or true by virtue of their embodiment or echoing of universal experience. "Universal" may be too strong a term, but it is not too much to say that a particular myth is the external and expressed mirroring of an internal experience that is both elemental within the consciousness and yet shared by a whole group.[6]

Through this distinction between "myth" and gospel Frei simply highlights the particularity of the gospel. The gospels are not stories about elemental human experience, but rather stories that render the identity of a particular person whose life, death, and resurrection accomplish God's purposes for the world.

Thus, what is important for Christian preaching is not "stories" in general or even "homiletical plots," but rather a specific story that renders the identity of a particular person. The ascriptive logic of the gospels provides both constraints and guidance for Christian preaching. On the one hand, Frei's "narrative theology," like all good theology,

6. Frei, *Identity,* 139.

serves a critical function in judging articulations of the story of Jesus in the church's preaching.[7] Preaching that ignores the ascriptive logic of the gospels — grammatically, preaching in which Jesus is not the subject of his own predicates — comes in for critique. On the other hand, Frei's "narrative theology" suggests the positive directions that preaching, including "narrative preaching," should take. Such preaching should adhere to the ascriptive logic of the gospels and dare to preach Jesus of Nazareth in all his particularity by rendering him as the subject of his own predicates.

Borrowing from the contemporary homiletical debate over "inductive" and "deductive" preaching, one could describe the ascriptive logic of the sermon in a different way. According to current understandings, deductive preaching begins with general propositions and moves to particular applications, while inductive preaching begins with the particulars of human experience and moves to general conclusions. However, within the context of Frei's work, this dichotomy is seen to be misguided. Rather, within the "paradigm" of the church's reading of Scripture, "inductive" preaching properly begins with the particularity of Jesus of Nazareth and moves from there to the church in and for the world.[8] The story of Jesus, not the particulars of human experience, is the fundamental reality and starting point. Indeed, to begin with human experience is almost immediately to run the risk of using the story of Jesus as a myth; Jesus easily becomes simply the predicate of some human experience, and the ascriptive logic at the heart of the gospels is lost.

Homiletical Examples

Lest this emphasis on ascriptive logic seem too abstract and formal, I will demonstrate the importance of Frei's insights by briefly examining two sermons, the first of which represents a "mythological" use of a gospel story, the second of which embodies Frei's understanding of ascriptive logic. The first sermon, "Angels, But Satan and Wild Beasts," by Wayne Bradley Robinson, is based on the story of Jesus' temptation (Mark 1:9-15)

---

7. Frei, *Types*, 124.

8. In the next chapter I will discuss the movement of the sermon to the church in and for the world.

and represents an approach to narrative different from Frei's, but typical of narrative homiletics.[9] Unlike Frei, Robinson bases his theory of narrative on the parables. In the essay that accompanies his sermon in *Journeys Toward Narrative Preaching,* Robinson uses the parable of the good Samaritan as a model for narrative preaching.[10] The result is a focus on plot, on the narrative structure of the sermon. Based on the parables, Robinson argues that the key to narrative preaching is the movement of the sermon from "identifying the issue" to "exploring the issue" to "reframing the issue" to "resolving the issue."[11] This movement, rather than the character of Jesus, is primary, and the results are instructive.

Robinson's sermon opens with an account of the plight of Dan Jensen in the 1988 Olympics. Jensen's sister died of leukemia the week of his speed-skating races, and in the midst of that trauma, after years of training, Jensen fell in both of his races and failed to win a medal. This story "identifies the issue" in the sermon — the problem to be solved: Why do bad things happen to good people?[12] However, this opening also raises the suspicion that Jesus will be identified in terms of a human experience embodied in Dan Jensen's story — a suspicion that is confirmed in the course of the sermon.

After identifying the issue, Robinson next turns to "explore the issue." He examines the "human condition" through his own personal reflections, insights from the "Peanuts" comic strip, and, finally, reflection on MacLeish's play *J.B.* and the book of Job.[13] Through his reflection on *J.B.* and the book of Job, Robinson "reframes the issue." "Why do bad things happen to good people?" turns out to be the wrong question. Rather, Robinson concludes, the appropriate question is "What can we do *when* bad things happen to us or to others we know or care about?"[14]

9. Wayne Bradley Robinson, "Angels, But Satan and Wild Beasts," in *Journeys Toward Narrative Preaching,* ed. Wayne Bradley Robinson (New York: Pilgrim Press, 1990), 101-5.

10. Wayne Bradley Robinson, "The Samaritan Parable as a Model for Narrative Preaching," in *Journeys Toward Narrative Preaching,* ed. Wayne Bradley Robinson (New York: Pilgrim Press, 1990), 85-100.

11. Robinson, "Samaritan Parable," 92-95. Although stated in different language, Robinson's model is almost identical to Lowry's homiletical plot. He also links his approach to Fred Craddock's inductive method (Robinson, "Samaritan Parable," 89, 91).

12. Robinson, "Angels," 101.

13. Robinson, "Angels," 101-3.

14. Robinson, "Angels," 103-4.

At this point in the sermon Jesus finally comes onto the scene with the "solution" to the problem. Jesus' "experience" in the wilderness provides the answer to the reframed question.[15] In this final portion of the sermon, Robinson explores the presence of wild beasts, Satan, and the angels at the temptation and shares what Jesus learns from this experience. The presence of the *wild beasts* teaches Jesus (and the hearers) "that there are things in the world over which no one has control, not us, not God's special child, not, it seems, even God! Freedom and chance are built into the system and cannot be selectively removed."[16] The presence of *Satan* teaches the hearers that Jesus was not spared the kind of testing that we undergo.[17] Most important, however, is the presence of the *angels*. Jesus was not left alone to face the wild beasts and Satan in the wilderness; through the angels, the caring presence of God was with him — and is also with us.[18]

Learning from Jesus' experience with wild beasts, Satan, and angels, Robinson concludes that we can respond in two ways when bad things happen to us. We can, first of all, affirm the option of love that is always there — a "permanent option built into life itself."[19] And, second, "we can use the bad things as occasions to grow." Robinson ends the sermon on this point:

> In the words of Rabbi Kushner, "We do have a lot to say about what suffering does to us, what sort of people we become because of it. Pain makes some people bitter and envious. It makes others sensitive and compassionate." The choice is ours. We can snuff out the coal of the heart and retreat in bitterness, or we can blow on the coal of the heart and let it become the source of new energy to grow in love. We don't seem to get to choose whether bad things will happen, but we do get to choose how we will act and whom we will become when they do.[20]

---

15. Robinson, "Angels," 104. As numerous interpreters have done with the parables, Robinson here treats the temptation story as a symbolic expression of Jesus' "religious experience."

16. Robinson, "Angels," 104.

17. Robinson, "Angels," 104.

18. Robinson, "Angels," 104-5.

19. Robinson, "Angels," 105.

20. Robinson, "Angels," 105.

Not surprisingly, by this point in the sermon Jesus, after a very brief appearance as a rather incidental character, has disappeared completely, for Robinson's sermon is basically a mythical story in Frei's terms. The unsubstitutable identity of Jesus is lost as he becomes simply a representative of a "common human experience," a symbolic embodiment of general principles about life. The story of the temptation is no more essential to the sermon than the story of the blooming forsythia bush in *J.B.* (though using the story of Jesus may carry a little extra authority in the church). Jesus is not a unique subject independent of us, but is rather absorbed into human experience and general "truths" about life; he is not the subject of his own predicates, but is in fact the predicate of another subject: "human experience." The only essential characters in the story seem to be the angels.

In addition, the focus of the sermon is not on the enacted intentions of Jesus, but on his "inner life," on what he surely must have learned from his "experience" in the wilderness. Such an approach stands in sharp contrast to that of Frei, for whom the temptation story depicts Jesus' active embodiment of God's reign in the world. According to Frei, Jesus is identified here as the obedient one, who rejects "the satanic temptation to tempt God" and moves from this temptation to the enactment of his mission.[21] Unlike in Robinson's sermon, in Frei's work Jesus is not simply an example of general human experience, but a unique agent enacting a unique mission.

The absence of the ascriptive logic of the gospel narratives is readily apparent in Robinson's sermon. Rather than preaching the unique, unsubstitutable identity of Jesus Christ, Robinson falls into a mythological use of the biblical story.[22] This happens because, to borrow Frei's terminology, Robinson is too concerned with Jesus' immediate meaningfulness. He does not take the time to render Jesus' identity before turning to Jesus' significance for contemporary hearers. As a consequence, Jesus of Nazareth evaporates into thin air.

---

21. Frei, *Identity*, 108-9.

22. Frei argues that Jesus becomes a unique person only in the narrative of the passion and resurrection. In the second stage of the narrative he is still depicted in terms of the coming of God's reign. However, once his unique identity is established at the resurrection, I think one must also affirm his uniqueness in the earlier portions of the narrative. Certainly he is unique as an embodiment of God's reign. Thus, I have no trouble using the phrase "unique, unsubstitutable identity" for Jesus throughout the narrative from the perspective of the resurrection.

This fact becomes even clearer when Robinson's sermon is viewed next to a sermon by Walter Brueggemann, "Pain Turned to Newness," based on Mark 5:24b-34.[23] Unlike Robinson's sermon, Brueggemann's does not follow a general, stereotyped plot movement from issue to resolution. Rather, Brueggemann simply follows the movement of the biblical story itself, seeking a "dramatic reenactment" of the story for the hearers.[24] He begins with the story, not with human experience. In fact, Brueggemann's sermon represents a kind of dramatic, expository preaching, in which text, exposition, and application are inseparably and dramatically woven together in the sermon.[25]

The sermon begins with a brief overview of the story within its larger context. Brueggemann highlights the intrusive, inconvenient character of the woman with the flow of blood, whose story interrupts that of the powerful, influential leader of the synagogue. Then, before moving to his reenactment of the story itself, Brueggemann invites the hearers into the story, suggesting that the woman's story might be ours as well. "Listen to her story as a tale about your own life and our life."[26] Brueggemann's move is subtle here, but important. He does not invite the hearers to "find their stories" in the biblical story — as if the hearers knew what their stories were apart from Scripture. Rather, he suggests that the biblical story may in fact redescribe the hearers' stories. In Lindbeck's terms, Brueggemann "does not suggest, as is often said in our day, that believers find their stories in the Bible, but rather that they make the story of the Bible their story."[27]

After this brief overview of the story Brueggemann moves to re-enact the dramatic encounter between Jesus and the woman with the flow of blood. Like a drama, Brueggemann's sermon moves through several scenes. He begins with a description of the woman as a "carrier of pain," using anachronisms to give the story a contemporary ring and

---

23. Walter Brueggemann, "Pain Turned to Newness," TMs [photocopy]. I am grateful to Walter Brueggemann for his permission to include this sermon in the Appendix to this volume. Page references are to the Appendix.

24. Walter Brueggemann, *Texts under Negotiation: The Bible and Postmodern Imagination* (Minneapolis: Fortress Press, 1993), 69.

25. Although it is not my purpose to argue for a specific sermon form based on Frei's work, Brueggemann's sermon embodies one possible form.

26. Brueggemann, "Newness," 260.

27. George Lindbeck, *The Nature of Doctrine: Religion and Theology in a Postliberal Age* (Philadelphia: Westminster Press, 1984), 118.

to enable the hearers to relate to the woman's story.[28] The woman is presented as a "type" of a person in pain, but without losing her "distinctively contingent or random individuality."[29] This scene ends with the woman's desperate action; she touches Jesus — "pain touching power" — and is healed. Jesus is not yet mentioned directly, but is himself at this point simply a "type" or embodiment of "power."

In the second scene Jesus appears directly, speaking to the crowds around him, asking who had touched him. Though presented as a powerful healer in this scene, once Jesus comes onto the stage his unique unsubstitutable identity almost immediately begins to become apparent. In particular, hints begin to surface that he is not simply a "type" of power or a powerful healer, but rather a person who embodies this power and healing in a unique way. The strange and unique conjunction of power and powerlessness in Jesus' person begins to become apparent, not only in Brueggemann's description of Jesus, but in the presence of both active and passive verbs throughout this scene.

> Only now does Jesus speak, only after he has been touched. The healing happened by his presence, without his knowing it. He is so saturated with the power for life that the power spills over to those around him. . . . [However,] Jesus, the powerful one, is changed by contact with pain. He is changed in ways commensurate with her. He is not an unmoved mover or an unnoticing power. He is impacted decisively by her touch. . . . It is an amazing moment between this pained woman and this powerful healer.[30]

The scene concludes with the woman, empowered by her new freedom and courage, presenting herself to Jesus — but in fear and trembling.

> She comes in fear and trembling. How odd. Why is that? Because she knew she had intruded on him improperly. Because she expected to

---

28. Brueggemann, "Newness," 260.

29. This use of character types is one of the characteristics of realistic narrative highlighted by Frei (Hans W. Frei, *The Eclipse of Biblical Narrative: A Study in Eighteenth and Nineteenth Century Hermeneutics* [New Haven: Yale University, 1974], 15).

30. Brueggemann, "Newness," 261-62. Here Brueggemann captures the "pattern of exchange" that Frei argues is at the heart of the gospel. This one story becomes in essence the gospel — the story of Jesus — in miniature.

be shamed or scolded, because she was used to being abused and "man handled" by men, for pain is always frightened in the presence of power.[31]

Although Brueggemann has given hints that Jesus is different, the woman still views him as simply an embodiment of "power"; so she approaches him with fear and trembling.

In the next scene Jesus speaks to the woman and emerges fully as a unique, unsubstitutable person. In speaking and acting toward the woman, Brueggemann writes, Jesus "acts out and models a new way of power towards pain."[32] As a thoroughly active subject in this scene, Jesus authorizes the woman for a new possibility by addressing her, celebrating her faith, and dismissing her with a blessing.[33] Through this story the world's configurations of power and powerlessness are redefined, not in terms of any abstract propositions, but in the conjunction of power and powerlessness enacted in the unique, unsubstitutable person, Jesus of Nazareth. Indeed, Brueggemann closes his reenactment of the story with a telling comment: "The woman is now forever a key character in *the story of Jesus*. . . . She becomes someone she was not, as she moved into the circle of Jesus' lifegiving power."[34]

In the final scene of the sermon Brueggemann carries the story into the time of his contemporary hearers. Again, he invites them to become characters in the story of Jesus, suggesting that there are various places they might stand in the story.[35] The story redescribes the world and calls the hearers to discipleship:

> Those who trust this story do not willingly settle for the old, weary patterns of "haves" and "have-nots," for the usual arrangements of

---

31. Brueggemann, "Newness," 262.
32. Brueggemann, "Newness," 262-63.
33. Brueggemann, "Newness," 263.
34. Brueggemann, "Newness," 263-64; italics mine.
35. Brueggemann, "Newness," 264. Although Brueggemann mainly explores personal identifications with individual characters or groups of characters in the story, he does also move ecclesiologically; he suggests that the church itself carries forward the story of Jesus in a unique way: "We are not Jesus but we do as baptized folk share in his power and in his capacity to heal, to let ourselves be touched so that some of our God-given power can flow to the lives of other bleeding outsiders" ("Newness," 264).

strength and weakness, power and powerlessness. This story offers to us a different map of reality, a different option, a different life.[36]

Brueggemann concludes with a restatement of Jesus' words to the woman, now addressed to the contemporary congregation: "Go in peace, be healed of your disease, by your faith be whole."[37]

Contrary to Robinson's sermon, Brueggemann's dramatic reenactment of the biblical story captures the unique, unsubstitutable agent, Jesus of Nazareth, who enacts a new social reality and redefines the relationship between power and powerlessness. Jesus is not absorbed into general human experience, but the hearers are invited to "move into his circle," to become characters in his story. Nor is the focus of the sermon on the inner life of Jesus, on either his self-understanding or his consciousness. Rather, Jesus *enacts* the way of God in the world; in Frei's terms, as an embodiment of the reign of God, Jesus is what he does and undergoes.[38] Indeed, apart from Jesus' enactment of God's reign, the old power arrangements remain intact and unchallenged. Unlike Robinson's sermon, Brueggemann's sermon risks everything on the assertion that Jesus embodies and enacts the reign of God; apart from Jesus of Nazareth Brueggemann simply has nothing to say in this sermon. In numerous ways, then, Brueggemann's sermon captures precisely the ascriptive logic of the gospel narratives.

As these two sermons illustrate, Frei's turn from parabolic plot to the story of Jesus has important implications for preaching, including narrative preaching. Frei's work directs preachers beyond general matters of narrative form to the particular ascriptive logic of the gospel stories. Further, as these two sermons suggest, a respect for the ascriptive logic of the gospels will contribute to more radical preaching in the church. In light of the work of John Dominic Crossan and others, who have examined the domesticating character of myth, it is probably no accident that Brueggemann's sermon is radical and revolutionary while Robinson's offers little more than comforting moralisms.[39] It is certainly no accident that Brueggemann's sermon seeks to form an alternative community, a "contrast society," while Robinson's simply helps middle-class individuals to cope.

36. Brueggemann, "Newness," 264.
37. Brueggemann, "Newness," 264.
38. Frei, *Identity,* 130-32.
39. John Dominic Crossan, *The Dark Interval: Towards a Theology of Story* (Niles, Illinois: Argus Communications, 1975), 59.

Admittedly, other things besides ascriptive logic contribute to the difference between the two sermons. And, of course, Jesus' identity could have been construed quite differently from the way Brueggemann construes it. However, when the unique, unsubstitutable subject, Jesus of Nazareth, evaporates into general human experience, one would rarely expect anything very radical — or even very interesting — to be preached. On the other hand, if preachers would linger with the identity of Jesus before moving too quickly to his meaningfulness, they might be surprised.

In this respect the ascriptive logic of the gospels serves as one kind of "hermeneutic of suspicion" with regard to the use of Scripture in preaching. This logic can serve as a check on tendencies to preach wisdom gleaned from "general human experience." The ascriptive logic of the gospels serves as a check upon the pallid, mythological preaching of which the church has heard so much. When preachers take seriously this logic amidst the diversity of the fourfold gospel, the truly disruptive power of Jesus becomes a reality not only in the individual gospel narratives, but in Jesus' refusal to be contained by any one story. When Jesus is preached in his unique, unsubstitutable identity, the church might be surprised and even startled by what it hears.

Frei's turn from parable to gospel and from plot to character thus has significant implications not only for preaching in general, but for narrative preaching in particular. Frei's work suggests that the narrative dimensions of preaching go beyond matters of form to matters of content, particularly matters of Christology. The ascriptive logic of the gospel narratives suggests helpful theological guidelines for preparing and analyzing sermons, including narrative sermons, at a level much deeper and more profound than that of sermon form. Moreover, when the character of Jesus, rather than sermonic plot, becomes central to preaching, some interesting consequences also emerge with reference to sermon form itself.

The Story of Jesus and Sermon Form

Several years ago, James Kay argued that the homiletical consequences of Frei's work are disastrous.[40] According to Kay, Frei's work constrains the

---

40. James F. Kay, "Theological Table Talk: Myth or Narrative," *Theology Today* 48 (October 1991): 326-32. See also James F. Kay, *Christus Praesens: A Reconsideration of*

preacher to do nothing more than simply recite verbatim the biblical narratives: ". . . there really remains no logical need for preaching in any sense other than narrative recitation."[41] Although Kay never convincingly demonstrates why such recitation is bad, he is nevertheless mistaken about the homiletical implications of Frei's work. In fact, Frei's work actually offers resources not only for moving beyond mere rote recitation, but also beyond a simplistic reliance on stories or narrative form. Within Frei's work are suggestions that highlight the complexity of the relationship between the story of Jesus and sermon form, including suggestions that may help "non-narrative" preachers preach the story of Jesus more faithfully.

As has become abundantly clear by now, Frei had no real stock in narrative form or stories per se. His concern was the particular story of Jesus in the gospels, and, in the fullest sense, the story of God in the entire Bible. Frei knew that Christians do not worship a particular genre, but rather the One whose identity is rendered through the story. Frei's concerns in this regard became apparent in the way he distanced himself from many forms of "narrative theology" toward the end of his life.

Throughout Frei's work Jesus is more important than narrative form; in fact, Frei repeatedly suggests that the "logic" of the biblical narratives can be captured in non-narrative form, though always with some distortion and always with the need to return to the biblical story.[42] For example, at several points in his work Frei notes that the epistles are legitimate commentaries on the story of Jesus; they capture the "logic" or grammar of the story in faithful ways, even though often in discursive form.[43] Frei will even use the epistles to support and clarify his interpreta-

---

Bultmann's Christology (Grand Rapids, Michigan: Wm. B. Eerdmans Publishing Co., 1994), 139-40.

41. Kay, "Myth or Narrative," 330.

42. See Frei, "Barth and Schleiermacher," 72; also Frei, *Types*, 90, 124-26.

43. Frei, *Identity*, 59; 104-5; 110. The phrase "the logic of the story" requires some qualification. I do not mean to suggest that, beyond the basic ascriptive logic, there is a single, uniform logic to the gospel narratives (though I will not deny that at times Frei, in his early work, seemed to suggest as much). In addition, I do not mean to affirm that a logic of the gospels exists independently of the interpretive communities reading Scripture. This section, including my discussion of Richard Hays's work, should not be read in isolation from a consideration of the role of communal practices in reading Scripture (see Chapter 9). Here I am simply suggesting a complex relationship between narrative logic and discursive sermon form, and I use the phrase "the logic of the story of Jesus" in this limited sense.

tion of the gospel narratives or to sum up the pattern of Jesus' identity.[44] Although Frei's treatment of this issue is not fully developed, he does at least suggest possible connections between the gospels and the epistles, between the story of Jesus and discursive forms of interpreting it.

In addition, Frei's own sermons did not take an explicitly narrative form — something Kay neglected to consider. Rather, Frei liked the form of colonial Puritan sermons: exegesis and application.[45] Frei's sermons would not be considered "narrative preaching," much less a simple recitation of the biblical stories. With respect to sermon form, Frei himself seemed most concerned to move from biblical text to contemporary situation, rather than "inductively" from human experience to the text. And, of course, this kind of sermon is consistent with the central convictions of Frei's work, which emphasize not narrative form per se, but the particular story of Jesus Christ.

I do not want to overstate the case here.[46] Frei did stress the importance of the repeated recital and reenactment of the gospel story in the church. He also recognized the value of some contemporary stories in helping imaginatively to bring the gospel story to life, though he fundamentally thought the gospel story should be the one to bring our stories to life.[47] Nevertheless, his own preaching suggests that Frei did not see a necessary connection between this essential repetition of the gospel story and a particular narrative form for the sermon.

Moreover, in "Theological Reflections" and *The Identity of Jesus Christ* Frei suggests the complexity of the relationship between the story of Jesus and the homiletical appropriation of it. Despite Frei's emphasis on the narrative rendering of Jesus' identity, both of these works reach their climax in an *argument* that Frei gleans from the "logic" of the gospel narratives, a fact that is easily overlooked by persons fixated on narrative.

In a sense (if I may put it in a manner totally uncongenial to them) the synoptic Gospel writers are saying something like this: "Our ar-

---

44. Frei, *Identity,* 104.

45. Personal letter from John Woolverton, September 19, 1991.

46. In this section I am not in any way trying to argue against "narrative preaching," particularly the kind that moves through the biblical story in the manner of Brueggemann's sermon just discussed. I am simply trying to note the complexity of the issue and suggest some ways of thinking about it based upon Frei's work.

47. Frei, *Identity,* 168-70.

gument is that to grasp what *this* identity, Jesus of Nazareth, is, is to believe that, in fact, he has been raised from the dead. . . ."

It may be dubious wisdom to make Luke or John speak like a late eleventh-century theologian. But something like this argument seems to me to be present in the resurrection account.[48]

Although Frei recognizes that this discursive way of speaking would have been uncongenial to the gospel writers, he nevertheless affirms that this argument captures the "logic" of the resurrection narratives.

In addition, Frei's use of the identity category of "self-manifestation" suggests that his work does not simplistically relegate preaching to the recitation of the linear sequence of events in the gospels. Frei's category of self-manifestation seeks to account for the unity of Jesus that emerges in the narrative.[49] Whereas the intention-action category focuses on specific sequential events in the narrative, the self-manifestation category emphasizes the unity and continuity of the person of Jesus who emerges in the entirety of the narrative. While organically inseparable from the cumulative interaction of character and incident in the narrative, a wholeness does emerge, a pattern of identifying Jesus that does not simplistically require a mere recitation of the sequence of events in the story. For example, Frei can speak of Jesus' unique identity in terms of an overall "pattern of exchange" characteristic of Jesus' self-enactment. Here Frei is not simply repeating a narrative sequence of events, but rather seeking to capture the "logic" of the narrative in relation to the unity of Jesus' identity rendered therein.[50] Frei thus indirectly suggests an overall pattern to the story of Jesus that may inform other kinds of discourse about him.

Frei's work in this regard has similarities to that of Northrop Frye, who distinguishes between the *mythos* and *dianoia* of stories.[51] According

48. Hans W. Frei, "Theological Reflections on the Gospel Accounts of Jesus' Death and Resurrection," *The Christian Scholar* 49 (Winter 1966): 299; Frei, *Identity*, 145-46.

49. Although, as I noted earlier, Frei became increasingly uneasy with the category of "self-manifestation," he nevertheless contended that some way of affirming the unity of a person was essential in identity description. I am using "self-manifestation" here simply because Frei never proposed an alternative. I am more interested in what Frei seeks to capture than in the possible limitations of his particular conceptuality.

50. Frei, *Identity*, 74-84.

51. My discussion here is dependent on Richard Hays, *The Faith of Jesus Christ*, Society of Biblical Literature Dissertation Series 56 (Chico, California: Scholars Press, 1983), 21-23. Hays draws on Frye's distinction between *mythos* and *dianoia* as the

to Frye (pay close attention to spelling here!), *mythos* refers to the plot or linear sequence of events depicted in the narrative. *Dianoia,* however, refers to the "theme" of the narrative or the plot examined as a simultaneous unity; it is the entire shape or pattern of the narrative that becomes "clear in our minds." This "theme" is an organic property of the narrative, inseparable from it, but *dianoia* represents the particular narrative elements in relation to a unity rather than merely in terms of suspense and linear progression.[52] Frei's distinction between an intention-action analysis of Jesus' identity, which focuses on specific linear sequences, and a "self-manifestation" analysis, which focuses on the continuity of the whole, captures the same distinction as Frye's *mythos* and *dianoia.* However, Frei's categories are more appropriate to the gospel narratives because, as categories of personal identity, they are less likely to lose Jesus as the center of the story than are categories such as "theme," which are not necessarily focused on the central character of the gospel stories.

At this point Frei's work can be viewed in relation to Richard Hays's detailed examination of the narrative substructure of Galatians 3:1-4:11. In his important study, *The Faith of Jesus Christ,* which has unfortunately been neglected by homileticians, Hays draws on Frye's distinction between *mythos* and *dianoia* and argues that "there can be a continuity between the language of story and discursive language, that the relationship between the two can be, in at least some cases, organic rather than artificial."[53] More specifically, Hays demonstrates that Paul's discursive argument in Galatians 3:1–4:11 is grounded in a narrative substructure and follows a "narrative logic"; Paul expounds the *dianoia* of his story of Jesus through the form of a discursive argument. While Hays's work is not dependent on Frei's, Hays does demonstrate clearly and convincingly the role of "narrative logic" in a discursive argument based on the story of Jesus. Hays's work represents both a consistent development of Frei's rather cryptic suggestions and also a challenge to simplistic moves from narrative Scripture to

---

theoretical basis for his exploration of the way in which Paul's discursive argument in Galatians 3:1–4:11 is dependent on a narrative substructure. Hays also refers to Ricoeur's distinction between the sequential and configurational dimensions of narrative and to Funk's analysis of the language of "primary reflectivity" (Hays, *Faith,* 23-27). However, in the course of his study Hays uses Frye's distinction most often. I will discuss Hays's work and its connection with Frei's more fully below.

52. Hays, *Faith,* 21-23.
53. Hays, *Faith,* 20.

narrative sermon form in contemporary homiletics. A brief look at Hays's
work will clarify the complexities of the relationship between narrative and
sermon that Frei's emphasis on the "logic" of the gospel stories suggests.

The implications of Hays's work for preaching are evident in the
explicit connection he draws between sermons and the Pauline letters,
noting that both take the form of "primary reflectivity."[54]

> Galatians must *not* be interpreted as if it were "foundational
> language." Paul writes in the mode of "primary reflectivity," and we
> understand the text properly only when we understand it as the expli-
> cation of something else. A helpful analogy may be found in the relation
> between text and sermon. A sermon does not retell the story told in the
> text upon which it is based, but the story is pervasively presupposed by
> the sermon. To understand a sermon, therefore, we need to know not
> only something about the rhetorical conventions of the sermon genre
> and about the congregational situation to which the sermon is
> addressed but also about the text which the sermon seeks to explicate.
> Galatians is not exactly a sermon (although it may well have been
> intended to be read aloud to the Galatian congregations), but it does
> stand close to the sermon on Funk's spectrum of language modes,
> clearly within the category of primary reflectivity. It is neither self-
> sufficient nor purely self-referential; instead, it constantly presupposes
> and elucidates the gospel story of Jesus Christ. . . .[55]

In Hays's view, there is a close relationship between sermons and Paul's
letter to the Galatians.

Within this homiletical understanding of Galatians, Hays defends
the integral relationship between the story of Jesus and the logic of
Paul's discursive arguments:

> . . . in certain key theological passages in his letters, the framework
> of Paul's thought is constituted neither by a system of doctrines nor

---

54. Hays borrows the term "primary reflectivity" from Robert Funk; it refers to
language that reflects not on previous reflection, but on the foundational language of the
community. Unlike for Hays and Frei, for Funk this foundational language is found in the
parables. For Hays's discussion and critique of Funk at this point, see Hays, *Faith*, 24-28.

55. Hays, *Faith*, 264-65; see also 1. Even narrative sermons belong in this category;
they too are "primary reflections" on Scripture. At another point in the book Hays makes
a distinction between the gospel that Paul "preached" and his letters. However, consistent
with my argument, what Paul preached was the *story of Jesus* (Hays, *Faith*, 7).

by his personal religious experience but by a "sacred story," a narrative structure. In these texts, Paul "theologizes" by reflecting upon this story as an ordering pattern for thought and experience; he deals with the "variable elements" of the concrete situation (for instance, the challenge of his opponents in Galatia) by interpreting them within the framework of his "sacred story," which is a story about Jesus Christ. . . . Paul does not, of course, simply retell the story in his letters, although he alludes to it constantly. He assumes that his readers know the gospel story, and his pervasive concern is to draw out the implications of this story for shaping the belief and practice of his infant churches. . . . It is possible, however, to identify Paul's allusions to his story of Jesus Christ, to discern some features of its narrative "shape," and to examine the way in which this story operates as a constraint governing the logic of Paul's argumentation. . . . the story provides the foundational substructure upon which Paul's argument is constructed. It also provides, therefore, certain boundaries or constraints for the logic of Paul's discourse.[56]

What Hays proposes is a kind of discursive speech that moves neither deductively from abstract, cognitive propositions nor inductively from human experience, but rather operates within the "paradigm" of a story.[57] Paul does not simply recite the sequence of events in his story of Jesus, but rather discursively expounds the *dianoia* of the story in a way shaped by the narrative itself. "Paul's thinking," Hays writes, "is shaped by a story in a way that not all thinking is. . . . Paul's thinking is shaped by a particular paradigmatic story about Jesus Christ."[58]

Hays defends this thesis in two stages. First, Hays identifies allusions to Paul's story of Jesus in the confessional formulae in Galatians 4:3-6 and 3:13-14.[59] He discerns in those texts a single, coherent story

56. Hays, *Faith*, 5-6.
57. Hays does not argue that Paul had access to one of the written gospels, but that he draws upon a story that is well known to the congregation — the story of Jesus that Paul himself had preached.
58. Hays, *Faith*, 19.
59. Frei would not have been interested in Hays's use of structuralist analysis. However, Hays uses Greimas's structural model in a "low-level" descriptive way, rather than making large, universal claims for the model. Hays suggests that what he is really doing is using certain analytical tools to think through the way in which the church has generally read these two confessional texts, despite scholarly arguments about the contradictions between them (Hays, *Faith*, 120).

outline, which he summarizes as follows: "Paul's gospel presents Jesus Christ as the protagonist sent by God whose faithful action brings deliverance and blessing to humanity."[60] Second, having discerned this general narrative structure, Hays examines in detail the way in which this story of Jesus serves as the "narrative substructure" that provides both warrants and constraints for Paul's argument in Galatians 3:1–4:11. He demonstrates that Paul's argument is not based on "logical necessities" or cognitive propositions, but rather functions within a "narrative logic" shaped by the story of Jesus. To put it another way, the coherence of Paul's argument is governed not by the "necessary truths of reason," but by a particular story of the Messiah.

Although it is both impossible and unnecessary to present all the details of Hays's study, a few points will help to clarify both the connections between his work and Frei's and the implications of his work for preaching. Hays reaches several conclusions about the "narrative logic" in Paul's argument. First, this "narrative logic" is not that of "logical necessities" and propositions, but rather embodies the contingencies of narrative itself. There is a "fitness" to narrative logic, like the fitness of the movement of a story; an argument within the structure of a narrative is quite different from an argument that moves inexorably from proposition to conclusion. Within the framework of a single story,

---

60. Hays, *Faith*, 176. Later in the book, after examining Paul's argument, Hays provides a fuller explication of this story: "The Messiah, in obedience to God's will, bears the curse and dies vicariously on behalf of others (3:13). Because of his faithfulness, however, he is vindicated by God and given life (3:11) and the inheritance of God's blessing, which has been promised to Abraham (3:16). In receiving this promise, he remains a representative figure: just as others received the benefits of his death, so also they participate with him in the inheritance, which they have 'in' him (3:14)" (Hays, *Faith*, 209).

The interpretation of the phrase, "faith of Jesus Christ," plays a central role in the book, as the title suggests. Hays determines that the phrase should be read as a subjective genitive, rather than an objective genitive. The "faith of Jesus Christ" does not mean "that believers receive the promise by the subjective act of placing their faith in Jesus Christ; instead, it must mean that Jesus Christ, by the power of faith, has performed an act which allows believers to receive the promise" (Hays, *Faith*, 124). Like Frei, Hays points beyond a kind of relationalism that makes salvation a "work" of human faith to a strong emphasis on the unique, unsubstitutable identity of Jesus Christ. Importantly, Hays does not emphasize Jesus' faith as merely an internal state apart from obedience; in Frei's terms, one might say that faith and obedience are as inseparable as intention and action.

numerous different arguments are possible because narrative itself is polyvalent.[61]

Second, the story of Jesus serves fundamentally as the *warrant* for Paul's arguments.[62] Rather than arguments based upon "universal truths of reason" or on general human experience, Paul's arguments are warranted by a particular, contingent story of Jesus. To borrow Frei's terminology, the unique subject, Jesus of Nazareth, is the unsubstitutable warrant in Paul's argument. This characteristic of Paul's "narrative logic" is clearly illustrated in Hays's discussion of Paul's treatment of the Law. According to Hays, Paul does not reject the salvific power of the Law because of a general human inability to fulfill it. Rather, as Hays writes,

> The Messiah defines the "pattern" for justification and life; consequently, since *he* lived and died and was raised *ek pisteōs,* justification through keeping the commandments must be *in principle* (not merely *de facto*) impossible. . . .
>
> Paul rejects the Law not because of an empirical observation that no one can do what it requires but because its claim to give life . . . is incompatible with the gospel story, which says that Christ had to die in order to give life to us. . . .[63]

The story of Jesus, not human experience or human reason, serves as a contingent and particular warrant for Paul's argument concerning the Law. In fact, if Paul had rejected the Law and turned to Jesus primarily because of a human inability to fulfill the Law, Jesus would have simply become the predicate of human needs or human experience. Paul's avoidance of this move reaffirms the importance of the ascriptive logic of the story of Jesus. Apart from the unique, unsubstitutable identity of Jesus, Paul's argument is impossible.

Third, Hays notes the way in which the "pattern of exchange" constrains and shapes Paul's argument. This pattern governs the logic of Paul's argument and shapes Paul's "participationist soteriology."[64] Hays even suggests a connection between his findings in Galatians and Frei's interpretation of the "pattern of exchange" in the gospel

61. Hays, *Faith,* 223-24.
62. Hays, *Faith,* 85, 235, 247, 257.
63. Hays, *Faith,* 207.
64. Hays, *Faith,* 208, 213.

narratives — thus suggesting also a link between the gospels and the epistles, between the narrative and discursive portions of the New Testament.[65]

Fourth, the language of Paul's argument is rich with allusions to the underlying narrative.[66] For example, Paul's references to the cross allude to the entire story of Jesus of which the crucifixion is a part:

> In Galatians, the gospel message is manifested in a kind of shorthand through allusive phrases such as "Jesus Christ crucified" (3:1). My thesis is that these allusive phrases are intended to recall and evoke a more comprehensive narrative pattern. . . .[67]

Importantly, the allusiveness of Paul's language required a people trained to listen. In order to follow Paul's argument people needed something more than reason or experience; they needed to know the story of Jesus.[68]

Finally, Hays argues, Paul's language is poetic and tensive, even though discursive. Grounded in the logic of a narrative and filled with allusions to that story, Paul's language is rich and polyvalent, like a story itself. Unlike many arguments, which are viewed as univocal, Paul's language is rich with multiple meanings, inviting the participation and involvement of the hearers.[69] Paul's discursive speech is thus very different from the deductive, propositional arguments rightly criticized by many contemporary homileticians.

Although I have not done justice to Hays's study, I have tried to make clear the ways in which he demonstrates that a narrative logic underlies Paul's discursive writing in this central section of Galatians.

65. Hays, *Faith,* 258. Hays even uses Frei's work to describe this "pattern of exchange" (Hays, *Faith,* 258).

66. In his book *Echoes of Scripture in the Letters of Paul* (New Haven: Yale Univ. Press, 1989), Hays has developed in more detail his insights into the allusive character of Paul's letters.

67. Hays, *Faith,* 7.

68. Hays, *Faith,* 196. Hays takes an approach diametrically opposed to that of Craddock. As I noted in Chapter 5, Craddock argues in *Overhearing the Gospel* that Paul used direct, discursive speech largely because of the missionary context in which he had to provide people with information about the gospel. Hays, however, argues that Paul can use his narratively structured argument precisely because the people *already know* the story of Jesus that Paul had preached.

69. Hays, *Faith,* 264-66.

Through his exploration of this narrative logic, Hays also indirectly suggests some new ways for thinking about sermon form. As in Paul's letter, so in sermons there may be a continuous and organic, rather than artificial, relation between the language of story and discursive language.[70] Like Paul, preachers need to explore kinds of discursive speech that move neither "deductively" from abstract, cognitive propositions nor "inductively" from human experience, but rather operate within the narrative logic of the story of Jesus. The relationship between narrative text and sermon form is more complicated than many contemporary narrative homileticians have suggested.

Contrary to James Kay's assertions, Frei's work, as developed by Hays, does not relegate preaching to a mere recitation of the biblical stories. Rather, just the opposite is the case. Frei's work suggests the rich and complex ways in which the story of Jesus and sermons may be related. Frei's focus on the character of Jesus and the "logic" of the gospel narratives directs preachers not only beyond a simple recitation of the biblical story, but also beyond a simplistic move from "narrative Scripture" to "narrative sermon." In the move from text to sermon, the narrative logic of the story of Jesus, not general considerations of narrative structure, provides the crucial connection between sermon form and content, whether the story of Jesus functions as a contingent and particular "substructure" of an argument or as the center of a narrative sermon. Far from constricting the relationship between biblical narrative and sermon form, Frei's work suggests more complex and expansive ways of exploring this relationship.

The Story of Jesus and the Homiletical Performance of Scripture

Frei's emphasis on the logic of the story of Jesus has implications not only for the form and content of the sermon, but also for the act of preaching itself, including its ethical dimensions. As I noted in Chapter Four, within a cultural-linguistic model of Christianity, biblical interpretation for preaching cannot be limited to the ways the preacher gleans meaning from the text or seeks to "translate" the text into the modern world. Rather, biblical interpretation also includes the ways in which

70. Hays, *Faith*, 20.

the church's practice of preaching itself is an interpretive *performance* of Scripture — a public enactment of the story of Jesus. From this perspective, new interpretive questions arise for the preacher, which are more fundamental than questions of meaning or "relevance": How does the practice of preaching itself publicly enact an interpretation of Scripture, particularly the story of Jesus? What are the implications of this enactment for the way we preach? And how does the performance of Scripture in preaching help to form the church's life after the pattern of Jesus' story?

One way of addressing these questions is provided by contemporary narrative homileticians, who have focused on the parables and on Jesus as a model preacher. Within this model, the preacher becomes primarily a "storyteller" or "narrative artist."[71] The preacher "performs Scripture" by being, like Jesus, a parabolic storyteller, either through the use of actual stories or through the overall plotlike shape of the sermon.

However, when one turns attention with Frei to the story of Jesus in the gospel narratives as a whole, this understanding of Jesus' implications for preaching becomes much too limited. Within the framework of Frei's work, the preacher is not called primarily to model her preaching formally upon Jesus' parables. Rather, the preacher is called to be a disciple, in whom the pattern of Jesus' storied identity is followed "at a distance" even in the practice of preaching. The significant thing for the preacher is not Jesus as a model preacher, but rather the identity of Jesus rendered in the gospels, which provides the pattern for the life of discipleship. In light of Jesus' identity, a view of the discipleship of preaching as simply "storytelling" or "narrative artistry" seems at best simplistic, at worst ridiculous.

Frei's work suggests a different way to reflect on the homiletical performance of Scripture. In *The Identity of Jesus Christ*, where Frei develops his specific reading of the story of Jesus, a significant pattern emerges, with important consequences for the practice of preaching. The key to this pattern lies in Frei's analysis of Jesus' movement from his ministry to his crucifixion and resurrection.

71. Edmund Steimle, Morris Niedenthal, and Charles Rice, *Preaching the Story* (Philadelphia: Fortress Press, 1980), ix, 12; Eugene Lowry, *The Homiletical Plot: The Sermon as Narrative Art Form* (Atlanta: John Knox Press, 1980), 6, 14.

According to Frei, in his ministry Jesus both witnesses to and embodies the reign of God in the world. The fulfillment of God's coming reign both *is witnessed to* and *takes place in* Jesus' preaching and mighty works.[72] During this period of active ministry Jesus is a powerful and authoritative figure, with freedom and scope of movement.[73]

In the course of this ministry, however, Jesus' preaching and deeds offend the "forces of history." These "forces" are the ones that the gospel writers discern acting powerfully against Jesus — "his accusers, judges, the complicated vested interests they represent, and back of them the vast mass of humanity."[74] Another way of putting this is that Jesus' ministry challenges and offends the "powers" of the world, which predictably turn against him and seek to destroy him through the violent means that are their *modus operandi*.[75] The powers simply cannot sit by and allow a challenge to their dominion to exist.[76]

At this point in the narrative, Jesus' transition from power to powerlessness occurs. Through his decision to go to Jerusalem and the cross, Jesus himself determines to enter into this powerlessness;[77] he rejects the option of fighting the "forces of history" with military power — even with divine "legions":

> Staying the hand that would defend him against arrest, Jesus asks: "Do you think I cannot appeal to my Father, and he will at once send me more than twelve legions of angels? But how then should the scriptures be fulfilled, that it must be so?" (Matt. 26:53-54). Jesus affirms the will of God obediently by both initiating and consenting

---

72. Frei, *Identity,* 130-32. For Frei this "stage" of the narrative runs from Jesus' baptism up till the time when he predicts his crucifixion and turns to go to Jerusalem.

73. Frei, *Identity,* 114.

74. Frei, *Identity,* 116. The actions of the forces are complicated by the fact that somehow God's activity is involved here too; the forces of history are not completely independent of God's ordering, but ironically carry out God's purposes (Frei, *Identity,* 117).

75. Frei, *Identity,* 131. Frei's understanding of the "forces of history" is compatible with the understanding of the "powers" developed by John Howard Yoder in *The Politics of Jesus,* 2nd ed. (Grand Rapids, Michigan: Wm. B. Eerdmans Publishing Co., 1994), 134-61.

76. For another excellent discussion of the "powers" and Jesus' engagement with them, see Walter Wink, *Engaging the Powers: Discernment and Resistance in a World of Domination* (Minneapolis: Fortress Press, 1992).

77. Frei, *Identity,* 105.

to the shape of the events that now develop in their mysterious
logic.[78]

Jesus intentionally rejects the way of violence and coercion, for the
purposes of God cannot be fulfilled by violent means. In obedience to
God Jesus makes a transition from ministry to crucifixion, from authoritative power to helplessness.[79] Consequently, as Jesus moves toward
the cross, his embodiment of God's reign appears increasingly tenuous
and ironic.[80]

Nevertheless, this transition from power to powerlessness is essential to Jesus' salvific role. In fact, Jesus' powerlessness always coexists
mysteriously with his power. Frei repeatedly cites the ironic truth of the
words of the priests and scribes: "He saved others; he cannot save
himself" (Mark 15:31). As Frei writes of this "pattern of exchange,"

> Indeed, the narrative points simultaneously to the pattern of coex-
> istence and transition between power and powerlessness. Jesus
> enacted the good of men on their behalf in both ways. It is his
> vicarious identification with the guilty and, at the climax of the story,
> his identification with the helplessness of the guilty that provide the
> Gospel's story of salvation. Yet this helplessness is his power for the
> salvation of others. Something of his power abides and is accentuated
> as he becomes helpless. The pattern of exchange becomes the means
> of salvation. . . . if Jesus had not forsaken the power to save himself,
> he could not have saved others. Thus, the transition from power to
> helplessness is at the same time the realization of his saving power.[81]

In determining and deciding for powerlessness before the hostile "forces
of history," Jesus mysteriously brings salvation to the world.

What is odd here, however, is that Frei makes no narrative connection between Jesus' ministry and this "transition to powerlessness,"
between Jesus' ministry and his crucifixion and resurrection. It is as if
in the final section of the story Jesus leaves behind his activity of witnessing to and embodying the reign of God. In particular, what Frei
fails to note is the way in which Jesus' refusal to take the military option,

---

78. Frei, *Identity*, 110.
79. Frei, *Identity*, 112-14.
80. Frei, *Identity*, 133-36.
81. Frei, *Identity*, 104.

his decision for "powerlessness" in the face of the hostile forces of history, is in fact his most profound challenge to those forces and his most crucial witness to and embodiment of God's reign. Frei does suggest this possibility. According to Frei, through the resurrection God vindicates Jesus' way in the world; the connection between Jesus and God's reign is reestablished, with Jesus now identifying the kingdom rather than vice versa.[82] However, Frei never explores the implications of this "reconnection" between Jesus and God's reign. He never explores the continuity between Jesus' ministry and his crucifixion and resurrection.

Nevertheless, Frei's work does at least suggest the important narrative connection between Jesus' ministry and his Passion. That connection is Jesus' intentional enactment of the way of nonviolent resistance. Jesus' ministry, particularly his preaching and his gathering of a people, offered a nonviolent alternative and challenge to the powers of the world.[83] When those powers sought to destroy Jesus, he did not suddenly undergo a transition from power to powerlessness, but he obediently carried forward his nonviolent witness to and embodiment of God's reign; the "transition" from power to powerlessness is not the result of a change in Jesus' mission, but a consequence of the violent response of the "forces of history." In his intentionally enacted nonviolence, Jesus resists the way of the "*forces* of history." He, in short, *performs* the Sermon on the Mount. Moreover, in his refusal to "fight them on their own terms," Jesus both exposes and defeats the powers.[84] And in the resurrection God confirms Jesus' nonviolent way as the way of the kingdom.

In terms of the "pattern of exchange," Jesus did what was impossible for humanity enslaved to the powers, and he consequently enabled the people of God to participate through baptism in the freedom from those powers.[85] Although Jesus accomplished this salvific act "once and for all," the church is now called to embody "at a distance"

---

82. Frei, *Identity,* 136.

83. On the centrality of nonviolence in Jesus' mission of gathering a people as a "contrast society," see Gerhard Lohfink, *Jesus and Community,* trans. John P. Galvin (Philadelphia: Fortress Press, 1984), 124, 173.

84. Yoder, 147-50.

85. For a narrative interpretation of baptism as the "inception of resurrection morality," see McClendon, *Ethics,* 255-59.

this pattern in its life in and for the world. As Frei argues, just as Jesus' identity was centered in a "moral action," so now the clue to our relationship to Jesus lies not in a "profound self-grasp," but in moral obedience patterned after that of Jesus.[86] At the center of that "moral obedience" is the church's nonviolent resistance to the powers of the world.

As a form of discipleship shaped by the identity of Jesus Christ, preaching is not primarily storytelling or narrative artistry, but rather an act of moral obedience. Like Jesus, who embodied the reign of God and challenged the powers of the world, but refused to use violence or coercion in that effort, so the preacher, always at a distance, is engaged in this same nonviolent resistance to the powers in his or her preaching. Not only is the preacher's *message* shaped by the story of Jesus, as I have argued in the earlier parts of this chapter, but the very *act* of preaching itself is a performance of Scripture, an embodiment of God's reign after the pattern of Jesus. The preacher witnesses boldly, announcing the coming of God's reign in Jesus Christ and challenging the powers of the world that oppose God's way. Indeed, the preacher may seem assertive, even pushy at times; for Christian preaching is not a form of passivity, but an active engagement with the powers. Such preaching may even create conflict, not only with the "forces of history" outside the church, but even among persons within the church, who in many instances are as much beneficiaries as victims of the "powers that be."

As disciples of Jesus, however, faithful preachers not only reject passivity, but also refuse to coerce belief or resort to violent domination, even in the face of conflict, disbelief, and rejection.[87] Preachers accept a strange kind of powerlessness, which finally relies on God to make effective not only individual sermons, but the very practice of preaching itself; like the Word made flesh, the preacher's words must be "redeemed by God" to be effective. Nevertheless, precisely through that powerlessness, preachers resist and challenge the way of the "forces of history" — the way of domination, coercion, and violence.

Faithful preaching thus enacts on behalf of the entire church an interpretive performance of the story of Jesus. In the practice of preach-

---

86. Frei, *Identity,* 108.

87. In *Engaging the Powers* Wink argues that Jesus' "third way" involves neither passivity nor violence, but rather nonviolent resistance to the powers. See pp. 175-93.

ing, the preacher enacts the way of Jesus in the world — the way of nonviolent engagement with the powers. Apart from all words spoken, the practice itself proclaims that the church does not resort to violence in the name of truth, but rather witnesses.[88] At the very point at which the church seeks to speak truth, the church also enacts its refusal to coerce belief. Indeed, in the act of witnessing to Jesus, the church is reminded that a resort to violence would be a contradiction of the One who is preached. In moral obedience shaped by the pattern of Jesus, the preaching of the church takes the path of nonviolence, rather than coercion or domination, in the face of those who resist God's reign. In this way the practice of preaching both constitutes the people of God as a people of nonviolence and calls the church to be such a people. As a performance of Scripture, preaching helps to form the church's life after the pattern of Jesus' identity; it seeks to "build up" the church to enact publicly the way of peace in and for the world.

Preaching is thus an odd thing in a world in which people seek to get their way and impose their truths through violent means. And this oddness should not be overlooked; it is part and parcel of preaching as a performance of the story of Jesus. Preaching is a strange, risky way for the church to spread the gospel and nurture people in the way of Jesus; it is a countercultural practice in a world in which attempts to control and manipulate the future through violence often rule the day. But preaching is odd because it participates in the odd way of Jesus in the midst of a violent world.

I am not claiming that preachers are always nonviolent. Preaching can and often does participate in the world's structures of domination. The church is not yet free from the powers, and preachers often succumb to uses of language and authority that partake of violence.[89] However, as a

88. Stanley Hauerwas, "The Church as God's New Language," in *Christian Existence Today* (Durham, North Carolina: Labyrinth Press, 1988), 53, 64 n. 17.

89. Narrative homileticians have also called preaching beyond coercive forms. Fred Craddock, in particular, has emphasized this point. In addition, the emphasis of narrative preaching on the participation of the hearers points in this direction. Nevertheless, narrative itself is certainly no guarantee against violence. As Wayne Booth has argued, all narratives seek to persuade and are thus as susceptible to violent kinds of manipulation as any other form. See Wayne Booth, *The Rhetoric of Fiction* (Chicago: Univ. of Chicago Press, 1961). A straightforward, direct argument can be less violent or manipulative than stories that yank people all over the place emotionally. In addition, much of the emphasis on noncoercive preaching among contemporary homileticians draws not on the non-

performance of the story of Jesus, the practice of preaching continually calls both the preacher and the church to follow the pattern of Jesus' nonviolent resistance to the powers. The practice of preaching itself challenges the use of the pulpit in the service of violence or domination; it morally constrains the uses to which Scripture may be put in the church. And this fact has important implications for the actual practice of preaching.

Most basically, faithful preaching will resist using the pulpit to support violent solutions to problems, particularly the violent solution of war — something many preachers have unfortunately forgotten from the Crusades to the Gulf War. The support of warfare from the pulpit stands in fundamental contradiction to the practice of preaching as an enactment of the story of Jesus. Similarly, this understanding of preaching challenges sermons that support or aid the kinds of systemic violence — for example, racism — that participate in the structures of domination. Christian preaching, patterned after the story of Jesus, stands with the victims against the powers.

This understanding of preaching also invites preachers to examine their use of language. Part of the preacher's resistance to the powers is resistance to certain kinds of speech. Michael Warren, for example, has explored the way certain images serve as lenses through which we view the world; and he has suggested that the image of domination and subordination has become a comprehensive metaphor through which many in our society see the world.[90] This image tends to break personal and social reality into the basic categories of superior and inferior. Moreover, this basic image finds expression in popular speech, in which "certain individuals are named 'losers' and others 'winners.' Winners are those who successfully dominate; they are the ones on top."[91] Consider the simple word "one," Warren suggests, in two very different celebrations:

---

violence of the gospel, which dares to speak truth and challenge the powers, but rather on a kind of pallid liberalism, which is intent on making no daring claims in order to respect each person's right to think what he or she wants. On the relationship between peacemaking, truth telling, conflict, and forgiveness, see Stanley Hauerwas, "Peacemaking: The Virtue of the Church," in *Christian Existence Today: Essays on Church, World, and Living in Between* (Durham, North Carolina: Labyrinth Press, 1988), 89-97.

90. Michael Warren, "Culture, Counterculture, and the Word," *Liturgy* 6 (Summer 1986): 90.

91. Warren, 90.

In sports, the word "one" usually means number one, the victors, those who have dominated their inferiors. The winners of a contest prance around and shout ecstatically, "We're number one!" In the eucharistic liturgy, however, the word "one" signifies the human unity of those joined by the Spirit of Jesus. Here "one" means communion and unity.[92]

As an enactment of the story of Jesus, Christian preaching calls for a counter-imagery, a counter-speech, which both resists and challenges the cultural imagery of domination and subordination.

Moreover, this understanding of preaching directs preachers beyond matters of hermeneutical method and homiletical technique. In this kind of preaching the character of the preacher becomes important, for one cannot preach nonviolently without developing the virtues, habits, and disciplines of nonviolence in one's own life. No mere technique is adequate for such preaching. Rather, the story of Jesus invites preachers to discern the violence in their own lives and to participate in communities within which the skills of peaceableness are practiced and learned.

Some of the disciplines of peaceableness may be simple; they may seem almost trivial. However, it is within the small, daily, "trivial" activities of our lives that peaceable characters are formed.[93] As Stanley Hauerwas has written,

> . . . learning the discipline to wait, to be at rest with ourselves, to take the time to be a friend and to be loved, are all . . . practices that are meant to free us from the normalcy of the world. Through them we are slowly recalled from the world of violence that we might envisage how interesting a people at peace might be.[94]

Other disciplines may be more dramatic, including even the practices of those communities engaged in the tactics of nonviolent political resistance.

In significant ways, then, Frei's reading of the gospel narratives

---

92. Warren, 90.

93. See Stanley Hauerwas, "Taking Time for Peace: The Ethical Significance of the Trivial," in *Christian Existence Today*, 253-66.

94. Stanley Hauerwas, *The Peaceable Kingdom* (Notre Dame: Univ. of Notre Dame Press, 1983), 150.

takes homiletics beyond Jesus as a model preacher and contributes to a broad understanding of the discipleship of preaching in the church. Frei's shift from parables to gospels and from plot to character has significant implications not only for the practice of preaching, but also for the life of the church. As a performance of Scripture, the church's preaching not only embodies a practice of nonviolent resistance to the powers, but also calls the church that is constituted by the Word to enact this same resistance in its life in and for the world. The story of Jesus not only shapes the content and form of the sermon, but also directs preachers to the larger life of the community of faith of which preaching is a part.

Chapter Nine

Building Up the Church

In Chapter Five I discussed the individualistic orientation of the contemporary homiletical emphasis on experiential events. Contrary to this general tendency, Frei's cultural-linguistic model of Christianity moves preaching in a more communal direction. Guided by Frei's work, the preacher's task must be seen not as that of creating experiential events for individual hearers, but rather as that of building up the church. In "grammatical" terms, one might say that God in Jesus Christ is not primarily the predicate of individual human needs or experience, but rather the active subject who gathers and builds up the eschatological people of God in and for the world.[1] Within the context of Frei's postliberal theology, this grammar governs the peculiar speech of preaching.[2] The function of preaching is not that of locating individual human needs and then offering God as an answer or solution to them — the issue in liberal, problem-solution preaching (including some of

---

1. For a discussion of Jesus' gathering of the eschatological people, see Gerhard Lohfink, *Jesus and Community,* trans. John P. Galvin (Philadelphia: Fortress Press, 1984), 7-74. In using the phrase "the church in and for the world," I mean to dispel any suggestion that "building up the church" involves a kind of narcissistic ecclesiastical navel gazing. Participating in Jesus Christ and shaped by the pattern of his life, death, and resurrection, the church lives in service to the world for which Jesus died. However, central to that service is the church's life as a distinctive people, a "contrast-society."

2. I have borrowed the phrase "peculiar speech" from William H. Willimon, *Peculiar Speech: Preaching to the Baptized* (Grand Rapids, Michigan: Wm. B. Eerdmans Publishing Co., 1992). Frei also uses this phrase in his discussion of the opening paragraph of Barth's *Church Dogmatics* (Hans W. Frei, *Types of Christian Theology,* ed. George Hunsinger and William C. Placher [New Haven: Yale Univ. Press, 1992], 78-79).

its newer narrative and inductive forms). Rather, the sermon moves from the identity of Jesus Christ to the "upbuilding" of the church.[3]

Before delineating the ways in which Frei's work moves homiletics in this communal direction and suggesting some of the concrete implications for preaching, I need to clarify my choice of the image "building up," which I am intentionally using instead of the more popular term, "formation." "Building up" *(oikodomein/oikodomē)* is an important image in the biblical idiom; it is part of the peculiar speech the church needs to learn to speak. Because of its communal, messianic, eschatological, and apocalyptic dimensions, *oikodomein* is not translated very well into the more domesticated term, "formation."

Although it is not my purpose to provide a complete exegetical study of *oikodomein*, a general look at some characteristics of the use of the word in Scripture may be helpful.[4] The Old Testament roots of the image go back to the prophets, particularly Jeremiah, and emphasize the building up of the people of Israel, usually within an eschatological context.[5] The image is often used in parallel to the image of planting and in contrast with that of tearing down or pulling up.

In the gospels, which draw on this Old Testament background, the image is thoroughly communal and takes on strong messianic and eschatological dimensions. *Oikodomein* is an eschatological act of the

---

3. The issue here is a critical one, reflecting the difference between a modern and a postmodern approach to preaching. Preaching focused on individual experiential events, in which the primary function is the eventful transformation of individuals, still operates within a basically modern, not to mention liberal, American framework. My account operates from a fundamentally different assumption: the community is logically prior to the individual, and the individual exists only within the context of relationships and roles played in a particular community. This understanding of preaching does not ignore the individual, but rather views the individual within the context of a faithful community. In fact, this approach does not even ignore the needs of individuals. Rather, it assumes that the fundamental need of persons is to be faithful disciples in a truthful community; and it assumes that this is the reason people are listening to sermons in the first place.

4. My discussion is based mainly on Otto Michel, *"oikodomeō,"* in Gerhard Friedrich, ed., *Theological Dictionary of the New Testament,* vol. 5, trans. Geoffrey Bromiley (Grand Rapids, Michigan: Wm. B. Eerdmans Publishing Co., 1967), 136-44. See also Lohfink, 99-106. My discussion takes the form of a "word study" approach to Scripture, which can be helpful, but is in itself inadequate. I will return to the image of "building up" later in this chapter when I discuss communal practices; a full understanding of "building up" is inseparable from its social embodiment in the community of faith.

5. Jeremiah 1:10; 12:14-17; 24:5-7; 31:27-28; Amos 9:11.

Messiah, who will build up the future temple and the new community.[6] The stress is on the activity of the Messiah, with some tension between the final building up at the time of the *parousia* and the present building up through the eschatological power of the resurrection. This tension is the eschatological tension between the "already" and the "not yet."

In Acts the image takes on a strong "ecclesiastical ring" and is used somewhat differently from the synoptics. The messianic emphasis is not as strong; God, rather than the Messiah, does the building; and the image of the "heavenly building" is not central. Nevertheless, the communal and eschatological dimensions remain. "The subject is God and the object is Israel or the community. The reference is to a fellowship. The totality grows and is built up with a spiritual and eschatological reference."[7]

The image really comes to the fore in the Pauline literature, where it not only serves as an image for Paul's apostolic activity, which involves establishing and building up the community, but also is highlighted as a task of the entire church.[8] The gifts of the Spirit are given for the upbuilding of the church, and the image is used particularly with reference to preaching and exhortation.[9] This "building up" is "the content and purpose of the [church's] liturgical life and its meetings."[10] Here the tensive character of *oikodomein* is evident. "Building up" is not only the work of God through the power of the resurrection and the activity of the Spirit, but also the task of the community of faith through the gifts of the Spirit. Another frequent translation is "edification," but this term, because of its associations with individual spiritual growth, also fails to capture very well the eschatological and communal dimensions of *oikodomein*.[11] While the

6. Mark 14:58; Matthew 16:18.

7. Michel, 139. See, e.g., Acts 9:31; 15:16; 20:32. One could also cite the eschatological work of the Spirit in gathering and building up the community of faith. Michel cites Acts 2 as a parallel to the power of resurrection in building up the community (Michel, 139). See also Lohfink, 81-82. This understanding of the relationship between the risen Christ and the Spirit is precisely the relationship that Frei seeks to capture in his work.

8. For references to "building up" as an image of Paul's apostolic activity, see 2 Corinthians 10:8; 12:19; 13:10; with reference to the entire community, see 1 Corinthians 14; 1 Thessalonians 5:11.

9. 1 Corinthians 14; 3:10-15; 8:1; 10:23; 14:3-4; 1 Thessalonians 5:11.

10. Michel, 141.

11. Lohfink, 102.

object of this building up includes the individual, its purpose is the incorporation of that individual brother or sister into the life of the community.[12]

Recently, a growing body of literature dealing with the ecclesial "household" (oikos/oikia) has highlighted the social, economic, and political dimensions of the community of faith.[13] The upbuilding of the church thus should not be considered simply a spiritual matter, but rather involves the building up of a concrete, publicly enacted society — a genuinely political community, or polis.[14]

My use of "building up" thus seeks to capture the richness of preaching in an eschatological, communal context, which is precisely the context in which preaching takes place among the baptized people of God gathered for worship on the Lord's Day. In addition, my use of "building up" serves as a reminder of the richness and distinctiveness of the biblical idiom, which is not easily translated into contemporary terminology. "Building up" is an image that finds its proper use not in the language of American culture, but in the particular story of God's active creation of a people — past, present, and future. Engaging in this "building up" is one of the primary ways the church participates in and carries forward that story.

In addition, the image of "building up" helps to clarify the practice of preaching at its most basic level. Preaching is basically a "practice of constituting a people." As MacIntyre writes, ". . . the creation and sustaining of human communities — of households, cities, nations — is generally taken to be a practice in the sense in which I have defined it."[15] Approaching preaching as this kind of communal practice will go

---

12. As Lohfink demonstrates, the communal dimension of the image is made abundantly clear through its close association with the pronoun "one another" (allēlōn) (Lohfink, 99-106). One of the most well known passages using this image is the baptismal text in 1 Peter 2:5, in which the new community is described as the eschatological oikos of God. For a more thorough discussion of this image, see John H. Elliott, A Home for the Homeless: A Sociological Exegesis of I Peter, Its Situation and Strategy (Philadelphia: Fortress Press, 1981).

13. Along with Lohfink, see, e.g., Michael H. Crosby, House of Disciples: Church, Economics, and Justice in Matthew (Maryknoll, New York: Orbis Books, 1988); Elliott.

14. I am using "political" here in a broad sense to refer to the "polity" or "social practices" of a particular community of people. Such distinctive, alternative political practices are essential to the church as a "contrast-society."

15. Alasdair MacIntyre, After Virtue, 2nd ed. (Notre Dame, Indiana: Univ. of Notre

a long way toward reshaping homiletical theory and Sunday-morning sermons.[16]

Moreover, Frei suggests that this upbuilding of the church is the central function of preaching. As I noted in Chapter Two, in *The Identity of Jesus Christ* Frei moves immediately from his rendering of the identity of Jesus to a discussion of the publicly enacted identity of the church. Jesus' presence and action in the world, which is the presence and action of God, is indirectly embodied in the church through the presence and action of the Spirit. The church is now the spatial and temporal basis of the presence of Jesus in the world.[17] The church, that is, embodies Jesus' indirect presence in and for the world. Or, as Frei thinks is better, "the church is simply the witness to the fact that it is Jesus Christ and none other who is the ultimate presence in and to the world. . . ."[18] In Frei's thought there is an integral, narratively rendered relationship between Jesus and the church.[19]

Dame Press, 1984), 187-88. MacIntyre's now classic definition of a "practice" shapes my use of the term: "By a practice I am going to mean any coherent and complex form of socially established cooperative human activity through which goods internal to that form of activity are realized in the course of trying to achieve those standards of excellence which are appropriate to, and partially definitive of, that form of activity, with the result that human powers to achieve excellence, and human conceptions of the ends and goods involved, are systematically extended" (MacIntyre, *After Virtue,* 187).

16. If Jesus were viewed as a "model preacher," this approach would look to the Sermon on the Mount, rather than the parables, as the key example of Jesus' preaching. As Hauerwas has written of the Sermon on the Mount, "the sermon is the constitution of God's kingdom people for their journey between the ages." Stanley Hauerwas, "Living the Proclaimed Reign of God: A Sermon on the Sermon on the Mount," *Interpretation* 47 (April 1993): 155. However, as Hauerwas notes, the Sermon on the Mount itself prevents one from making Jesus simply a model preacher, for the sermon depends on Jesus' personal enactment of it as the one who challenged the powers and inaugurated the reign of God in his life, death, and resurrection, apart from which the church cannot be constituted as an eschatological people. Apart from the enacted identity of Jesus Christ, the Sermon on the Mount makes no sense.

17. Hans W. Frei, *The Identity of Jesus Christ: The Hermeneutical Bases of Dogmatic Theology* (Philadelphia: Fortress Press, 1975), 157-58.

18. Frei, *Identity,* 158-59. The indirectness of this presence serves as a constant reminder that the church remains a "frail human instrument," not to be identified with Jesus or the reign of God. The church always follows Jesus "at a distance."

19. Frei, *Identity,* 160. The narratively rendered connection between Israel, Jesus, and the church is the source of Frei's use of typology or figural interpretation, which I will discuss more fully below.

Richard Hays has nicely captured the substance of Frei's thought at this point. In the "final sequence" of the story, Hays writes, the Christian community becomes the subject of the narrative, not imitating Jesus' action, which was once and for all, but embodying "in him" the pattern of his story in the world until the not-yet-visible consummation.[20] Similarly, Stanley Hauerwas has written,

> To be sure, like Israel, the church has a story to tell in which God is the main character. But the church cannot tell that story without becoming part of the tale. The church as witness to God's work for us in Israel and Jesus of Nazareth means that here the teller and the tale are one. For this is not just another possible story about the way the world is, it is the story of the world as created and redeemed by God. That story, the story of the world, cannot be told rightly unless it includes the story of the church as God's creation to heal our separateness.[21]

This intimate, narratively rendered relationship between the identity of Jesus and the church can be seen in the way Frei applies the same categories of identity description to the church that he uses in his identity description of Jesus. The church's identity is derived from Jesus' identity and is enacted publicly in the world as Jesus' was. Although Frei does make two important distinctions between Jesus and the church, each of these distinctions actually serves to emphasize the inseparable relationship between the two and to highlight Frei's move from Jesus to the community of faith. First, the church must be a follower, rather than a complete reiteration of Jesus.[22] Jesus has enacted the good of all people on their behalf once and for all; the church has no need to play the role of Christ figure. Rather, the church is called to be a "collective disciple," to "follow at a distance" the pattern of Christ's intentional

---

20. Richard Hays, *The Faith of Jesus Christ*, Society of Biblical Literature Dissertation Series 56 (Chico, California: Scholars Press, 1983), 260-63. Because the church is the subject of the story only "in Christ," there is a "complex overlay of two Subjects": "The Spirit given as our Helper effects a mysterious personal union with Christ. Thus the story does not simply shift from Christ as Subject in one sequence to humanity as Subject in the next. Instead, there is a complex overlay of two Subjects. . . ." (Hays, *Faith*, 262-63).

21. Stanley Hauerwas, "The Church as God's New Language," in *Christian Existence Today* (Durham, North Carolina: Labyrinth Press, 1988), 53-54.

22. Frei, *Identity*, 160.

action that is narrated in the gospels. Second, the church's intention-action pattern differs from that of Jesus because the church's story is not yet finished.[23]

Frei thus moves in *Identity* from the narratively rendered identity of Jesus to the church, which is the embodiment of and witness to Jesus' indirect presence in and for the world. Frei does not move to the private, affective life of individuals; indeed, he says almost nothing about individuals. Nor does Frei turn to general human experience as the key correlate of the gospel message. Nor, except through the church's relation to humanity as a whole, does he move to society at large. Rather, Frei moves from the narratively rendered identity of Jesus Christ to the publicly enacted "collective discipleship" of the church. The church, as the embodiment of the indirect presence of Jesus Christ in and for the world, becomes a central character in the ongoing story of Jesus. Further, according to Frei, Word and sacrament "constitute" the church; they provide the temporal and spatial basis for Christ's indirect presence and for the church's ongoing role as a publicly enacted character in the story.[24]

Homiletically, Frei's move is crucially important. Grammatically, God in Jesus Christ is not simply the predicate of individual human experience or needs, but is an active subject building up a people to embody and witness to Jesus' presence in and for the world. Stanley Hauerwas has noted the soteriological implications of this grammar: "Salvation cannot be limited to changed self-understanding or to insuring meaningful existence for the individual. Salvation is God's creation of a new society which invites each person to become part of a time that the nations cannot provide."[25] Similarly, Richard Hays has summed up the ethical implications of this position:

> The church is a counter-cultural community of discipleship and this community is the primary addressee of God's imperatives. The biblical story focuses on God's design for forming a covenant *people.* Thus the primary sphere of moral concern is not the character of the individual but the corporate obedience of the church.[26]

23. Frei, *Identity,* 160.
24. Frei, *Identity,* 159.
25. Hauerwas, "The Church as God's New Language," 48.
26. Richard B. Hays, "Scripture-Shaped Community: The Problem of Method in New Testament Ethics," *Interpretation* 44 (January 1990): 47.

In short, as David Steinmetz has written, "The church and not human experience as such is the middle term between the Christian interpreter and the biblical text."[27]

Frei's work thus directs preaching beyond individual, experiential events to the building up of the church as a people who embody and witness to Jesus Christ's indirect "presence" and thereby God's reign in the world. This orientation is further emphasized and clarified in Frei's turn to a cultural-linguistic model of Christianity in his later work. The communal orientation of this cultural-linguistic model has been clearly stated by Wayne Meeks, whose influence on Frei I have noted in previous chapters:

> The goal of a theological hermeneutics on the cultural-linguistic model is not belief in objectively true propositions taught by the text nor the adoption by individuals of an authentic self-understanding evoked by the text's symbols, but the formation of a community whose forms of life correspond to the symbolic universe rendered or signaled by the text.[28]

In this regard Walter Brueggemann has written that preaching helps to provide an "infrastructure" for the corporate life of the community.

> I use the term "infrastructure" to refer to the system or network of signs and gestures that make social relationships possible, significant, and effective. The social infrastructure is the almost invisible system of connections that gives life functioning power and provides connections and support systems. I take it that the most elemental human infrastructure is a network of stories, sacraments, and signs that give a certain nuance, shape, and possibility to human interaction. An evangelical infrastructure is one that mediates and operates in ways that heal, redeem, and transform.[29]

27. David C. Steinmetz, "Theology and Exegesis: Ten Theses," in *A Contemporary Guide to Hermeneutics*, ed. Donald McKim (Grand Rapids, Michigan: Wm. B. Eerdmans Publishing Co., 1987), 27.

28. Wayne Meeks, "A Hermeneutics of Social Embodiment," *Harvard Theological Review* 79 (January, April, July, 1986): 184-85.

29. Walter Brueggemann, *Texts under Negotiation: The Bible and Postmodern Imagination* (Minneapolis: Fortress Press, 1993), 27. In his book *Homiletic: Moves and Structures* (Philadelphia: Fortress Press, 1987), David Buttrick also emphasizes the role of preaching in communal formation. However, his emphasis is on a rather esoteric and

Within Frei's cultural-linguistic model of Christianity, this communal function of helping to "build up" a distinctive "infrastructure" within the church becomes fundamental to preaching — and leads to a quite different understanding of preaching from that which focuses on private, individual, experiential events.[30]

The implications of this different understanding of preaching may be seen by looking at a couple of concrete ways in which this communal approach can inform the actual practice of preaching. One concrete way this "upbuilding" can take place through preaching is when the preacher redescribes theologically the common practices of the church, usually in contrast to the descriptions offered by the culture. For example, American culture would describe the welcoming of a new member into the church through baptism as the addition of an individual to a voluntary institution, which is a collection of individuals. In contrast to this description, the preacher's task is to redescribe the practice of baptism as an episode in the ongoing story of God's active gathering and building up of an eschatological people who carry forward Jesus' story in and for the world. Such repeated redescriptive use of the church's peculiar speech is vitally important for building up "a visible people who have listened to a different story from that of the world."[31]

Moreover, only as the church is built up in this way will believers begin to see the character of the world in a truthful light. Only in relation to the church can the world be known as world, as a realm that is

---

ethereal thing he calls "communal consciousness." Buttrick does not sufficiently emphasize the political, enacted dimension of the community. Brueggemann's "infrastructure" offers a better description in this regard, not the least because it fits very nicely with *oikodomein.*

30. Part of this "infrastructure" is, of course, the biblical story that is retold in preaching and gives the community its identity, memory, and hope. This role of the biblical story in forming community is mentioned by many writers, but none has spelled out how preaching functions in this regard, other than by creating experiential events for individual hearers. I am not dwelling at this point on the rather obvious assertion that the community is formed by the biblical story. I am rather trying to focus on other dimensions, which nevertheless presuppose this basic assumption.

31. Stanley Hauerwas and William Willimon, "Embarrassed by the Church: Congregations and the Seminary," *The Christian Century* (Feb. 5-12, 1986): 120. Hauerwas and Willimon provide other concrete examples of this kind of redescription related to such "common" activities as reroofing a building and having a communal meal after worship on Sunday.

disobedient to God.[32] For example, only as the Eucharist becomes a meal where barriers are broken down between races, classes, and genders will Christians see the world clearly as a place of domination where, in opposition to the way of Jesus, these barriers distort and corrupt human relationships. In this way the redescription of the church's practices inevitably includes a redescription of the world and shapes the church's service and resistance to the world.

Another concrete implication of this communal approach can also be noted. It consists quite simply of letting the church be the "middle term" as the preacher moves from text to sermon. Rather than asking how texts connect with predetermined individual needs or how they connect with "general human experience" or how they are relevant to American society, preachers should quite consciously ask what the Spirit is saying to the *church* through the church's Scripture.[33] The focus is not simply on what a text "means" but on how a particular passage of Scripture functions to "build up" the people of God in and for the world. The movement, again, is from the narratively rendered identity of God in Jesus Christ to the identity of the church as a character in that ongoing story.

This approach may sound rather simple, but it is foreign to many preachers in an individualistic, liberal society. Most of the sermons I hear focus either on the needs of individuals in the congregation or on issues in American society. This twofold movement is typical of American liberalism, reflecting a story that divides life into the "private" and the "public," with no room for the church (and with Christianity in-

---

32. Hauerwas, "Church as God's New Language," 53-54.

33. Richard Lischer gives some typical examples of what happens when the church is lost as the middle term in interpretation: "Thus the prodigal son was as callow as your typical 17-year old spoiled brat. The disciples in the boat with Jesus were as anxious as any person thrown into the 'storm' of a personal crisis. The early workers in the vineyard were angry, just as I am when a lazy student receives a better grade than mine. The cleansing of the temple reminds me that it's ok to vent my anger at unjust institutions. Jesus' temptations are like our craving for personal possessions in our wilderness of materialism. And so on. The New Testament texts are brimming with ecclesial and eschatological clues to their interpretation, but the symbols and allusions that have enriched the church for centuries and, indeed, seemed so clear in New Testament class, simply do not find a voice in our preaching" (Richard Lischer, *A Theology of Preaching: The Dynamics of the Gospel*, rev. ed. [Durham, North Carolina: Labyrinth Press, 1992], 87).

creasingly relegated to the private realm because of its lack of influence on the public). In ethical terms, such liberal preaching moves between an "ethics of interiority" and an "ethics of society."[34] In contrast, the move to the church is radically different, placing both preacher and congregation in a different story from that of American liberalism. Learning to ask the "hermeneutical question" in this communal way is another crucial element in a "hermeneutic of suspicion," which preachers need to remember in a liberal, individualistic society.[35] Such communal interpretation provides one concrete means of building up the church as an alternative community.

Frei thus directs preaching beyond individual experiential events to the upbuilding of the church. Other aspects of Frei's work help to flesh out this communal emphasis, particularly his cultural-linguistic focus on the language and practices of Christian communities and his emphasis on the figural interpretation of Scripture.

Preaching as Linguistic Improvisation

Within Frei's cultural-linguistic model of Christianity, the key to being a Christian is neither a set of cognitive propositional truths nor an individual religious experience. Rather, the key is the language and practices of the Christian community, which are understood as a set of skills to be learned. Coming to be a Christian involves the acquisition of particular skills, which are behavioral and dispositional as well as linguistic and conceptual.[36] As Frei writes, "To learn the language of the Christian community is not to undergo a profound 'experience' of a privileged sort, but to make that language one's own, in faith, hope, and love."[37] Only within this framework of language

34. James William McClendon, *Systematic Theology: Ethics* (Nashville: Abingdon Press, 1986), 210.

35. Later in this chapter I will discuss the way Frei suggests making this move through the use of figural interpretation. I am not suggesting here that preaching never deals with individuals or society. It certainly does and must, though usually the individual will be addressed as a part of the church and society will be addressed in relation to the church's presence in and for the world.

36. Frei, *Types*, 4.

37. Frei, *Types*, 54.

and practices are certain experiences even possible and certain cognitive propositions even discussable.[38]

Within a postliberal, cultural-linguistic model, then, faith is not
primarily an individual, existential, experiential event, but rather a journey into the language and practices of a particular community. People
enter this distinctive community through the practice of baptism, which
inaugurates their journey into the language and practices of the church.
And on the Lord's day the people of God are gathered as this distinctive
community in a peculiar time — the eschatological day of resurrection
and new creation.[39] Within Frei's postliberal theology, this distinctive
cultural-linguistic community becomes crucial to the Christian faith —
and to preaching.

Within this model, preaching does not seek primarily to present
cognitive propositions; here a postliberal homiletic accepts the criticism
of cognitive-propositional preaching that has been developed by contemporary narrative homileticians. However, unlike much of contemporary homiletics, the postliberal alternative also does not emphasize
the individual experiential event. Rather, the focus is on learning the
distinctive language and practices — the infrastructure — of the Christian community, which then make certain ideas and experiences
possible.

The difference between a postliberal homiletic and one focused
on the individual experiential event can be seen clearly in the emphasis
on language *use* in the cultural-linguistic model. As George Lindbeck
has noted, within a cultural-linguistic model, language is not understood primarily as a collection of symbols that are expressive or evocative of private, affective experience. Rather, language is fundamentally
a public instance of communally ruled behavior.[40] As Murphy and
McClendon have argued, this "postmodern" understanding of language
focuses not on its representational or expressive dimensions, but on the
public, communal *use* of language:

38. Frei, *Types*, 74.
39. On the meaning of the Lord's Day, see H. B. Porter, *The Day of Light: The
Biblical and Liturgical Meaning of Sunday* (Greenwich, Connecticut: Seabury Press, 1960;
reprint, Washington, D.C.: The Pastoral Press, 1987).
40. George Lindbeck, "Ebeling: Climax of a Great Tradition," *Journal of Religion*
61 (1981): 313.

How may we use the word "God," and how does this use restrain or shape ideas about God and even our experience of God? Putting it in an oversimplified form, whereas for classical Greek thought, *ideas* determined both reality and language, and for moderns, at least with the rise of empiricism, *experience* determined ideas, which determined language, in postmodern thought the tables are turned and *language* makes possible both ideas and experience.[41]

This language use is shaped by the beliefs, institutions, and practices of the community, as Alasdair MacIntyre has demonstrated:

> The conception of language . . . is that of a language as it is used in and by a particular community living at a particular time and place with particular shared beliefs, institutions, and practices. These beliefs, institutions, and practices will be furnished expression and embodiment in a variety of linguistic expressions and idioms; the language will provide standard uses for a necessary range of expressions and idioms, the use of which will presuppose commitment to those same beliefs, institutions, and practices. . . . Moreover, the learning of the language and the acquisition of cultural understanding are not two independent activities.[42]

Within the cultural-linguistic view of language, learning a community's "peculiar speech" and being initiated into that community's traditions, beliefs, and practices are one and the same initiation.[43]

When language is thus understood as a public, communal instance of ruled behavior, rather than as a collection of evocative and expressive symbols, the implications for preaching are significant. In general, the purpose of preaching becomes not to explain the meaning (much less prove the "truth") of the Christian gospel in terms of cognitive propositions. Nor does preaching seek primarily to create an existential, experiential event for individual hearers (though there is nothing to prevent this from happening from time to time). Rather, preaching models the use of Christian language and thereby plays a role in nurturing believers in that

41. Nancey Murphy and James William McClendon, "Distinguishing Modern and Postmodern Theologies," *Modern Theology* 5 (April 1989): 202-3.

42. Alasdair MacIntyre, *Whose Justice? Which Rationality?* (Notre Dame, Indiana: Univ. of Notre Dame Press, 1988), 373-74.

43. MacIntyre, *Whose Justice?* 382.

language usage. Sermons become a means through which the Christian community enters more deeply into its own distinctive speech, so that Christian ideas, beliefs, and experience become possible. Preaching seeks to recreate a universe of discourse and put the community in the middle of that world — instructing the hearers in the use of the language by showing them how to use it.[44] As Frei remarked to George Lindbeck in response to Lindbeck's concern about the issue of truth in *The Nature of Doctrine*, "Go on, George, show people how to use Christian language properly and that will take care of the question of truth."[45] Within a cultural-linguistic model, this "showing how to use" becomes one of the fundamental purposes of preaching, as Stanley Hauerwas has concisely noted: ". . . the sermon [is] the communal action whereby Christians are formed to use their language rightly."[46]

At the heart of learning this distinctive language is the ability to "go on," as Wittgenstein puts it, the ability to use the language innovatively in all its richness in new situations and contexts.[47] Alasdair MacIntyre has also described this dimension of language use very well. Distinguishing between knowing a language and being able to use a foreign-language phrase book, MacIntyre not only clarifies the character of "going on" with a language, but relates that ability to authoritative texts and traditions. A lengthy quotation is warranted here:

> What cannot be learned from the matching of sentence with sentence and of sentence with context, no matter how sophisticated the phrase book writer, is . . . how a grasp of a language-in-use enables a competent language user to move from one kind of use of expression in the context of one sentence to another notably different kind of use of the same expression in the context of another and perhaps then go on to innovate by inventing a third kind of use for that very

44. This is a paraphrase of Frei's description of the work of Karl Barth (Hans W. Frei, "An Afterword: Eberhard Busch's Biography of Karl Barth," in *Karl Barth in Review: Posthumous Works Reviewed and Assessed*, ed. H.-Martin Rumscheidt, Pittsburgh Theological Monograph Series 30 [Pittsburgh: Pickwick Press, 1981], 100).

45. Hans W. Frei, "Epilogue: George Lindbeck and *The Nature of Doctrine*," in *Theology and Dialogue*, ed. Bruce Marshall (Notre Dame, Indiana: Univ. of Notre Dame Press, 1990), 279.

46. Hauerwas, "Church as God's New Language," 60.

47. Ludwig Wittgenstein, *Philosophical Investigations*, 3rd ed., trans. G. E. M. Anscombe (New York: MacMillan Publishing Company, 1989), 56-89.

same expression in yet another sentential context. It is this knowing how to go on and go further which is the badge of elementary linguistic competence. Someone who knows that it is appropriate to assent to "Snow is white" if and when snow is white does not as yet thereby evidence a grasp of "white" in English. Such a grasp would be evidenced by being able to say, for example, "Snow is white and so are the members of the Ku Klux Klan, and white with fear is what they were in snow-covered Arkansas last Friday." That is the kind of thing you cannot learn how to say from phrase books or indeed from any recursively enumerable set of individual English sentences.

Knowing how to go on and go further in the use of the expressions of a language is that part of the ability of every language-user which is poetic. The poet by profession merely has this ability in a preeminent degree. It is in hearing and learning and later in reading spoken and written texts that the young in the type of society with which we are concerned learn the paradigmatic uses of key expressions at the same time and inseparably from their learning the model exemplifications of the virtues, the legitimating genealogies of their community, and its key prescription. Learning its language and being initiated into their community's tradition or traditions is one and the same initiation. When asked in such a society "What is 'x'?" or "What does 'x' mean?" one standard way of answering is to quote a line or two from a poem. So the meanings of key expressions are fixed in part by reference to standard authoritative texts, which also provide the paradigmatic examples used in instructing the same young as to how to extend concepts, to find new uses for established expressions, and to move through and on from that multiplicity of uses, acquaintance with which provides the background for introducing such distinctions as those between the literal and the metaphorical, the joking, the ironic, and the straightforward, and later, when the going becomes theoretical, the analogical, the univocal, and the equivocal. All tradition-informed language-use tends thereby in some measure toward the condition of multiple meanings. . . .[48]

What MacIntyre demonstrates is that "translation" may be appropriate for a few isolated words or phrases, but it is an inadequate way of understanding the use of a language as a whole. One does not "translate"

---

48. MacIntyre, *Whose Justice?* 382-83.

a language-in-use, but rather learns to speak it, something "translation" models of preaching have neglected to consider.

As an exemplary part of the Christian community's language-in-use, preaching should be understood as modeling appropriate Christian speech based primarily on the Scripture that functions as the canon of the church. Preaching models ways of "going on," as the richness and "semantic depth" of the language are developed in new contexts and new situations. The preacher thus needs to be a person who preeminently knows the language of faith and is able to "go on" with it — a consideration that might shift the teaching of preaching away from learning certain methods and techniques to nurturing preachers in the language of the Christian community through immersion in Scripture.

Preaching, in this sense, is something like jazz improvisation. Starting with a basic "text" of music, jazz musicians do not translate that text into a new language, but rather "go on" with the language of the text in new ways for new contexts. Whether improvising rather conservatively on the theme of a piece of music or engaging in a more radical, nonthematic improvisation based on the chord progressions, jazz musicians develop the basic language of the "text" in new ways. Consistent with MacIntyre's description of language, jazz musicians often learn the art of improvisation by immersing themselves in the language and spirit of the tradition and by imitating classic pieces from the tradition. Through such immersion and imitation, jazz musicians are prepared to improvise, or "go on," with the music in new and creative ways. Improvisation is not simply spontaneous, but is the fruit of years of immersion in the "language" of jazz. Not surprisingly, African-American preaching, which improvises with the biblical idiom in such powerful ways, has been closely related to the jazz tradition.[49]

This kind of "going on" with the language of Scripture and tradition is what preaching (and the training of preachers) involves in a cultural-linguistic model. Week after week the preacher uses distinctive Christian speech both paradigmatically and innovatively as an instance of communal, public, ruled behavior within the language game of the worship of the baptized on the Lord's Day. While private, affective "experiential events" may occur from time to time for some members

---

49. For a comprehensive treatment of jazz improvisation, see Paul F. Berliner, *Thinking in Jazz: The Infinite Art of Improvisation*, Chicago Studies in Ethnomusicology (Chicago: Univ. of Chicago Press, 1994).

of the congregation, at a deeper and more significant level people are repeatedly hearing a peculiar speech used to redescribe contemporary life. In the process, preacher and hearers alike are learning how to use this language more richly and faithfully.

Further, learning Christian speech is not simply a conceptual or cognitive activity. Rather, it involves dispositions and behavior as well. Preaching is not just an abstract language, but is embodied in the character of the preacher, the tone and inflections of speech, and the manner of delivery, just as a piece of jazz improvisation is inseparably related to the character and spirit of the musician. As Paul Holmer has written of the language of preaching,

> . . . everyone must learn not simply the words and concepts, the names and places, but he must also acquire the knack, the outlook, the kind of life and spirit, which will give vitality and purpose to [Jesus'] name, His life, and all that goes with them. . . . Sermons are one way, a very important way, too, to teach people both the "what" and the "how."[50]

The crucial role of preaching in a cultural-linguistic model is thus not that of offering cognitive-propositional information, nor that of creating private, affective experiential events for individual hearers. Rather, the crucial role of preaching is the use of Christian speech so that the community may learn to use its language rightly. The focus of preaching is on learning a language, which is not simply a series of discrete existential "events," but a long, slow process of use and growth. In a time when the church is struggling with its identity within a secular society, this postliberal, cultural-linguistic model is a crucial one for the contemporary pulpit to take seriously. In fact, as should have become clear by now, this chapter and the previous one largely consist of suggestions about the appropriate "grammar" of Christian speech in the pulpit.

On the surface this understanding of the language of preaching may sound fairly pedestrian, much less interesting than the rather dramatic notion of preaching as a transformative, individual experiential event. However, this model of preaching does not deny some of the important emphases of the experiential model of preaching. Rather, it simply places these emphases in a larger framework — one that is more in tune with the

---

50. Paul Holmer, "The Logic of Preaching," *Dialog* 4 (Summer 1965): 208.

way preaching actually works week in and week out in the local church. For example, this model does not deny the performative, "eventful" character of homiletical speech. However, it locates the performative role of language at a different place from private, affective individual experience. In a sermon about preaching, Barbara Brown Taylor makes precisely this point: "It is enough to proclaim the Word and to believe that in doing so we change the world whether the world knows it or not — whether we know it or not — simply by standing and speaking the words that have been given to us. . . ."[51] After this comment Taylor simply proceeds to use in a powerful way the peculiar speech of Scripture and tradition:

> You don't need a grand pulpit; any old housetop will do. Even the sun room will do at the nursing home, where you stand by the piano surrounded by wheelchairs full of old people. Some of those old people are dozing, some whimpering, and less than half of them are aware you are there. Say, "Resurrection!" in their presence. Say, "Life everlasting!" Say, "Remember!" Just let those words loose in the room; just utter them in the light, and trust them to do their work.
>
> Speak to a support group for people with AIDS. Worship with them, laying hands on their heads and praying for their healing. Say, "Mercy!" to them. Say, "Comfort!" Say, "Beloved children of God!" Just let those words loose in the room; just utter them and trust in their power to make people whole.[52]

Taylor concludes with an image of the preacher as one who models the use of Christian language for the people of God, so they can go into the world and speak that language themselves: "Here's the plan: God showed Jesus how; Jesus shows us how; we show the whole people of God how; they show the world how."[53]

In her sermon Taylor is obviously not presenting a theory of performative language. She leaves much unsaid. However, this understanding of preaching is no less eventful or performative than an "experiential event." After all, "I now pronounce you husband and wife,"

---

51. Barbara Brown Taylor, "Words We Tremble to Say Aloud," *Preaching Today* Audiotape #91 (Carol Stream, Illinois: *Christianity Today* and *Leadership*, 1991).

52. Taylor.

53. Taylor. As will become clear in what follows, I think Taylor's statement is a bit too one-directional; the relationship between preacher and congregation is more dynamic than she suggests.

the classic example of performative speech, does not depe~~r~~
experience of the couple when the words are spoken. For Taylo~~ι~~ ~~͙~~
is not the experiential event, but language use — the peculiar speech of
the church. And the performative character of that language is not
diluted because it is independent of private, affective experiential events.
Nor does the performative character of the language have to be understood in *ex opere operato* fashion. Rather, Christian speech changes
situations by providing people with a language — a world of discourse
— that may be learned and come to shape the world for them, even if
no "experiential event" initially occurs. Once "resurrection" is spoken,
things cannot be the same again.

In addition, this understanding of the language of preaching does
not deny the transformative power of preaching. Rather, it places transformation in a larger temporal framework. Transformative events do
not happen every week. Rather, people are transformed over time as
they learn the language and participate in the practices of the Christian
community.[54] Walter Brueggemann has stressed this larger temporal
framework of transformation:

> . . . people change by the offer of new models, images, and pictures
> of how the pieces of life fit together — models, images, and pictures
> that characteristically have the particularity of narrative to carry them.
> Transformation is the slow, steady process of inviting each other into
> a counterstory about God, world, neighbor, and self. This slow, steady
> process has as a counterpoint the subversive process of unlearning or
> disengaging from a story we no longer find credible.[55]

Richard Lischer has affirmed a similar understanding of preaching,
arguing for a turn from the image of *event* to that of *journey:*

> As attractive as the *event* is as a metaphor for God's action in the sermon,

---

54. For example, repetition is a crucial part of learning a language. Not surprisingly, however, repetition receives little attention in homiletical positions that emphasize
experiential events; individual creativity and originality rule the day in those theories.

55. Brueggemann, *Texts,* 24. One could also speak here of growing in one's ability
to "go on" with a language or, in Kenneth Surin's terms, of increasing in appreciation
and understanding of the "semantic depth" of the language (Kenneth Surin, "The Weight
of Weakness: Intratextuality and Discipleship," in *The Turnings of Darkness and Light:
Essays in Philosophical and Systematic Theology* [Cambridge: Cambridge Univ. Press,
1989], 219).

it does not deliver the moral and theological formation necessary for God's people in the world. The alternative image of journey or pilgrimage suggests that the sermon does not merely strike the conscience or create an existential experience, but that preaching, as opposed to individual sermons, forms a community of faith over time.[56]

The transformative power of preaching is affirmed in the cultural-linguistic model, but it is located within a larger temporal framework, which is in fact more faithful to the way preaching works in local congregations.[57]

Finally, the participatory involvement of the hearers in the sermon is affirmed in this model in a variety of ways. To begin with, the hearers participate in the sermon through the ongoing conversation of the community of faith, which takes place in numerous ways outside the time of formal preaching. Indeed, as part of this ongoing conversation in the life of the church, the saints in the congregation may be expected regularly to correct and enrich the preacher's speech. In addition, persons who operate at different levels of language use — different abilities to "go on" — will necessarily hear different things in the sermon and be engaged in the sermon in different ways, just as a novice listening to jazz will hear differently from an experienced jazz aficionado. Further, the hard and innovative work of "going on" with the language in specific contexts and situations remains in the lives of the hearers both communally and individually. Preaching as language use within a cultural-linguistic model is not preaching that simply passes on information or spoon-feeds people simplistic answers. Rather, such preaching seeks to build up the church by training people in a skill — the skill of using their language rightly. And that process requires the active engagement and involvement of the hearers both during and beyond the sermons.

Thus, the performative, transformative, participatory character of preaching is retained in a postliberal homiletic. However, these aspects

56. Lischer, 88. For another discussion of the image of journey for preaching, see Charles L. Campbell, "Living Faith: Luther, Ethics, and Preaching," *Word and World* 10 (Fall 1990): 374-79.

57. In the local church people rarely remember individual, sermonic "events." Rather, preaching "does its work" over time, through hundreds of sermons that have an effect at a level beneath conscious knowledge and experience. I am suggesting that this level is that of learning to use a language in a particular cultural-linguistic community.

of preaching are understood within a larger communal framework, rather than in terms of private, individual experience. And these dimensions of preaching are developed within the larger temporal journey of learning a language, rather than simply in terms of immediate, existential experiential events. Moreover, in a cultural-linguistic model, these temporal and communal aspects of preaching are inseparable from specific practices that are essential to proper language use and crucial for the preaching and hearing of the gospel.

Preaching and Practice

Over the past few years I have been given a group of close friends. These friendships have been intentionally and self-consciously Christian ones, shaped by shared Christian convictions and purposes. The friendships have involved common worship and prayer, as well as lengthy, ongoing conversations about Scripture, theology, and even sermons. In fact, apart from shared Christian convictions and shared commitments to a common good, I doubt if several of these friendships would have developed. The only way I can characterize these friendships is to call them part of the practice of being the church.[58]

Several of these friends are single, and not by accident, but by choice. Their singleness and participation in a community of friends is part of their present calling to discipleship and ministry. These particular friendships, because they involve people quite different from myself, have required more intentional effort and elicited more self-conscious reflection than many of my previous friendships. And I knew these friendships were changing me. However, only recently did I realize how much.

58. On friendship see Aristotle, *Nicomachean Ethics,* Books 8 and 9; Paul J. Wadell, *Friendship and the Moral Life* (Notre Dame, Indiana: Univ. of Notre Dame, 1989); and Gilbert Meilaender, *Friendship: A Study in Theological Ethics* (Notre Dame, Indiana: Univ. of Notre Dame Press, 1981). On friendship as a practice within the framework of MacIntyre's definition of a practice, see McClendon, *Ethics,* 172-73. On the relationship between friendship and the church, see Stanley Hauerwas, "Companions on the Way: The Necessity of Friendship," *The Asbury Theological Journal* 45 (Spring 1990): 35-48; and Celia Allison Hahn, *Sexual Paradox: Creative Tensions in Our Lives and In Our Congregations* (New York: Pilgrim Press, 1991), 159-74. On the subversive character and possibilities of Christian friendship, see Rosemary Rader, *Breaking Boundaries: Male-Female Friendship in Early Christian Communities* (New York: Paulist Press, 1983).

Not long ago I was asked to perform the wedding of a colleague. When I sat down with the couple to look over marriage services, I was, for the first time in my life, appalled at the implications of the services. At best one might say the services were a bit extravagant in their exclusive claims for marriage. At worst, however, the services were idolatrous, implying that the only way to be a complete human being was through marriage. The couple and I concluded that we would have to rework the language of the services to take account of the positive character of singleness as a calling in the church. My practice of friendship with single Christians had shaped my reading of the marriage services.

This experience highlights the crucial role of communal practices in the reading and interpretation of texts, particularly Christian Scripture. In a recent essay Stanley Hauerwas both confirmed and named my experience. Writing about the failure of the church to take seriously the "anti-family" passages in Scripture, Hauerwas concludes,

> Such anti-family texts are ignored within mainstream contemporary Protestantism because of our commitment to the politics of democratic society and its idolization of the family. No amount of reading of the text as text can challenge that form of politics. Unless the church is constituted by a counterpolitics in which singleness is as valid a way of life as marriage, we will not be able to hear or preach the Church's apocalyptic judgment on this family. We will not be able to do so because we will lack the resources to see that Jesus challenges the family. On the contrary, we have been led to believe that Christianity is good for the nation because Christianity is good for the family. We therefore fail to stand under the authority of the Word because the Word is captured by practices and narratives that are more constitutive of that entity called America than that community called Church. Indeed the confusions of those narratives have made it impossible for us to rightly be proclaimers and hearers of the Word.[59]

As Hauerwas suggests, preaching is fundamentally a political activity because both the reading of Scripture and the preaching and

---

59. Stanley Hauerwas, "Political Preaching," in *Unleashing the Scripture: Freeing the Bible from Captivity to America* (Nashville: Abingdon Press, 1993), 42-43.

hearing of the gospel are inseparably related to the political practices of the church.[60] My experience with the marriage service reminded me of this fact in a poignant and powerful way. However, with the current emphasis on homiletical method and technique, contemporary homileticians fail to consider the significance of such practices as friendship for the preaching and hearing of the gospel. This fact reveals how narrowly circumscribed the discipline of homiletics has become today.

Frei's postliberal, cultural-linguistic theology directs homiletics beyond its current focus on technique to the larger communal context within which preaching takes place. Specifically, Frei's turn to the interpretative community as central to biblical interpretation points in this direction, particularly when one remembers that the community of interpretation — the church — is not a matter of ethereal consciousness or some invisible reality, but rather a publicly enacted community of concrete practices. Indeed, one implication of Frei's later work is that readers must be trained within the interpretive community to read Scripture rightly. Similarly, Frei's turn to a cultural-linguistic model of Christianity, which emphasizes the integral relationship between language use and "form of life," points in this direction. Within this model, the language and practices of the community are inseparably held together; one cannot be abstracted from the other, as Frei made clear as early as *The Identity of Jesus Christ,* which he concluded with a famous quote from Albert Schweitzer:

> He comes to us as one unknown, without a name, as of old, by the lakeside, He came to those men who knew him not. He speaks to us the same word: "Follow thou me!" and sets us to the tasks which He has to fulfill for our time. He commands. And to whose who obey Him, whether they be wise or simple, He will reveal Himself in the toils, the conflicts, the sufferings which they shall pass through in His fellowship, and, as an ineffable mystery, they shall learn in their own experience Who He is.[61]

---

60. For an excellent, extended account of the importance of communal practices in the reading of Scripture, see Stephen E. Fowl and L. Gregory Jones, *Reading in Communion: Scripture and Ethics in Christian Life* (Grand Rapids, Michigan: Wm. B. Eerdmans Publishing Co., 1991).

61. Albert Schweitzer, *The Quest of the Historical Jesus,* trans. W. Montgomery (New York: Macmillan Publishing Company, 1968), 403; cited in Frei, *Identity,* 171.

For Frei, one comes to know — and *experience* — the identity of Jesus Christ through the practice of discipleship. Similarly, the gospel is rightly preached and heard only where such discipleship is present. As Frei concludes, we are "in touch with the story" by being disposed to the story through the way of discipleship.[62] Although Frei does not examine particular communal practices of discipleship, his work points to this larger political context within which the gospel is rightly preached and heard.

Moreover, Frei is in good company here; he captures a significant emphasis within the tradition of preaching, which has generally been lost today. For example, Aristotle, whose work has influenced preaching through the centuries, wrote insightfully about the intimate relationship between ethics, rhetoric, and politics.[63] While Aristotle had a profound appreciation for the importance of language, even emphasizing the socio-linguistic nature of human beings, he knew that speeches alone, apart from the polity of the society and the related character of the hearers, were inadequate. In contemporary homiletical terms, Aristotle reminds us that "Word-events" alone are insufficient apart from the communal practices that contribute to the truthful hearing of the gospel.

Similar insights have come from the Christian tradition as well. In an article that raises important issues for preachers enamored with "story," Marianne Sawicki has argued that Matthew and Luke discount the value of stories apart from specific communal practices. Stories alone, Sawicki argues, cannot create the recognition or experience of the risen Christ. Rather, particular Christian practices are essential.

> *According to Luke-Acts,* what makes it possible to grasp resurrection is a community whose members can be hungry, recognize hungry persons, and fill their needs. *According to Matthew,* what is required is to put certain ethical teachings into practice. Both Gospels expressly link these conditions to recognition of the identity and significance

---

62. Frei, *Identity,* 171.

63. For a discussion of the interrelation between ethics, rhetoric, and politics in Aristotle, see Eugene E. Ryan, "Aristotle's *Rhetoric* and *Ethics* and the Ethos of Society," *Greek, Roman, and Byzantine Studies* 13 (1972): 291-308. For most of the Christian tradition the *Rhetoric* has been the central text of Aristotle appropriated in homiletics. However, in recent years his *Poetics* has become more important.

of Jesus, while at the same time they discount the efficacy of verbal identifications. This is highly ironic, for a text itself can hardly be anything other than words.[64]

Sawicki concludes, "These first evangelists find that they cannot bring anyone to the possibility of resurrection through the mere telling of a story." The gospel stories themselves are finally about "the futility of narrative."[65] Sawicki highlights in a provocative way the importance the gospels themselves place on Christian practices for hearing the story rightly and identifying and "experiencing" the resurrected Christ.[66]

Consistent with the gospels, many in the early church also highlighted the intimate relationship between Christian discipleship and the right hearing of the Word. Athanasius succinctly made this point at the conclusion of his classic work, *On the Incarnation:*

> . . . for the searching and right understanding of the scriptures there is need of a good life and a pure soul, and for Christian virtue to guide the mind to grasp, so far as human nature can, the truth concerning God the Word. One cannot possibly understand the teaching of the saints unless one has a pure mind and is trying to imitate their life.[67]

In many Protestant churches a similar emphasis can be discerned. For example, one strand of the Reformed tradition, generally associated with Martin Bucer and John Knox, has emphasized ecclesial discipline as a "mark" of the church along with the Word and sacraments.[68] As

64. Marianne Sawicki, "Recognizing the Risen Lord," *Theology Today* 44 (January 1988): 442.

65. Sawicki, 443.

66. Two other New Testament scholars have made this point more generally. Wayne Meeks has argued that "a hermeneutical strategy entails a social strategy" (Meeks, 183). Similarly, Richard Hays has written, "*Right reading of the New Testament occurs only where the Word is embodied. . . .* until we see the text lived, we cannot begin to conceive what it means. Until we see God's power at work among us we do not know what we are reading. Thus the most crucial hermeneutical task is the formation of communities seeking to live under the Word" (Hays, "Scripture-Shaped Community," 51).

67. Athanasius, *On the Incarnation,* rev. ed. (Crestwood, New York: St. Vladimir's Orthodox Theological Seminary, 1953), 96.

68. See *The Scots Confession,* Article 18. On Bucer see Kenneth R. Davis, "No Discipline, No Church: An Anabaptist Contribution to the Reformed Tradition," *Sixteenth Century Journal* 13, no. 4 (1982): 43-58.

this theological position suggests, apart from a disciplined community it is improbable that the Word will be rightly proclaimed and heard and the sacraments rightly administered. Preaching requires a people capable of hearing the Word rightly, and the communal practices of the church contribute to the upbuilding of that people.[69]

More recently William Willimon has sounded this same note:

> Some time ago I overheard two musicians at our Chapel discussing the possible performance of a particular piece of contemporary music. "Could we muster the orchestra and singers to tackle that piece?" asked one of the other.
>
> "Oh, sure. No problem getting the musicians," said the other. "The problem would be in finding the necessary audience. I don't think we have yet developed the tastes of the people of Durham to the point where we could ask the musicians to go through all that work and expect their efforts to be heard." It had not occurred to me how dependent musicians are on people who are trained to hear their music. . . .
>
> I have long suspected that many congregations get the preachers they deserve. Faithful preaching is frighteningly dependent on faithful listening.[70]

In their attention to homiletical method and technique, contemporary homileticians have given almost no attention to the communal practices that enable "faithful listening."[71]

I am not suggesting here in any way that Scripture exerts no force upon the church — that the church simply reads its will into Scripture. Rather, I am arguing that it is precisely when the church returns again and again to close readings of Scripture within the framework of faithful communal practices that Scripture exerts its most profound — and at

---

69. Hauerwas, "Church as God's New Language," 60.

70. William H. Willimon and Stanley Hauerwas, *Preaching to Strangers* (Louisville, Kentucky: Westminster/John Knox Press, 1992), 135. Willimon's use of an aesthetic example is significant. Many homileticians today draw on the aesthetic model. However, they never discuss the importance of training to see or hear the aesthetic object. Rather, they simply assert that each individual possesses the resources to participate fully and faithfully in the aesthetic experience.

71. For a treatment of this issue in relation to the liturgy as a whole, see Michael Warren, "The Worshiping Assembly: Possible Zone of Cultural Contestation," *Worship* 163, no. 1 (1989).

times disruptive — challenge to the church. In this process Scripture begins to be heard in its "semantic depth." Moreover, within this framework, the importance of preaching as a crucial practice and discipline of the church can be understood. Through the weekly gathering of the people of God to hear sermons, the rhythm of the church's life incorporates a regular return and submission to the authority of Scripture as constitutive of its life together.

In addition, I am not suggesting that God cannot use the sermon apart from all human discipline and preparation. After all, the centrality of discipline as a mark of the church has been emphasized in the Reformed tradition, which is quite serious in affirming the sovereignty of God and the primacy of grace. Rather, I am suggesting that technique — or homiletical method or sermon form — has been too naively entertained as the savior of contemporary preaching, as that which will enable a "new hearing" of the gospel. A genuinely new hearing will require more than the technique of the preacher; it will also require a disciplined community of hearers grounded in the practice of Scripture, sacrament, and discipleship. In other words, the Spirit works in the preaching and hearing of the Word not just in the discrete events on Sunday morning, but in all of the communal practices that build up the congregation within which the sermon is preached and heard.

Faithful preaching and hearing of the gospel are deeply embedded within this larger political context of the church — within the various activities, practices, and habits that shape the life of the community within which preaching takes place. In Raymond Williams's terms, the "manifest symbol system" of preaching is deeply embedded within the "realized symbol system" that is enacted in the everyday life of churches.[72] If the concern of homiletics is to enable a "new hearing," then far more than method and form (and even content) will need to be considered. Here again, Frei's cultural-linguistic understanding of Christianity, as well as his emphasis on the publicly enacted community of interpretation, points the discipline of homiletics beyond an emphasis on individual, experiential events (and the methods to create them) toward this larger communal context within which preaching occurs.

As a concrete example of the implications of this emphasis on

---

72. Raymond Williams, *The Sociology of Culture* (New York: Schocken Books, 1982), 208-10.

communal practices, consider again the practice of "building up" the church in relation to the training of preachers. As Lohfink has noted, the preacher does not engage in this practice either in isolation from the community as a whole or in a hierarchical fashion. Rather, "building up" the church is a practice engaged in by the entire community.[73] Preaching is simply one of the places where this practice occurs most publicly.[74] Moreover, this practice requires time for togetherness, as well as training to receive both admonition and forgiveness. As Lohfink writes of the admonition involved in building up the church,

> Proper admonition requires much of the one who admonishes, for instance, the courage to allow *oneself* to be corrected on another occasion, and the knowledge that in a truly fraternal community conflicts absolutely must be resolved, not suppressed or artificially concealed. The courage to admonish others fraternally and the humility to let oneself be corrected are among the most certain signs of the presence of authentic community and of consciousness of community.[75]

Apart from this larger communal practice of "togetherness," which involves both admonition and forgiveness, the use of the language of "building up" suffers because it is not embodied in the life of the people. Where this "building up" is not lived, preachers will not know what it means. As Nicholas Lash might put it, "building up" begins to deliver its meaning only insofar as it is "brought into play" through its interpretive performance.[76] The practice of admonishing and forgiving in the larger community is an essential part of the training that enables preachers to participate in the building up of the church through preaching.

---

73. Lohfink, 102.

74. As Lohfink suggests, the early church understood this upbuilding to be the calling of the entire community even within the service of worship, where various persons would participate and speak. A focus on preaching as "building up" the church may have radical implications indeed for the church's practice of preaching (Lohfink, 102-4).

75. Lohfink, 106. On the importance of being trained to receive forgiveness, see Hauerwas, "Living the Proclaimed Reign of God," 154.

76. Nicholas Lash, "Performing the Scriptures," in *Theology on the Way to Emmaus* (London: SCM Press, 1986), 41.

However, the institutional training of preachers often does not provide the time or space for this communal practice of "building up," which is so integral to the preaching and hearing of the gospel. In fact, in an important essay, Ronald Cram and Stanley Saunders have suggested that the institutional structures of the seminary may actually preclude the kind of space and time required for the communal practice of building up the church.[77] Seminaries shaped by the politics and economics of American culture may in their very training of preachers institutionally militate against the faithful preaching and hearing of the Word. The institutional structures themselves may exert pressure toward an emphasis on the method and technique of the individual preacher in the individual sermon. As Cram and Saunders write,

> A society's perception of space and time shapes in fundamental ways its evaluation of what kind of knowledge is of most worth. So long as the Church and its educational institutions operate by the American clock (dominated by media time, which suggests that life is a series of disconnected, self-contained episodes [i.e., discrete, sermonic, experiential events!]) and presume to occupy safe space within the Western economy, the kind of knowing and acting its practitioners express will be more American than Christian. The issue for theological education is how we can shape environments that will enable the rediscovery of a peculiarly Christian experience of time and space, its attendant economy, and the distinctive forms of learning and knowledge appropriate to it.[78]

Saunders and Cram challenge homileticians to examine the institutional structures that shape, possibly in detrimental ways, the production and reproduction of Christian culture — that is, the "building up" of the church.

However, in critiquing the institution one must not go so far as to ignore the Christian communal practices that do go on in the seminary, particularly in the residential seminary. Among pockets of students such practices do occur, and they can be even more significant

---

77. On the tendency of institutions to corrupt practices, see MacIntyre, *After Virtue*, 194.

78. Ronald H. Cram and Stanley P. Saunders, "Feet Partly of Iron and Partly of Clay: Pedagogy and the Curriculum of Theological Education," *Theological Education* 29 (Spring 1992): 44-45.

than class work. For example, it has been in the seminary context that I have discovered the practice of friendship that I mentioned at the beginning of this section. And the practice of "upbuilding" can also undoubtedly take place. While exploring and critiquing the institution, homileticians can also both name and nurture the practices within seminaries that contribute to the formation of preachers.

Almost thirty years ago Joseph Sittler wrote that

> . . . the expectation must not be cherished that, save for modest and obvious instruction about voice, pace, organization, and such matters, preaching as a lively art of the church can be taught at all. And therefore, seminary provisions for instruction in preaching, when these exist as separate curriculum items, should be re-examined.[79]

What I am suggesting is that Sittler is correct. Preaching cannot be taught. However, what I am also suggesting is that preachers can be formed. And this formation, as Cram and Saunders argue, is a communal process involving concrete practices; the process is much closer to the model of apprenticeship and the practice of building up the church than it is to current models of teaching homiletical method within discrete preaching classes. Frei's work ultimately suggests the need to reexamine not only the communal practices of our churches, but also the homiletics curricula of our seminaries.

Nurturing a Figural Imagination

The narrative and communal dimensions of Frei's work come together in his emphasis on the typological or figural interpretation of Scripture. In *The Eclipse of Biblical Narrative* Frei argues that typological interpretation has traditionally served two functions within the church. First, figural interpretation has served to unify the Scripture by highlighting the patterns that connect the various events, people, and institutions into a single story. Typology is a way of interpreting Scripture as a unified narrative, rather than merely as a collection of discrete, isolated vignettes.[80] Typo-

79. Joseph Sittler, *The Anguish of Preaching* (Philadelphia: Fortress Press, 1966), 7.
80. Hans W. Frei, *The Eclipse of Biblical Narrative: A Study in Eighteenth and Nineteenth Century Hermeneutics* (New Haven: Yale Univ. Press, 1974), 2, passim.

logical interpretation is thus intimately related to a narrative understanding of Scripture; it respects the particularity and integrity of the various events, people, and institutions in the story, serving essentially to connect them into narrative configurations.[81]

Second, figural interpretation serves not only to unify the biblical narrative, but also to incorporate the contemporary world, particularly the contemporary people of God, into that story; it is not just a way of reading Scripture, but a way of reading life.[82] Through typological interpretation, the world of the contemporary people of God is seen and described in terms of the patterns and connections discerned in the biblical narrative. The opposite of "translation," typology is one of the primary means of "intratextual" interpretation, which redescribes the contemporary world within the "storied world of the Bible."[83] The goal is to incorporate "extra-biblical thought, experience, and reality into the one real world detailed and made accessible by the biblical story — not the reverse."[84] In this second function figural interpretation is nothing less or more than a means of carrying forward the biblical story into the present and the future. It is, as George Lindbeck puts it, one crucial way we make the biblical story our story.[85] As such, typology's impli-

---

81. It is not my purpose to provide a detailed discussion of typological interpretation. Nor do I want to critique allegorical interpretation by contrasting it with typology. Indeed, David Dawson argues that a sharp contrast between the two is misguided (David Dawson, *Allegorical Readers and Cultural Revision in Ancient Alexandria* [Berkeley: Univ. of California Press], 15-17). Rather, I simply want to suggest the integral relationship between narrative and typology and the potential value of typological interpretation for contemporary preaching. Nevertheless, I do want to be very clear about what I do *not* mean by figural interpretation. I do not mean a simplistic kind of prophecy-fulfillment model, which makes the Old Testament obsolete now that the prophecies have been fulfilled and makes the pattern of Jesus' life, death, and resurrection irrelevant for the church's life because the story is completed in him. My understanding of figural interpretation, like Frei's, makes the story of Israel integral to that of the church, with Jesus serving as the pivotal link between the two. See Richard Hays's discussion of the metaphorical character of typology and of Paul's ecclesiocentric typological interpretation, in which Israel and the church are intimately related (*Echoes of Scripture in the Letters of Paul* [New Haven: Yale Univ. Press, 1989], 95-102, 161-62).

82. Frei, *Eclipse*, 3; Hans W. Frei, "The 'Literal Reading' of the Biblical Narrative in the Christian Tradition: Does It Stretch or Will It Break?" in *The Bible and the Narrative Tradition*, ed. Frank McConnell (New York: Oxford Univ. Press, 1986), 72.

83. Frei, *Eclipse*, 3.

84. Frei, *Eclipse*, 3.

85. Lindbeck, *Doctrine*, 118.

cations for preaching, particularly for narrative preaching, seem obvious, though these have not been explored in recent homiletical
thought.

This twofold function of typological interpretation is evident in
Scripture itself. A good example is the Exodus event, which serves as a
narrative pattern both for connecting various key events in the biblical
story and for incorporating the people of God into that ongoing story.
The Exodus provides the pattern for describing the Israelites' entry into
the promised land and then their return from exile.[86] The gospels then
locate the coming of Jesus within this same story and interpret his death
and resurrection as a continuation and fulfillment of this story, a pattern
that continues in the liturgical actions of baptism and Eucharist. All of
these typological moves serve not only to unify Scripture, but also to
incorporate the people of God (at many times and places) into God's
ongoing story.[87]

A contemporary liturgical example from the service of baptism
further highlights this twofold function of figural interpretation, as well
as highlighting the important role that typology has played in Christian
liturgy. One version of the Prayer of Thanksgiving over the Water runs
as follows:

> We give you thanks, Eternal God,
> for you nourish and sustain all living things
> by the gift of water.
> In the beginning your Spirit moved over the watery chaos,
> calling forth order and life.
>
> In the time of Noah,
> you destroyed evil by the waters of the flood;
> giving righteousness a new beginning.
>
> You led Israel out of slavery,
> through the waters of the sea,
> into the freedom of the promised land.

---

86. Joshua 3:7-17; Isaiah 40:3-5; 43:16-21.
87. For another biblical example of typological interpretation, see the discussion
of Stephen's sermon before the Sanhedrin (Acts 7) in Justo L. Gonzalez and Catherine G.
Gonzalez, *The Liberating Pulpit* (Nashville: Abingdon Press, 1994), 100-101.

In the waters of Jordan
Jesus was baptized by John
and anointed with your Spirit.
By the baptism of his own death and resurrection,
Christ set us free from sin and death
and opened the way to eternal life.

We thank you, O God, for the water of baptism.
In it we are buried with Christ in his death.
From it we are raised to share in his resurrection.
Through it we are reborn by the power of the Holy Spirit.

Send your Spirit to move over this water
that it may be a fountain of deliverance and rebirth.
Wash away the sin of *all* who *are* cleansed by it.
Raise *them* to new life,
and graft *them* to the body of Christ.
Pour out your Holy Spirit upon *them,*
that *they* may have power to do your will,
and continue forever in the risen life of Christ.
To you, Father, Son, and Holy Spirit, one God,
be all praise, honor, and glory,
now and forever.
Amen.[88]

In the prayer, figural interpretation not only unifies the biblical narrative, but carries that story forward into the present as the person is baptized into a distinctive community given its identity by the "storied world of the Bible." The "hermeneutical" move is precisely the reverse of that in the translation model.

In these examples another important characteristic of figural interpretation becomes apparent. Typology is fundamentally a Christological and ecclesial form of interpretation. That is, the movement is from events in the story of Israel through Jesus as the center and "archetype" of the story to the church as the ongoing bearer of the story.[89] As

88. Theology and Worship Ministry Unit, Presbyterian Church (U.S.A.), *Book of Common Worship* (Louisville, Kentucky: Westminster/John Knox Press, 1993), 410-11.
89. I have borrowed the term "archetype" from Justo and Catherine Gonzalez, 101. A lot of other terms have been used, but "archetype" captures most clearly Jesus'

Justo and Catherine Gonzalez write, making an integral connection between preaching and baptism,

> The fact that preaching is addressed to a baptized congregation should make a difference in the Biblical interpretation and the preaching. Scripture is a word already addressed to God's People — even the history of a dialogue between God and God's People. The congregation is not there to choose whether to be part of this people — they already are. Baptism is the sign of that inclusion. Therefore the word is for them. The preacher needs to make clear the connection of that ancient word to this present People of God. Typology assumes the continuity of the People of God, and therefore the word to that ancient people can readily be applied to the congregation now gathered.[90]

Preaching here is appropriately linked with the typological incorporation of people through baptism into a distinctive community with a distinctive story. The function of typological preaching is not primarily to connect individuals with the individual characters in different biblical stories, a means of interpretation that I have referred to as analogy. Rather, in typological preaching the move is from the story of Israel through Jesus Christ to the church. While there is obviously an analogical dimension to typological interpretation, it differs fundamentally from contemporary, individualistic uses of analogy, which neglect the Christological-ecclesial axis of typological interpretation.[91]

Here again, Frei's work is instructive. As I have already argued, according to Frei the proper move of the sermon is from the identity of Jesus to the community of faith. In *The Identity of Jesus Christ* he places this move in close relation to the story of Israel. In the gospel narratives Jesus is the embodiment or fulfillment of the history of Israel, as well as the one from whom the church receives its identity and patterns its life.[92] The story of Jesus stands as the pivot between the

---

pivotal role in defining the pattern of the entire story. The term should not be confused with the Jungian understanding of archetypes.

90. Gonzalez and Gonzalez, 113.

91. For a good example of typological interpretation that takes seriously the Christological-ecclesial axis, see the Gonzalezes' discussion of the David and Goliath story in *Liberating Pulpit*, 102-3.

92. Frei, *Identity*, 128-30.

story of two peoples; indeed, it connects those stories. A Christological-communal typology is thus inherent in Frei's reading of the gospel narratives in *The Identity of Jesus Christ*. Through such figural interpretation the church as the people of God is incorporated into the biblical story; the church receives a distinctive identity and carries the story forward.[93] Figural interpretation thus provides the crucial means for moving narratively from Israel to the identity of Jesus Christ to the "upbuilding" of the church.

In this respect, typological interpretation should not be viewed as a rather conservative, antiquated form of interpretation. In fact, the problem for contemporary hearers may be its radical character. As the Gonzalezes argue, typology in its full form thrived while the church was a persecuted, or at best tolerated, minority, but faded away during the Constantinian era, when interpretation tended to accommodate the Bible to the dominant culture and empire.[94] Typological interpretation was simply too particularistic, too radical for the Constantinian age; it functioned too much to "build up" a peculiar people, a "contrast-society," according to a different and distinctive story.

> [Typology] assumes the repetition in our lives of the pattern that is fully exemplified in the work of Jesus. . . .
>
> The added demand on us is one reason why typology disappeared in its full form after the fourth century. Christianity, now the official religion of the Roman Empire, was increasingly equated with expected, decent behavior, but hardly with the demands that put a Christian over against the general society. If you wanted a more rigorous class of Christianity you could join the monastic forms that began to flourish at this time. But one would hardly anticipate a cross in a Christian Empire. For this reason, the repetition in our lives of the type seen fully in Christ was not something to be expected.[95]

---

93. Typological interpretation is just as open to abuse as any other kind of interpretation. The Gonzalezes suggest three "checks" upon potential abuses: (1) the finality of Jesus Christ as the archetype; (2) the centrality of the cross; and (3) the importance of hearing many different voices within the community of faith, particularly those of the marginalized (Gonzalez and Gonzalez, 115-16). Frei himself points out the polyvalence inherent in typological interpretation, likewise suggesting the importance of hearing other voices (Frei, *Eclipse*, 6-7).

94. Gonzalez and Gonzalez, 103-4.

95. Gonzalez and Gonzalez, 114.

The Gonzalezes likewise note that today it is in fact within the marginal communities of society — Christian communities in Africa, Asia, and Latin America, as well as minorities in the North Atlantic — that figural interpretation thrives.[96] Such interpretation gives those communities a distinctive story — a peculiar memory, identity, and hope — in the midst of the dominant, oppressive culture. The Gonzalezes suggest that the mainline church may have to learn from these communities of "resident aliens" in an increasingly secular age. Typological interpretation, they argue, is a vehicle by which the church can recapture its distinctive identity and purpose.[97]

Figural interpretation is thus not only a means for incorporating the church into the "storied world of the bible," but a way in which the church can be "built up" to carry that story forward as a distinctive people. Indeed, perhaps it is the mainline church's need to "translate" the gospel into the terms of the "empire" that has contributed to the loss of figural interpretation in the church today. The neglect of typology highlights the fundamentally individualistic translation model that has governed narrative homiletics despite all its assertions about the formation of the community by the biblical story.

However, there may also be another reason for the neglect of typology in contemporary homiletics. Figural interpretation is not a hermeneutical technique or method that can be taught in the abstract apart from the practices of the Christian community.[98] Rather, figural interpretation is an act of the imagination, an act of seeing narrative patterns and connections between events, people, and institutions that are temporally separated.[99] Such interpretation is a primary way of "going on" with the language that follows no paint-by-numbers formula. As Hays writes,

> It is questionable . . . whether typology should be considered a method of interpretation; it is, rather, a framework of literary-historical sensibility that creates the hermeneutical conditions necessary for the metaphorical linkage of scriptural text and contemporary situation.[100]

96. Gonzalez and Gonzalez, 101-2; 106-7. Figural interpretation is so prevalent in African-American preaching as to need no elaboration.
97. Gonzalez and Gonzalez, 107-8.
98. Frei, *Eclipse*, 3.
99. Hays, *Echoes*, 100-101, 161-62.
100. Hays, *Echoes*, 161.

People learn to do figural "improvisation" not as a hermeneutical or homiletical technique, but through immersion in Scripture, participation in the liturgical practices of the church, and engagement in the alternative politics of the community of faith. A preacher, for example, does not come to "figure" the church's current situation as one of "exile" through any abstract methodological hermeneutic, but through living with Scripture as a part of the church in and for the world.[101] A figural imagination requires training and nurture; it is not the product of homiletical technique or hermeneutical method, but part of a communal journey into the language and practices of the Christian community. As the Gonzalezes write, reflecting on the preaching and martyrdom of Oscar Romero, "Perhaps there is a connection between being ready to see and live out the full implications of the Gospel and an excellent, true use of typology."[102] In Frei's terms, the connection between figural interpretation and "mode of life" is essential.[103]

In Frei's work, then, figural interpretation provides a critical link between the story of Jesus, the upbuilding of the church, and the practice of preaching. As an alternative to individualistic, "translation" models of preaching, typology offers a way for the church to recapture its distinctive identity within an increasingly secular culture. In conjunction with the other aspects of a postliberal homiletic, which I have discussed, figural interpretation can help Christian preaching contribute to the renewal of the church as a "collective disciple" of Jesus Christ in and for the world.

---

101. For a figural interpretation of the church's situation as one of exile, see Walter Brueggemann, "Preaching to Exiles," *Journal for Preachers* 16 (Pentecost 1993): 3-15. As is obvious in Brueggemann's essay, a figural interpretation of the church necessarily involves an interpretation of the world as well; if the church is in exile, the culture within which the church exists is also "figured" in a particular way.

102. Gonzalez and Gonzalez, 118.

103. Frei, *Eclipse,* 3.

Appendix

"Pain Turned to Newness"

Mark 5:24b-34

Walter Brueggemann
Columbia Theological Seminary
May 9, 1992

The woman in Mark 5 almost did not make the text, almost did not have a story. She is at the edge of the crowd as Jesus approaches. Even in the larger gospel narrative, she has to muscle her way into the text. She is an intruder who does not belong there, for her action takes place in the middle of a better, more impressive story about a more impressive character. In the verses just before her intrusive narrative (vv. 21-24a), a leader of the synagogue, a big, impressive, influential man, persuades Jesus to make a sick call on his ailing daughter. And just after this woman's intrusive narrative, the story of the big synagogue man is resumed and completed (vv. 35-43). This story of the woman is an inconvenience that disrupts only briefly the better story of the man. I will wager that not only is her Bible story an inconvenience, but she herself was endlessly an inconvenience as well to those around her.

But then, the Bible and life itself are like that, little stories of insignificant people who are unworthy, who crowd in upon better stories and demand their fifteen minutes of fame, and if not fame, then fifteen minutes of well-being. The wonder, of course, is that the woman made it into the text at all. As we shall see before we finish, we may be very

259

glad she made it in, because her story might turn out to be our story as well. Listen to her story as a tale about your own life and our life.

I

The woman is a pitiful character, a surplus member of the crowd, a "non-person." She stands at the edge of the crowd and watches. The first thing we learn about her, the most important fact about her, the fact that establishes her identity, is that her body is a mess. She is a carrier of pain. Her pain comes at us in three layers:

- She has been hemorrhaging for twelve years. That's a lot of blood that has been lost, as the life ebbed out of her. We can imagine her all in bandages, in smelly bandages, unattractive, for a bleeder in a crowd is at best unwelcome.
- She had "endured much under many physicians." She had been in frantic pursuit of health, spending her days helplessly in clinics, waiting rooms, emergency rooms, overwhelmed by technology, filling out endless forms, passed along through the medical bureaucracy, poked at and questioned by lots of medical experts and a few medical students, some gentle, some uncaring.
- The end result is, she had spent all that she had. She had no health insurance, so that all her wherewithal was used up in a futile pursuit of health care, but still she bled. Now she is bloody and broke.

She is like lots of folks at the edge of the crowd, carrier of pain, pain from bleeding, pain from medical indifference, pain from economic exhaustion, without health, without money, without hope, pitiful!

She makes one last, desperate effort for her future. She still has the imagination and courage to try one last option. Her desperate action is fueled by faith. She reaches out to touch power. Her frail, extended hand enacts the drama of *pain touching power*. She said, "If I can only touch his clothes, I will be made well." She enacts bold, body-to-body, person-to-person contact that cuts through her poverty, brokenness, despair, and shame. She is indeed "reaching out and touching someone," but it is not a nice, innocuous suburban touch. This is a real touch, undertaken by an untouchable, that shatters the neat division between the well and the sick, the acceptable and the disreputable. She overrides all the categories that belong to her disability. Her eagerness to touch is an act of desperate hope, like the eagerness of a child to touch, extending hands in order to be safe with mother. It is like the heavy-veined, pulsating hands in a nursing home, reaching out to touch the child that has just entered. It is exhausted, forlorn life touching full, powerful life, and power is transferred by the touch from the one to the other. This is the human act of "laying on of hands" that transfers possibility. This is the real "apostolic succession," as the continuity of human power and human possibility is enacted.

The outcome happens just as she had hoped for the woman. She touches, and immediately (this is Mark's favorite word, *euthus*, straightway, promptly, in this very moment), immediately, the bleeding stops, and she is healed. Pain touches power and all things are new!

II

Only now does Jesus speak, only after he has been touched. The healing happened by his presence, without his knowing it. He is so saturated with the power for life that the power spills over into those around him. Immediately (the same preferred word of Mark again), Jesus knew power had been transferred from him. This was a bold, concrete human transaction. We cannot tell if Jesus is upset at the intrusion of the woman, or anxious for his own body, or compassionate toward the needy one. He wants to identify the one with whom he has been coupled in a holy transformation from sickness to health.

Jesus has a quick conversation with his entourage. He asks his disciples, "Who touched?" Maybe his word is a command, "find her." But his disciples resist. They are not as intense about the matter as is he. They give a casual response, as though the touch did not matter. They do not know how important the touch is between pain and power, even if Jesus knows. They say, "It's a big crowd, it could have been anyone. It is foolish to try to locate the toucher in this mass." They think in generalities. Jesus, however, is much more intense, caring, concerned,

and specific than his best friends. Not only does the woman know she
has gained new power for healing. Jesus is also aware that his body has
been exposed to pain, and that exposure has redefined him as well as
her. Jesus, the powerful one, is changed by contact with pain. He is
changed in ways commensurate with her. He is not an unmoved mover
or an unnoticing power. He is impacted decisively by her touch.

While his disciples have no concern or interest in the matter,
because they are not direct players in this drama of pain and power,
Jesus continues to notice, to wonder, and to care. He looks. He surveys
the crowd. Even in all his power, however, he is not able to identify the
woman.

She takes the initiative. She announces herself, which reflects her
new-found courage and freedom, which comes from being healed. The
narrator says, ". . . knowing what had happened to her, the woman came
in fear and trembling, fell down before him and told him the whole
truth." It is an amazing moment between this pained woman and this
powerful healer. She knows irreducibly what had happened to her. By
his power she had been healed. But she also knows she has taken an
inappropriate initiative on her own behalf. She had pushed in where
she did not belong. She had touched him when one does not properly
touch the powerful. She told him about her pain and the truth about
his power, which had now become power for life, truth about the transformation that her courage had instigated, about which he knew nothing.

She comes in fear and trembling. How odd. Why is that? Because
she knew she had intruded upon him improperly. Because she expected
to be shamed or scolded, because she was used to being abused and
"manhandled" by men, for pain is always frightened in the presence of
power.

III

Now Jesus speaks to her for the first time. He finally has found his
partner in creating a new possibility. This is a confrontation between
power and pain, out of which something new can be wrought. He speaks
as the powerful one. He surprises her and no doubt the onlookers as
well. He does not scold or shame or abuse her. He acts out and models

a new way of power towards pain. He is not unhappy that they have converged in this uncommon way. He does not measure if his power has been diminished or trivialized by her touch. His mind is completely off himself and his own authority. He is able to think not of his own interests, but of "the interests of others" (cf. Phil. 2:4).

He is focused fully and intensely upon her and upon her future. She had hardly dared entertain the thought that she might have a future. But he authorizes her for a new possibility:

- He addresses her: "daughter." It is close to a name, as close as she has ever been to a real identity. He gives her a title of regard and acknowledgement, perhaps even of affection. He counts her a full member of his family of faith and obedience. He names her in a way that honors her.
- He celebrates her faith. "Your faith has made you well." He does not even claim to have done anything for her. Her faith was in part her passion for Jesus and her confidence in his lordly capacity. But her faith was also about herself, refusing to accept the sorry state in which the doctors and bankers had left her disabled. Her faith is the courage and freedom to take an initiative for well-being. She had faith in her capacity to reach out, to touch, to take, to receive, to be changed, to benefit from the touch of power. Her faith is her conviction that her future did not need to be only more of the same dreary past tense.
- Finally he dismisses her with a blessing: "go in peace." Go in holiness, go in *shalom,* no more bleeding, no more hemorrhaging loss of life, no more manhandling by doctors who would not help her, no more poverty from exhausted finances, but now full, healthy, joyous human life. She has become a full, liberated character in her life story.

End of story. That is enough. Now Mark, in his telling, goes back to the better, bigger story of the leader of the synagogue. Even then, however, Jesus does the same for the powerful man and his daughter as he did for this pitiful woman. Nothing more. The nameless woman is given her life as well as is the leader of the synagogue. The woman is now forever a key character in the story of Jesus, because of her need, and her fear and trembling, and her courage and caring. She becomes

someone she was not, as she moved into the circle of Jesus' life-giving
power.

IV

You recognize, do you not, your own place in this story. We are all
hemorrhaging women, with life bleeding out of us, tired of being
abused, with exhausted resources, scarcely able one more time to reach
out for a touch. We are all of us part of the busy disciples, too busy with
numbers to notice, too important and preoccupied. We are not Jesus
but we do as baptized folk share in his power and in his capacity to heal,
to let ourselves be touched so that some of our God-given power can
flow to the lives of other bleeding outsiders. We are also the by-standing
folk who watch in astonishment. We watch because this hurting woman
and this caring agent of God, this odd text, provide a new shape for
social relations. It is a shape that generates new possibility, new chances
for communion, and new patterns of social power.

We are dazzled. Who would have thought

a) that we would be here so many years later, talking about one
   feeble reach for new life that succeeded?
b) that this pitiful woman would generate a totally new model of
   life and reality?

Those who trust this story do not willingly settle for the old, weary
patterns of "haves" and "have-nots," for the usual arrangements of
strength and weakness, power and powerlessness. This story offers to
us a different map of reality, a different option, a different life. This is
a new life we receive by touching and sharing power. It is a new life we
give by being touched. The word is for us and for all our fellow bleeders:
"Go in peace, be healed of your disease, by your faith be whole."

Bibliography

Allen, Ronald. "Agendae in Homiletics." In *Papers of the Annual Meeting of the Academy of Homiletics*, 32-46. Fuller Theological Seminary, December 5-7, 1991.

————. "New Directions in Homiletics." *Journal for Preachers* 16 (Easter 1993): 20-26.

Anselm, *Proslogion*. In *St. Anselm: Basic Writings*. 2nd ed., 1-33. Translated by S. N. Deane. Lasalle, Ill.: The Open Court Publishing Company, 1962.

Aristotle. *The Rhetoric and the Poetics of Aristotle*. Translated by Rhys Roberts and Ingram Bywater. Edited by Friedrich Solmsen. The Modern Library. New York: Random House, 1954.

Athanasius. *On the Incarnation*. Rev. ed. Crestwood, N.Y.: St. Vladimir's Orthodox Theological Seminary, 1953.

Auerbach, Erich. "Figura." Translated by Ralph Manheim. In *Scenes from the Drama of European Literature*. New York: Meridian Press, 1959; reprint, Minneapolis: University of Minnesota Press, 1984.

————. *Mimesis: The Representation of Reality in Western Literature*. Translated by Willard R. Trask. Princeton: Princeton University Press, 1953; Princeton Paperback Edition, 1974.

Barr, James. "Revelation through History in the Old Testament and in Modern Theology." *Interpretation* 17 (April 1963): 193-205.

————. "Story and History in Biblical Theology." *The Journal of Religion* 56 (January 1976): 1-17.

Barth, Karl. *Anselm: Fides Quaerens Intellectum*. Translated by Ian W. Robertson. Pittsburgh Reprint Series. London: SCM Press, 1960.

————. *Church Dogmatics*. Vol. I, part 1, *The Doctrine of the Word of God*. Edited by G. W. Bromiley and T. F. Torrance. Translated by G. W. Bromiley. Edinburgh: T. & T. Clark, 1975.

————. *Church Dogmatics*. Vol. II, part 2, *The Doctrine of God*. Edited by G. W. Bromiley and T. F. Torrance. Translated by G. W. Bromiley et al. Edinburgh: T. & T. Clark, 1957.

————. *Church Dogmatics*. Vol. IV, part 1, *The Doctrine of Reconciliation*. Edited by G. W. Bromiley and T. F. Torrance. Translated by G. W. Bromiley. Edinburgh: T. & T. Clark, 1956.

————. *Homiletics*. Translated by Geoffrey W. Bromiley and Donald E. Daniels. Louisville: Westminster/John Knox Press, 1991.

————. "An Introductory Essay." Translated by James Luther Adams. In Ludwig Feuerbach, *The Essence of Christianity, x-xxxii*. Translated by George Eliot. New York: Harper and Row, 1957.

————. "No!" In *Natural Theology*. Translated by Peter Fraenkel, 65-128. London: Centenary Press, 1946.

Bass, George M. "The Evolution of the Story Sermon." *Word and World* 2 (Spring 1982): 183-88.

Bennett, Billy Joe. *The Development of a Story-Form Homiletic, 1958 to 1985: Retelling the Story of God in Community*. Ann Arbor, Mich.: University Microfilms International, 1988.

Berliner, Paul F. *Thinking in Jazz: The Infinite Art of Improvisation*. Chicago Studies in Ethnomusicology. Chicago: University of Chicago Press, 1994.

Booth, Wayne. *The Rhetoric of Fiction*. Chicago: University of Chicago Press, 1961.

Brilioth, Yngve. *A Brief History of Preaching*. Translated by Karl E. Mattson. Philadelphia: Fortress Press, 1965.

Brown, Robert McAfee. *The Spirit of Protestantism*. New York: Oxford University Press, 1965.

Brueggemann, Walter. "Preaching to Exiles." *Journal for Preachers* 16 (Pentecost 1993): 3-15.

————. *Texts Under Negotiation: The Bible and Postmodern Imagination*. Minneapolis: Fortress Press, 1993.

Brunner, Emil. "Nature and Grace." In *Natural Theology*, 15-64. Translated by Peter Fraenkel. London: Centenary Press, 1946.

Buechner, Frederick. *Telling the Truth: The Gospel as Tragedy, Comedy, and Fairy Tale*. New York: Harper and Row, 1977.

Bultmann, Rudolf. *Jesus Christ and Mythology.* New York: Charles Scribner's Sons, 1958.

Busch, Eberhard. *Karl Barth: His Life from Letters and Autobiographical Texts.* Translated by John Bowden. Philadelphia: Fortress Press, 1976.

Buttrick, David. *Homiletic: Moves and Structures.* Philadelphia: Fortress Press, 1987.

————. *The Mystery and the Passion: A Homiletic Reading of the Gospel Traditions.* Minneapolis: Fortress Press, 1992.

————. *Preaching Jesus Christ: An Exercise in Homiletical Theology.* Philadelphia: Fortress Press, 1988.

Campbell, Charles L. "Living Faith: Luther, Ethics, and Preaching." *Word and World* 10 (Fall 1990): 374-79.

Childs, Brevard. *Biblical Theology in Crisis.* Philadelphia: Westminster Press, 1970.

————. "The *Sensus Literalis* of Scripture: An Ancient and Modern Problem." In *Beiträge Zur Alttestamentlichen Theologie,* 80-95. Edited by Herbert Danner, Robert Hanhart, and Rudolf Smend. Göttingen: Vandenhoeck and Ruprecht, 1977.

Chopp, Rebecca. *Power to Speak.* New York: Crossroads Publishing Company, 1991.

Comstock, Gary L. "Truth or Meaning: Ricoeur Versus Frei." *Journal of Religion* 66 (April 1986): 117-40.

Cox, Harvey. *The Secular City.* New York: Macmillan, 1965.

Craddock, Fred B. *As One Without Authority: Essays on Inductive Preaching.* 3rd ed. Nashville: Abingdon Press, 1979.

————. *Overhearing the Gospel.* Nashville: Abingdon Press, 1978.

————. *Preaching.* Nashville: Abingdon Press, 1985.

————. "The Sermon as a Twice-Told Tale." Sprunt Lectures, Union Theological Seminary in Virginia, February 4-6, 1991. Reigner Recording Library, Union Theological Seminary in Virginia.

Cram, Ronald H., and Stanley P. Saunders. "Feet Partly of Iron and Partly of Clay: Pedagogy and the Curriculum of Theological Education." *Theological Education* 29 (Spring 1992): 21-50.

Crites, Stephen. "The Narrative Quality of Experience." *Journal of the American Academy of Religion* 39 (September 1971): 291-311.

Crosby, Michael H. *House of Disciples: Church, Economics, and Justice in Matthew.* Maryknoll, N.Y.: Orbis Books, 1988.

Crossan, John Dominic. *The Dark Interval: Towards a Theology of Story.*
    Niles, Ill.: Argus Communications, 1975.

———. *In Parables.* San Francisco: Harper and Row, 1973.

Daniélou, Jean. *The Bible and the Liturgy.* University of Notre Dame
    Liturgical Studies. Notre Dame, Ind.: University of Notre Dame
    Press, 1956.

Davis, H. Grady. *Design for Preaching.* Philadelphia: Fortress Press, 1958.

Davis, Kenneth R. "No Discipline, No Church: An Anabaptist Contribu-
    tion to the Reformed Tradition." *Sixteenth Century Journal* 13, no.
    4 (1982): 43-58.

Dawson, David. *Allegorical Readers and Cultural Revision in Ancient
    Alexandria.* Berkeley: University of California Press, 1992.

Doan, Gilbert. "Preaching from a Liturgical Perspective." In *Preaching
    the Story,* 95-106. Edited by Edmund Steimle, Morris Niedenthal,
    and Charles Rice. Philadelphia: Fortress Press, 1980.

Dodd, C. H. *The Parables of the Kingdom.* New York: Charles Scribner's
    Sons, 1961.

Donahue, John R. *The Gospel in Parable: Metaphor, Narrative, and The-
    ology in the Synoptic Gospels.* Philadelphia: Fortress Press, 1988.

Eagleton, Terry. *Literary Theory: An Introduction.* Minneapolis: Univer-
    sity of Minnesota Press, 1983.

Ebeling, Gerhard. *Theology and Proclamation: Dialogue with Bultmann.*
    Translated by John Riches. Philadelphia: Fortress Press, 1966.

Ellingsen, Mark. *The Integrity of Biblical Narrative: Story in Theology
    and Proclamation.* Minneapolis: Fortress Press, 1990.

Elliott, John H. *A Home for the Homeless: A Sociological Exegesis of I Peter,
    Its Situation and Strategy.* Philadelphia: Fortress Press, 1981.

Eslinger, Richard. *Narrative and Imagination: Preaching the Worlds That
    Shape Us.* Minneapolis: Fortress Press, 1995.

———. *A New Hearing: Living Options in Homiletic Method.* Nashville:
    Abingdon Press, 1987.

Ferm, William Deane. "American Protestant Theology, 1900-1970." *Re-
    ligion in Life* 44 (Spring 1975): 59-72.

Fish, Stanley. *Doing What Comes Naturally: Change, Rhetoric, and the
    Practice of Theory in Literary and Legal Studies.* Durham, N.C.:
    Duke University Press, 1989.

———. *Is There a Text in This Class? The Authority of Interpretive
    Communities.* Cambridge, Mass.: Harvard University Press, 1980.

Ford, David. "Hans Frei and the Future of Theology." *Modern Theology* 8 (April 1992): 203-14.

Fowl, Stephen E., and L. Gregory Jones. *Reading in Communion: Scripture and Ethics in Christian Life.* Grand Rapids: Wm. B. Eerdmans Publishing Company, 1991.

Frei, Hans W. "An Afterword: Eberhard Busch's Biography of Karl Barth." In *Karl Barth in Re-View: Posthumous Works Reviewed and Assessed,* 95-116. Edited by H.-Martin Rumscheidt. Pittsburgh Theological Monograph Series, no. 30. Pittsburgh: Pickwick Press, 1981.

————. "Analogy and the Spirit in the Theology of Karl Barth." TMs [photocopy].

————. "Barth and Schleiermacher: Divergence and Convergence." In *Barth and Schleiermacher: Beyond the Impasse?* 65-87. Edited by James O. Duke and Robert F. Streetman. Philadelphia: Fortress Press, 1988.

————. "Conflicts in Interpretation." *Theology Today* 49 (October 1992): 344-56.

————. "David Friedrich Strauss." In *Nineteenth Century Religious Thought in the West,* vol. 1, 215-60. Edited by Ninian Smart et al. New York: Cambridge University Press, 1985.

————. *The Doctrine of Revelation in the Thought of Karl Barth, 1909-1922: The Nature of Barth's Break With Liberalism.* Ann Arbor, Mich.: University Microfilms, 1956.

————. *The Eclipse of Biblical Narrative: A Study in Eighteenth and Nineteenth Century Hermeneutics.* New Haven: Yale University Press, 1974.

————. "Epilogue: George Lindbeck and *The Nature of Doctrine.*" In *Theology and Dialogue,* 273-81. Edited by Bruce Marshall. Notre Dame, Ind.: University of Notre Dame Press, 1990.

————. "Feuerbach and Theology." *Journal of the American Academy of Religion* 35 (September 1967): 250-56.

————. "German Theology: Transcendence and Secularity." In *Postwar German Culture,* 98-112. Edited by Charles E. McClelland and Stephen P. Scher. New York: E. P. Dutton Publishing Company, 1974.

————. "H. Richard Niebuhr on History, Church, and Nation." In *The-*

ology and Narrative: Selected Essays. Edited by George Hunsinger and William C. Placher. New York: Oxford University Press, 1993.

———. *The Identity of Jesus Christ: The Hermeneutical Bases of Dogmatic Theology.* Philadelphia: Fortress Press, 1975.

———. "In Memory of Robert L. Calhoun, 1896-1983." *Reflection* 82 (November 1984): 8-9.

———. "Karl Barth: Theologian." In *Karl Barth and the Future of Theology: A Memorial Colloquium Held at the Yale Divinity School, January 28, 1969,* 5-12. Edited by David L. Dickerman. New Haven: Yale Divinity School Association, 1969.

———. "The 'Literal Reading' of the Biblical Narrative in the Christian Tradition: Does It Stretch or Will It Break?" In *The Bible and the Narrative Tradition,* 36-77. Edited by Frank McConnell. New York: Oxford University Press, 1986.

———. "The Mystery of the Presence of Christ." Unit I. *Crossroads* (January-March 1967): 69-96.

———. "The Mystery of the Presence of Christ." Unit II. *Crossroads* (April-June 1967): 69-96.

———. "Narrative in Christian and Modern Interpretation." In *Theology and Dialogue,* 145-57. Edited by Bruce Marshall. Notre Dame, Ind.: University of Notre Dame Press, 1990.

———. "Niebuhr's Theological Background." In *Faith and Ethics: The Theology of H. Richard Niebuhr,* 9-64. Edited by Paul Ramsey. New York: Harper and Brothers, 1957.

———. "Religion: Natural and Revealed." In *A Handbook of Christian Theology: Definition Essays on Concepts and Movements of Thought in Contemporary Protestantism,* 310-21. Edited by Marvin Halverson and Arthur A. Cohen. Cleveland: World Publishing Company, 1958.

———. "Remarks in Connection with a Theological Proposal." In *Theology and Narrative: Selected Essays.* Edited by George Hunsinger and William C. Placher. New York: Oxford University Press, 1993.

———. "Response to 'Narrative Theology: An Evangelical Appraisal.'" *Trinity Journal* 8 (Spring 1987): 21-24.

———. Sermon based on John 15:1-8. AMs [photocopy].

———. "Theological Reflections on the Gospel Accounts of Jesus' Death and Resurrection." *The Christian Scholar* 49 (Winter 1966): 263-306.

————. *Theology and Narrative: Selected Essays.* Edited by George Hunsinger and William C. Placher. New York: Oxford University Press, 1993.

————. "Theology and the Interpretation of Narrative: Some Hermeneutical Considerations." In *Theology and Narrative: Selected Essays.* Edited by George Hunsinger and William C. Placher. New York: Oxford University Press, 1993.

————. "The Theology of H. Richard Niebuhr." In *Faith and Ethics: The Theology of H. Richard Niebuhr,* 65-116. Edited by Paul Ramsey. New York: Harper and Brothers, 1957.

————. *Types of Christian Theology.* Edited by George Hunsinger and William C. Placher. New Haven: Yale University Press, 1992.

Funk, Robert W. *Language, Hermeneutic, and Word of God.* New York: Harper and Row, 1966.

Geertz, Clifford. *Interpretation of Cultures.* New York: Basic Books, 1973.

Gilkey, Langdon. "Cosmology, Ontology, and the Travail of Biblical Language." *The Journal of Religion* 41 (July 1961): 194-205.

Goldberg, Michael. *Theology and Narrative.* Nashville: Abingdon Press, 1982.

Gonzalez, Justo L., and Catherine G. Gonzalez. *The Liberating Pulpit.* Nashville: Abingdon Press, 1994.

Green, Garrett, ed. *Imagining God: Theology and the Religious Imagination.* San Francisco: Harper and Row, 1989.

————. *Scriptural Authority and Narrative Interpretation.* Philadelphia: Fortress Press, 1987.

Greer, Rowan. "The Christian Bible and Its Interpretation." In James L. Kugel and Rowan Greer, *Early Biblical Interpretation.* Philadelphia: Westminster Press, 1986.

Hahn, Celia Allison. *Sexual Paradox: Creative Tensions in Our Lives and in Our Congregations.* New York: Pilgrim Press, 1991.

Hauerwas, Stanley. *Christian Existence Today: Essays on Church, World, and Living in Between.* Durham, N.C.: Labyrinth Press, 1988.

————. *A Community of Character: Toward a Constructive Christian Social Ethic.* Notre Dame, Ind.: University of Notre Dame Press, 1981.

————. "Companions on the Way: The Necessity of Friendship." *The Asbury Theological Journal* 45 (Spring 1990): 35-48.

————. "Living the Proclaimed Reign of God: A Sermon on the Sermon on the Mount." *Interpretation* 47 (April 1993): 152-58.

————. *The Peaceable Kingdom: A Primer in Christian Ethics.* Notre Dame, Ind.: University of Notre Dame Press, 1983.

————. "Political Preaching." In *Unleashing the Scripture: Freeing the Bible from Captivity to America.* Nashville: Abingdon Press, 1993.

————. *Resident Aliens: Life in the Christian Colony.* Nashville: Abingdon Press, 1989.

————, and Steve Long. "Interpreting the Bible as a Political Act." *Religion and Intellectual Life* 6 (Spring/Summer 1989): 134-42.

————, and William Willimon. "Embarrassed by the Church: Congregations and the Seminary." *The Christian Century,* 5-12 February 1986, 117-20.

Hays, Richard B. *Echoes of Scripture in the Letters of Paul.* New Haven: Yale University Press, 1989.

————. *The Faith of Jesus Christ.* Society of Biblical Literature Dissertation Series, no. 56. Chico, Calif.: Scholars Press, 1983.

————. "Scripture-Shaped Community: The Problem of Method in New Testament Ethics." *Interpretation* 44 (January 1990): 42-55.

Henry, Carl F. H. "Narrative Theology: An Evangelical Appraisal." *Trinity Journal* 8 (Spring 1987): 3-19.

Hobbie, Wellford. "Out of the Shadows: The Resurgence of Homiletics/Preaching Since the Sixties." *Affirmation* 1 (1980): 21-37.

Holbert, John C. *Preaching Old Testament: Proclamation and Narrative in the Hebrew Bible.* Nashville: Abingdon Press, 1991.

Holmer, Paul. "The Logic of Preaching." *Dialog* 4 (Summer 1965): 205-13.

Hughes, Robert G. "Narrative as Plot." In *Journeys Toward Narrative Preaching,* 48-61. Edited by Wayne Bradley Robinson. New York: Pilgrim Press, 1990.

Hunsinger, George. "Beyond Literalism and Expressivism: Karl Barth's Hermeneutical Realism." *Modern Theology* 3, no. 3 (1987): 209-23.

————. "Hans Frei as Theologian: The Quest for a Generous Orthodoxy." *Modern Theology* 8 (April 1992): 103-28.

Jensen, Richard. *Telling the Story: Variety and Imagination in Preaching.* Minneapolis: Augsburg Press, 1980.

Jeremias, Joachim. *The Parables of Jesus.* Translated by S. H. Hooke. 2nd ed. New York: Charles Scribner's Sons, 1972.

Kay, James F. "Theological Table Talk: Myth or Narrative?" *Theology Today* 48 (October 1991): 326-32.

Kelsey, David. "Biblical Narrative and Theological Anthropology." In *Scriptural Authority and Narrative Interpretation,* 121-43. Edited by Garrett Green. Philadelphia: Fortress Press, 1987.

————. *The Uses of Scripture in Recent Theology.* Philadelphia: Fortress Press, 1975.

Kerr, Fergus. *Theology after Wittgenstein.* Oxford: Basil Blackwell Publishers, 1986; paperback edition, 1988.

Lampe, G. W. H., and K. J. Woollcombe. *Essays on Typology.* Naperville, Ill.: Alec R. Allenson, Inc., 1957.

Lash, Nicholas. "How Large Is a Language Game?" *Theology* 87 (January 1984): 19-28.

————. "Performing the Scriptures." In *Theology on the Way to Emmaus.* London: SCM Press, 1986.

Lewis, Ralph L., and Gregg Lewis. *Learning to Preach Like Jesus.* Westchester, Ill.: Crossway Books, 1989.

Lindbeck, George. "Ebeling: Climax of a Great Tradition." *Journal of Religion* 61 (1981): 309-14.

————. "Hans Frei and the Future of Theology in America." 2 December 1988. TMs [photocopy].

————. *The Nature of Doctrine: Religion and Theology in a Postliberal Age.* Philadelphia: Westminster Press, 1984.

————. "Scripture, Consensus, and Community." *This World* 23 (Fall 1988): 5-24.

Lischer, Richard. "The Limits of Story." *Interpretation* 38 (January 1984): 26-38.

————. *A Theology of Preaching.* 2nd ed. Durham, N.C.: Labyrinth Press, 1992.

Loewe, Raphael. "The 'Plain Meaning' of Scripture in Early Jewish Exegesis." *Papers of the Institute of Jewish Studies in London* I, 140-85. Jerusalem, 1964.

Lohfink, Gerhard. *Jesus and Community.* Translated by John P. Galvin. Philadelphia: Fortress Press, 1984.

Long, Thomas G. *Preaching and the Literary Forms of the Bible.* Philadelphia: Fortress Press, 1989.

————. *The Witness of Preaching.* Louisville: Westminster/John Knox Press, 1989.

Louth, Andrew. *Discerning the Mystery: An Essay on the Nature of Theology*. Oxford: Clarendon Press, 1983.

Lowry, Eugene. *Doing Time in the Pulpit: The Relationship Between Narrative and Preaching*. Nashville: Abingdon Press, 1985.

————. *The Homiletical Plot: The Sermon as Narrative Art Form*. Atlanta: John Knox Press, 1980.

————. *How to Preach a Parable: Designs for Narrative Sermons*. Nashville: Abingdon Press, 1989.

Lukacs, George. *Studies in European Realism*. Translated by Edith Bone. London: Hillway Publishing Company, 1950.

McClendon, James William. *Systematic Theology: Ethics*. Nashville: Abingdon Press, 1986.

McClure, John. "Narrative and Preaching: Sorting It All Out." *Journal for Preachers* 15 (Advent 1991): 24-29.

McFague, Sallie. *Speaking in Parables: A Study in Metaphor and Theology*. Philadelphia: Fortress Press, 1975.

MacIntyre, Alasdair. *After Virtue*. 2nd ed. Notre Dame, Ind.: University of Notre Dame Press, 1984.

————. *Whose Justice? Which Rationality?* Notre Dame, Ind.: University of Notre Dame Press, 1988.

Meeks, Wayne. *The First Urban Christians: The Social World of the Apostle Paul*. New Haven: Yale University Press, 1983.

————. "A Hermeneutics of Social Embodiment." *Harvard Theological Review* 79 (January, April, July 1986): 176-86.

————. "On Trusting an Unpredictable God: A Hermeneutical Meditation on Romans 9–11." In *Faith and History: Essays in Honor of Paul Meyer*, 105-24. Edited by John T. Carroll, Charles H. Cosgrove, and E. Elizabeth Johnson. Atlanta: Scholars Press, 1990.

————. "The Polyphonic Ethics of the Apostle Paul." In *The Annual of the Society of Christian Ethics, 1988*, 17-29. Edited by D. M. Yeager. Washington, D.C.: Georgetown University Press, 1988.

Michel, Otto. "*oikodomeō*." In *Theological Dictionary of the New Testament*, vol. 5, 136-44. Edited by Gerhard Friedrich. Translated by Geoffrey Bromiley. Grand Rapids: Wm. B. Eerdmans Publishing Company, 1967.

Moore, Stephen D. "Are the Gospels Unified Narratives?" In *Society of Biblical Literature Seminar Papers, 1987*, 443-58. Edited by Kent Howard Richards. Atlanta: Scholars Press, 1987.

Murphy, Nancey, and James William McClendon. "Distinguishing Modern and Postmodern Theologies." *Modern Theology* 5 (April 1989): 191-214.

Newbigin, Lesslie. *Foolishness to the Greeks: The Gospel and Western Culture.* Grand Rapids: Wm. B. Eerdmans Publishing Company, 1986.

Niebuhr, H. Richard. *Christ and Culture.* New York: Harper and Row, 1951; Harper Colophon Edition, 1975.

————. *The Meaning of Revelation.* New York: Macmillan Publishing Company, 1941; Macmillan Paperbacks Edition, 1960.

Niebuhr, Reinhold. *The Nature and Destiny of Man.* 2 vols. New York: Charles Scribner's Sons, 1941-43.

Niedenthal, Morris. *Preaching the Presence of God.* Ann Arbor, Mich.: University Microfilms International, 1969.

Ogden, Schubert, and Van Harvey. "How New Is the 'New Quest of the Historical Jesus'?" In *The Historical Jesus and the Kerygmatic Christ: Essays on the New Quest of the Historical Jesus,* 197-242. Edited by Carl E. Braaten and Roy A. Harrisville. Nashville: Abingdon Press, 1964.

Placher, William C. *Narratives of a Vulnerable God: Christ, Theology, and Scripture.* Louisville: Westminster/John Knox Press, 1994.

————. "Paul Ricoeur and Postliberal Theology: A Conflict of Interpretations?" *Modern Theology* 4, no. 1 (1987): 35-52.

————. *Unapologetic Theology: A Christian Voice in a Pluralistic Conversation.* Louisville: Westminster/John Knox Press, 1989.

Poland, Lynn M. *Literary Criticism and Biblical Hermeneutics: A Critique of Formalist Approaches.* American Academy of Religion Series, ed. Carl A. Raschke, no. 48. Chico, Calif.: Scholars Press, 1985.

————. "The New Criticism, Neoorthodoxy, and the New Testament." *Journal of Religion* 65 (1985): 459-77.

Porter, H. B. *The Day of Light: The Biblical and Liturgical Meaning of Sunday.* Greenwich, Conn.: Seabury Press, 1960; reprint, Washington, D.C.: The Pastoral Press, 1987.

Preuss, James Samuel. *From Shadow to Promise: Old Testament Interpretation from Augustine to Young Luther.* Cambridge, Mass.: Belknap Press, a Division of Harvard University Press, 1969.

Reynolds, David S. "From Doctrine to Narrative: The Rise of Pulpit

Storytelling in America." *American Quarterly* 32 (Winter 1980): 479-98.

Rice, Charles. *Interpretation and Imagination: The Preacher and Contemporary Literature.* The Preacher's Paperback Library. Philadelphia: Fortress Press, 1970.

——. "Shaping Sermons by the Interplay of Text and Metaphor." In *Preaching Biblically: Creating Sermons in the Shape of Scripture,* 101-20. Edited by Don M. Wardlaw. Philadelphia: Westminster Press, 1983.

Ricoeur, Paul. "Interpretative Narrative." Translated by David Pellauer. In *The Book and the Text,* 237-57. Edited by Regina Schwartz. Cambridge, Mass.: Basil Blackwell Publishers, 1990.

——. "The Narrative Function." In *Hermeneutics and the Human Sciences,* 274-96. Edited and translated by John B. Thompson. Cambridge: Cambridge University Press, 1981.

Robinson, James M. *A New Quest of the Historical Jesus.* London: SCM Press, 1959; reprint, Philadelphia: Fortress Press, 1983.

——, and John B. Cobb, eds. *New Frontiers in Theology.* Vol. 2, *The New Hermeneutic.* New York: Harper and Row, 1964.

Robinson, John A. T. *Honest to God.* Philadelphia: Westminster Press, 1963.

Robinson, Wayne Bradley. "Angels, But Satan and Wild Beasts." In *Journeys Toward Narrative Preaching,* 101-5. Edited by Wayne Bradley Robinson. New York: Pilgrim Press, 1990.

——. "The Samaritan Parable as a Model for Narrative Preaching." In *Journeys Toward Narrative Preaching,* 85-100. Edited by Wayne Bradley Robinson. New York: Pilgrim Press, 1990.

Rose, Lucy. "The Parameters of Narrative Preaching." In *Journeys Toward Narrative Preaching,* 23-41. Edited by Wayne Bradley Robinson. New York: Pilgrim Press, 1990.

Ryan, Eugene E. "Aristotle's *Rhetoric* and *Ethics* and the Ethos of Society." *Greek, Roman, and Byzantine Studies* 13 (1972): 291-308.

Ryle, Gilbert. *The Concept of Mind.* London: Hutchinson Press, 1949; reprint, Chicago: University of Chicago Press, 1984.

Sawicki, Marianne. "Recognizing the Risen Lord." *Theology Today* 44 (January 1988): 441-49.

Schner, George P. "*The Eclipse of Biblical Narrative:* Analysis and Critique." *Modern Theology* 8 (April 1992): 149-72.

Scholes, Robert, and Robert Kellogg. *The Nature of Narrative.* New York: Oxford University Press, 1966.

Schwartzentruber, Paul. "The Modesty of Hermeneutics: The Theological Reserves of Hans Frei." *Modern Theology* 8 (April 1992): 181-96.

Sittler, Joseph. *The Anguish of Preaching.* Philadelphia: Fortress Press, 1966.

Steimle, Edmund. "Preaching and the Biblical Story of Good and Evil." *Union Seminary Quarterly Review* 31 (Spring 1976): 198-211.

————, Morris Niedenthal, and Charles Rice. *Preaching the Story.* Philadelphia: Fortress Press, 1980.

Steinmetz, David C. "Theology and Exegesis: Ten Theses." In *A Contemporary Guide to Hermeneutics,* 27. Edited by Donald McKim. Grand Rapids: Wm. B. Eerdmans Publishing Company, 1987.

Stout, Jeffrey. "Hans Frei and Anselmian Theology." Paper presented at the annual meeting of the American Academy of Religion, Boston, 1987. TMs [photocopy].

————. "The Relativity of Interpretation." *The Monist* 69 (January 1986): 103-18.

————. "What Is the Meaning of a Text?" *New Literary History* 14 (Autumn 1982): 1-12.

Stroup, George. Review of *The Bible and the Narrative Tradition,* ed. Frank McConnell. In *Homiletic* 12, no. 1 (1987): 24.

————. "Theology of Narrative or Narrative Theology? A Response to *Why Narrative?*" *Theology Today* 47 (January 1991): 424-32.

Surin, Kenneth. "The Weight of Weakness: Intratextuality and Discipleship." In *The Turnings of Darkness and Light: Essays in Philosophical and Systematic Theology.* Cambridge: Cambridge University Press, 1989.

Tanner, Kathryn E. "Theology and the Plain Sense." In *Scriptural Authority and Narrative Interpretation,* 59-78. Edited by Garrett Green. Philadelphia: Fortress Press, 1987.

Taylor, Barbara Brown. "Words We Tremble to Say Aloud." *Preaching Today* Audiotape, no. 91. Carol Stream, Ill.: *Christianity Today* and *Leadership,* 1991.

Theology and Worship Ministry Unit, Presbyterian Church (U.S.A.). *Book of Common Worship.* Louisville: Westminster/John Knox Press, 1993.

Thiemann, Ronald F. *Revelation and Theology: The Gospel as Narrated Promise*. Notre Dame, Ind.: University of Notre Dame Press, 1985.

Thulin, Richard L. "Retelling Biblical Narratives as the Foundation for Preaching." In *Journeys Toward Narrative Preaching*, 7-18. Edited by Wayne Bradley Robinson. New York: Pilgrim Press, 1990.

Tillich, Paul. "You Are Accepted." In *The Shaking of the Foundations*. New York: Charles Scribner's Sons, 1948.

Tompkins, Jane. *Sensational Designs: The Cultural Work of American Fiction, 1790-1860*. New York: Oxford University Press, 1985.

Vanhoozer, Kevin J. *Biblical Narrative in the Philosophy of Paul Ricoeur*. Cambridge: Cambridge University Press, 1990.

——. "A Lamp in the Labyrinth: The Hermeneutics of 'Aesthetic' Theology." *Trinity Journal* 8 (Spring 1987): 25-56.

——. "The Semantics of Biblical Literature: Truth and Scripture's Diverse Literary Forms." In *Hermeneutics, Authority, and Canon*, 51-104. Edited by D. A. Carson and John D. Woodbridge. Grand Rapids: Academie Books, 1986.

Wadell, Paul J. *Friendship and the Moral Life*. Notre Dame, Ind.: University of Notre Dame Press, 1989.

Wardlaw, Don M. "Introduction: The Need for New Shapes." In *Preaching Biblically: Creating Sermons in the Shape of Scripture*, 11-25. Edited by Don M. Wardlaw. Philadelphia: Westminster Press, 1983.

Warren, Michael. "Culture, Counterculture, and the Word." *Liturgy* 6 (Summer 1986): 85-93.

——. "The Worshiping Assembly: Possible Zone of Cultural Contestation." *Worship* 163, no. 1 (1989): 2-16.

Webster, John. "Response to George Hunsinger." *Modern Theology* 8 (April 1992): 129-32.

West, Cornel. "On Frei's *Eclipse of Biblical Narrative*." Review of *The Eclipse of Biblical Narrative: A Study in Eighteenth and Nineteenth Century Hermeneutics*, by Hans W. Frei. In *Union Seminary Quarterly Review* 37, no. 4 (1983): 299-302.

White, Graham. "Karl Barth's Theological Realism." *Neue Zeitschrift für systematische Theologie und Religionsphilosophie* 26, no. 1 (1984): 54-70.

Wilder, Amos N. "Comment." *The Christian Scholar* 49 (Winter 1966): 307-9.

————. *Early Christian Rhetoric: The Language of the Gospel.* New York: Harper and Row, 1964; reissue, Cambridge, Mass.: Harvard University Press, 1971.

Williams, Daniel Day. "Comment." *The Christian Scholar* 49 (Winter 1966): 310-12.

Williams, Raymond. *The Sociology of Culture.* New York: Schocken Books, 1982.

Willimon, William H. *Peculiar Speech: Preaching to the Baptized.* Grand Rapids: Wm. B. Eerdmans Publishing Company, 1992.

————, and Stanley Hauerwas. *Preaching to Strangers.* Louisville: Westminster/John Knox Press, 1992.

Wink, Walter. *Engaging the Powers: Discernment and Resistance in a World of Domination.* Minneapolis: Fortress Press, 1992.

Wittgenstein, Ludwig. *Philosophical Investigations.* 3rd ed. Translated by G. E. M. Anscombe. New York: Macmillan Publishing Company, 1989.

Wood, Charles. *The Formation of Christian Understanding: An Essay in Theological Hermeneutics.* Philadelphia: Westminster Press, 1981.

Yoder, John Howard. "But We Do See Jesus." In *The Priestly Kingdom.* Notre Dame, Ind.: University of Notre Dame Press, 1984.

————. "The Hermeneutics of Peoplehood." In *The Priestly Kingdom.* Notre Dame, Ind.: University of Notre Dame Press, 1984.

————. *The Politics of Jesus.* 2nd ed. Grand Rapids: Wm. B. Eerdmans Publishing Company, 1994.

————. " 'What Would You Do If . . . ?' An Exercise in Situation Ethics." *Journal of Religious Ethics* 2 (Fall 1974): 81-105.

Permissions

The author and publisher gratefully acknowledge permission to reprint material granted by the following:

Book of Common Worship. © 1993 Westminster/John Knox Press. Used by permission of Westminster John Knox Press.

The Eclipse of Biblical Narrative, by Hans Frei, Yale University Press, 1974. Used by permission.

The Faith of Jesus Christ, by Richard B. Hays, Scholars Press, 1983. Used by permission.

The Identity of Jesus Christ, by Hans Frei, copyright © 1975 Fortress Press. Used by permission of Augsburg Fortress.

Theology and Narrative: Selected Essays, by Hans Frei, edited by George Hunsinger and William C. Placher. Copyright © 1993. Reprinted by permission of Oxford University Press.

Whose Justice? Which Rationality? by Alasdair MacIntyre. © 1988 by the University of Notre Dame Press. Used by permission.

Index

the church's worship and life, 112; as the central character in the gospels, 173, 182, 186, 205; in Christian preaching, 43-44, 141-42, 156, 171-73, 178-80, 189-93, 196, 198-201, 202-3, 212, 216, 222, 230; Jesus of history and Christ of faith, 15, 17-27; as known in the practice of discipleship, 243-45; life of, 22, 178, 192, 209, 237; ministry of, 135, 212-15; as model preacher, 178-80, 212, 220, 225n.16; pattern of exchange, salvation as, 60n.110, 204, 209, 214, 215; power and powerlessness in, 59n.108, 111, 191, 198-200, 213-15; presence of, 18, 19, 40, 43, 47, 48, 60, 61, 109, 142, 225, 227-28; as Redeemer, 54, 60n.110; in union with God, 58, 59. *See also* Ascriptive logic: of the gospel narratives; Character (narrative): Jesus as; Death of Jesus; Identity of Jesus; Resurrection of Jesus

Kant, Immanuel, 7, 36
Kay, James, 201-3, 211
Kellogg, Robert, 171, 173
Kierkegaard, Søren, 127, 134

Language: as a collection of evocative and expressive symbols, 131-32, 232-33; as communally ruled behavior, 131, 232-33; "going on" with, 234-35; language game, 66, 131, 236; as language-in-use, 96, 232-35, 243; performative, 79, 132, 238-39, 240
Language and theology: in the Biblical Theology Movement, 11; in Rudolph Bultmann, 36; in Hans Frei, 45-47, 52-54, 56, 61, 70-71, 73; in Charles Rice, 123; in Edmund Steimle, 137; in Paul Tillich, 42-43. *See also* Cultural-linguistic model of Christianity; Cultural-linguistic model of religion
Language of preaching: as a collection

of evocative, expressive symbols, 132, 143; as communally ruled behavior, 143, 236; as "going on" with language, 236, 239n.55, 240, 256; as language-in-use, 96, 153, 233-41; as linguistic improvisation, 231, 236, 257; and nonviolent resistance to the Powers, 218-19; as performative, 132, 238-39, 240; as poetic and metaphorical, 121, 210. *See also* Preaching: biblical idiom in
Lash, Nicholas, 103-4, 170, 248
Liberal theology (theological liberalism), 5, 7, 8, 28, 29-40, 48, 52, 56, 60, 72, 74, 112; in preaching, 40-44, 156, 165, 180
Liberalism, American, 143, 144, 230-31
Lindbeck, George, 3, 32n.11, 65-69, 71, 79, 80, 82, 95, 122, 123, 131-32, 135, 141, 197, 232, 234, 251
Lischer, Richard, 143n.118, 230n.33, 239
"The 'Literal Reading' of the Biblical Narrative in the Christian Tradition: Does It Stretch or Will It Break?": and *ad hoc* apologetics, 51; and the cultural-linguistic model of Christianity, 69; and the literal sense of Scripture, 69, 86; and narrative theology, 56
Literal sense *(sensus literalis)*, 39, 64, 69, 86-95, 98, 101, 105, 106-7, 109, 110, 173, 182. *See also* Scripture: literal reading of
Literary criticism: formalist, 85, 97, 98; Marxist, 74, 76; New Criticism, 63, 90n.23, 97, 168, 177, 183-84; of Scripture, 3-4, 12, 13, 14, 15, 16, 18, 27, 77-78, 80, 91, 93, 98, 112, 126
Loewe, Raphael, 88-89
Logic: of Christian belief, 18, 21-22, 43, 45, 48-49, 50, 94; of biblical narratives, 15, 18, 22, 39, 48, 54-55, 60n.109, 202, 203-4, 206, 211. *See also* Ascriptive logic; Grammar
Lohfink, Gerhard, 248n.74
Long, Thomas G., 141, 154n.23, 163